THE STOCCOS

Nino Bucci is an investigative reporter at the ABC. He was previously a journalist at *The Age* (where he first covered the Stoccos), at the *Canberra Times*, and at the *Bendigo Advertiser*. He lives in Melbourne. *The Stoccos* is his first book.

LIKE FATHER, LIKE SON

THE STOCCOS

THE EIGHT-YEAR MANHUNT THAT CAPTURED AUSTRALIA

NINO BUCCI

VIKING
an imprint of
PENGUIN BOOKS

VIKING

UK | USA | Canada | Ireland | Australia
India | New Zealand | South Africa | China

Penguin Books is part of the Penguin Random House group of companies
whose addresses can be found at global.penguinrandomhouse.com.

First published by Penguin Random House Australia Pty Ltd, 2018

1 3 5 7 9 10 8 6 4 2

Cover design by Adam Laszczuk © Penguin Random House Australia Pty Ltd
Cover photograph: Mark and Gino Stocco PR Handout Image provided by NSW Police/AAP;
Pinevale by Wolter Peeters/Fairfax
Map by Guy Holt
Typeset in Adobe Garamond by Midland Typesetters, Australia
Printed and bound in Australia by Griffin Press, an accredited ISO AS/NZS 14001
Environmental Management Systems printer.

A catalogue record for this
book is available from the
National Library of Australia

ISBN 978 0 14378 317 6

penguin.com.au

1

The highways are long and straight and grey. Like the barrel of a rifle. Five of them meet at St George, in western Queensland. Every now and again, something catches the sun and starts to glint. A minute or so later, a road train bangs past; forty-odd metres of steel and rubber and glass. And then you are alone again with the road, and the carcasses of roos and pigs and tyres. Beyond them are the farms; cotton and wheat mostly, some cattle.

Cubbie Station, about an hour south of St George, is the most famous farm of them all. It has the largest irrigation system in the southern hemisphere, with a 28-kilometre-long reservoir that could store all the water in Sydney Harbour and that reaches every corner of the 93 000-hectare property. Much of the water was in the Balonne River before it was sucked up.

The Balonne, wide and brown, with dead gums poking their limbs up from its middle like distressed swimmers signalling for help, runs parallel to St George's main street. St George is a town intimate with both drought and flood; a town with a verandahed pub, a water tower wearing a crown of mobile-phone antennas, and a carved emu egg museum with a $5 entry fee. Almost anywhere else it would be a small town, but in this patch of Australia, just where the deep green of the eastern seaboard starts to turn red, it is a regional centre, with council headquarters, and a post office and banks.

It is the sort of town you can imagine a person like Barnaby Joyce living in – and he did, for a decade, working as a local accountant at his firm Barnaby Joyce and Co. before he became a senator. In 2013, he quit the Senate and left St George, moving to Tamworth to run for a House of Representatives seat in New England. It was a bold play, leaving St George, and a smart one. Less than three years later, he was deputy prime minister and the leader of the National Party.

St George is a farming town and a frontier town. Surveyor Thomas Mitchell came through the region while trying to find a route from Sydney to the Gulf of Carpentaria in the 1840s. When he returned to Sydney two years later, word spread of the 'unclaimed' pastures almost 900 kilometres north. What followed was years of conflict between squatters and the local Indigenous population, the Mandandanji, who attacked every station in the region until their resistance was bloodily and mercilessly crushed. Almost all that was left of them was a river bearing the Mandandanji word for water, or running stream: Balonne. That's what Mitchell thought he heard, anyway, when it came to giving it a name.

If you're a cop in St George, it's those passing through, not those on farms, who cause the trouble. Most are cutting inland as they drive north–south, or south–north, as Mitchell did more than

170 years ago. Others drift from central Australia towards the east coast, or in the opposite direction. Some of those rolling through St George are moving something they shouldn't: drugs, mostly. For others, it is the movement itself that is the trouble: the vagrants or backpackers who will not be here long enough to be caught. They shoplift. And then there's the other source of trouble: those who cannot move. Those who are stuck here. Who have a lash at the bottle, or the glass pipe, or the bong, or the needle – or all four – before lashing out at each other.

On the afternoon of 14 June 2013, the local sergeant, Liam Duffy, got a phone call from Kim, the owner of the FoodWorks in town. Duffy had given his personal number to most St George business owners and told them to use it any time. He knew that if they had to report crime by coming into the station, or by waiting for someone to pick up the landline, then the crime would rarely be solved; whoever was responsible would be back on a highway and gone. Kim had just confronted a shoplifter, who simply ignored her and walked out. The supermarket was only 150 metres from the police station, so she called Duffy. He had spent the morning doing first-aid training, and had taken a break for lunch. Because of the training, there were more coppers rostered in the town that day than normal. They had come from tiny stations all across south-west Queensland to be trained. It was impractical for them to wear their utility belts, with handcuffs, pepper spray and handguns, during the training, but they were in uniform. The other officers had left the station for lunch when Kim called.

Duffy listened to her describe the man: he wasn't a local, looked like a backpacker – unkempt, bearded, dark features, probably early thirties – and he was walking towards the river. That meant he was walking towards the police station. Duffy walked out the back of the station and saw a bloke who looked exactly like the man Kim had described. He had bulging pockets and bulging eyes, which kept flicking over his shoulder towards the supermarket to check if he was being followed. Duffy told Kim he saw the suspect, and hung up the phone. His soft face, quick to smile, hardened as he bellowed, 'Stop, police!' and his thick arms and thicker legs started to pump, propelling his 100-kilogram and 190-centimetre frame towards the suspect.

Gino and Mark Stocco called it going shopping. The father and son walked into a shop, took what they wanted, and left without paying. They would go shopping for groceries. They would go shopping for farm machinery. They would go shopping for camping gear. Until they shopped too much in North Queensland and decided to leave their home town of Ingham. That was a dozen years, a couple of prison stints, a yachting adventure and tens of thousands of kilometres ago. They did not miss Ingham, and its whispers and its memories. The road was home now.

The Stoccos drove along a highway lined with tufts of cotton and dying weeds stuck in the red dirt, arriving in St George: a town with two supermarkets to shop in, and five highways to choose from after they did, so they could be on their way again.

The pair decided on the FoodWorks. It was smaller, likely to have fewer staff and customers, and was slightly closer to the edge of town. It was also on an intersection, so the pair could walk separate ways after shopping. Gino would do a lap of the block and go and fetch their ute, and then pick Mark up near the Balonne River.

The white automatic doors slid open and they strode inside. The supermarket was small, with only a few aisles down the middle, a deli along the right side, fridges and freezers along the left, and a fresh produce section at the rear. The pair separated, filling their pockets as they went. There were cameras in the store, but the Stoccos weren't bothered. Stealing came naturally to Gino. He had been doing it for most of his life. And, gradually, he had helped his son understand the importance of theft. It was not merely a means of survival: without taking back what was rightfully theirs, there was no way to even out 'the system', and the world would remain unjust.

As Mark started to walk towards the registers and out the door, he was stopped by the supermarket owner. She had seen him stealing, and told him so. Mark did what he had been taught to do by his old man. He just ignored the woman and kept on walking.

Mark crossed Victoria Street, the main drag, and kept walking down Scott Street, towards the Balonne. He was anxious, looking behind him, making sure the woman at the supermarket had not called someone on to him. His dad would be there soon in the ute. The ute Gino had stolen from his sister. *Keep walking*. Then Mark heard the shout, 'Stop, police!' and saw a brute of a copper running towards him.

Mark started to run, and then turned at the cop, grabbing a packet of pilfered spaghetti from his pocket and hurling it at him. But he kept coming. So Mark pulled out a bottle of olive oil and held it above his head, threatening the cop. But still he kept coming. So Mark threw that at him too.

Sergeant Liam Duffy was not stopped by the olive oil. Soon he was on the bloke he would later find out was Mark Stocco, grabbing him and wrestling him to the ground. After a brief struggle, Mark submitted. 'I don't want to fight with you,' he said. 'Well, stop resisting then,' Duffy answered.

Duffy had Mark pinned to the pavement with his hands secured, little more than 50 metres from the St George police station. But without his handcuffs, or anything else normally fixed to his utility belt, he faced the difficulty of getting up while keeping a firm hold on Mark, to walk him to the station. As he caught his breath and started working out what to do next, Duffy heard the distinct whir of a car being quickly reversed. And then he heard the driver pull up on the road behind him.

Duffy thought nothing of the reversing driver; perhaps it was a good Samaritan coming to help. Even if he had felt the need to look towards the sound, he would not have taken his eyes off the shoplifter he was straddling. Then he heard a voice: 'Let him go.'

Before he could register what it all meant, Duffy was being punched in the back of the head. The barrage was unrelenting, dull thud after dull thud in the soft area just behind the ears, near where his spine plugged into his brain. Duffy knew from his police training that he was being hit in an area called the knockout triangle: get punched here hard enough, or long enough, and you're out cold. So he stopped holding down the shoplifter and lifted his arms to either side of his head, elbows pointed straight ahead and forearms around his ears, hoping to block the onslaught. He still had his weight on the bloke, but as Duffy released his hands, Mark was able to get his arms free. And, as Duffy continued to be punched in the head, Mark started to push up from the concrete. Duffy went with it, getting to his feet by using Mark's momentum, as Gino continued hooking into his head.

Duffy was standing now, Gino to his back and Mark standing at his front. He charged again at Mark, hoping to push him into the low metal fence surrounding a house on a corner block that overlooked the Balonne. Moving forwards would also get him away from the punches. Duffy came at Mark until he lurched backwards over the fence and into the front yard. But Duffy went with him and was catapulted further over the fence and into a bush.

Duffy's vision was blurry now, his head swimming – as though he had dived deep into the Balonne and opened his eyes. He was in a tangle of dusty scrub under a willow, a frangipani and a yellow box. He could hear the doors of the vehicle slamming and it speeding away. He had never even seen the man who had tried to cave in the back of his head. Eventually he made his way to his feet and stumbled the short distance to the police station.

The extra police officers who had been in St George for first-aid training were quickly dispatched in all directions. It took a particularly vicious and desperate crook to belt the local sergeant on his lunchbreak within view of the police station. The officers would do everything they could to catch the two men who had felled one of their own. But Duffy knew it would be difficult to catch them; he had a description of the ute, but there were five major roads the men could have taken. And the roads south led to the New South Wales border, little more than 100 kilometres away, and freedom from the chasing pack of Queensland Police.

Duffy later said he reckons the efforts were hampered further by the fact the officers were not from the area, so did not immediately know in which direction to head. After a frantic few hours' driving, and with darkness closing in, the police conceded they had lost the pair. They had escaped, almost certainly driving through the border towns of Hebel or Mungindi, further east.

Police turned their attention to finding out who the men were. Their first stop was the FoodWorks, to look at the CCTV footage. They noticed another bloke in the supermarket doing the same thing as the man Duffy had caught. He was shorter and older, with a thicker beard. Kim, the supermarket owner, had not noticed this man at all; he may have slipped out while she was confronting the younger man. Then one of the officers looked at the men more closely. She thought she recognised them, so she looked up a database of outstanding warrants in Queensland. And Mark and Gino Stocco stared back at her.

As the Stoccos kept driving south, getting distance between them and the coppers, Duffy went to the hospital. He had only minor cuts and scrapes to his face, lumps on his head and grazed knees from wrestling on the footpath. His mind started to tick. He rued not wearing his utility belt, not being able to cuff the shoplifter as soon as he had chased him down. And he rued that he had not registered the sound of the reversing car as a threat, contemplating the strange things a mind can do, even one conditioned to be cautious and distrusting and alert. Duffy had been assaulted on the job before; in his first eight weeks as a cop, he was kicked in the head during schoolies week in Surfers Paradise. And as he quickly climbed the ranks, working as far south as the Gold Coast, to Weipa on Cape York, and at Innisfail and Aurukun in between, he had his fair share of other scrapes. But this one had shaken him.

'You could toe the macho line and say that it didn't, but it did,' he tells me. In later months, Duffy reflected on the dangers of patrolling alone and talked to junior officers about it. It rattled his confidence that he had not realised how dangerous the situation was when he had Mark pinned, and that the sound of the reversing car did not alarm him further. He eventually came to another disturbing conclusion: that it was probably a good thing he did not have his belt on, because the person behind him might have taken his gun from the holster and blown him away.

Something else lodged in Duffy's mind. It stayed long after his head stopped throbbing, and after the cuts became scabs and then slightly discoloured marks and then fully restored skin. It was the voice of the man he now knew was Gino Stocco. The way Gino had spoken, before swinging violently at his head. There was an utter absence of anger. No fear or distress. Just three words – 'Let him go' – delivered in a monotone. A perfect calm, before the storm of punches rained down on his skull.

2

Amid the boatloads of migrants fleeing a ravaged Europe at the end of the Second World War were a young couple from Veneto in north-eastern Italy: Pietro and Egidia Stocco.

Venice, the capital of the province, was one of the jewels of the continent. But most families in Veneto, which stretches from the Dolomites to the Adriatic Sea, led far from glamorous lives as farmers. The heart of agricultural activity was the Po Valley, where farmers harvested corn or wheat, or tended orchards or vineyards. The farmers had, in many instances, lived hand-to-mouth even before Fascist dictator Benito Mussolini thrust them into war, and it was certainly no better in the years immediately after he was overthrown.

When the Allies claimed victory in 1945, Australia threw open its doors. 'Australia wants, and will welcome, new healthy citizens who are determined to become good Australians,' Arthur Calwell, the minister for Immigration in the Chifley government, said at the time. The government would pay the boat fare of immigrants if they worked for two years in whatever job was given to them by the government once they arrived. The driving force of the policy was a need for labour, and it was hoped that filling this need would induce a new wave of prosperity. In the next three decades, the country's population would almost double, to 13 million people.

Italians had been arriving in Ingham since the 1860s. But strong undercurrents of racial tension and class division remained when Pietro and Egidia unpacked their suitcases there almost a century later, in 1954. It is unclear whether the couple chose to live in Ingham or the government sent them there as part of their conditions of settlement.

Ingham was built on sugar and the backbreaking work needed to harvest it. In 1874, a decade after the town was founded, William Bairstow Ingham, a colonialist who had ventured north from Tasmania looking for property to build his fortune, bought a 285-hectare sugar farm on the Herbert River. He became popular in the region, and the town was named in his honour. Three years later, Ingham and his crew were killed in New Guinea, after he had tried to smooth over a dispute between indigenous tribes and colonialists, who were there for gold. A survivor of the attack said that, within hours of being killed, Ingham and his men were roasted and eaten.

Within three decades of Ingham's fateful departure, the town's Italian population rapidly expanded. Businessman Chiaffredo Venerano Fraire was a northerner, like the Stoccos, hailing from the north-western city of Piedmont. In 1891, he orchestrated a migration scheme that saw about 335 Italians move to Ingham and other Queensland sugarcane towns, such as Bundaberg and Burdekin, according to historian Dr Catherine Dewhirst. Their arrival was not universally welcomed. 'Their presence from 1891 generated heated debate in parliament and the press about their capacity to assimilate,' Dewhirst wrote in the *Journal of Australia* in 2008. 'By 1907, racist rhetoric was being used by the *Bulletin* newspaper, for instance, to question the racial hygiene of Italians, calling them "bucolic", "dull-witted", "primitive" and "impoverished".'

Italians worked the cane fields with Indigenous Australians and Pacific Islanders who were mostly from Vanuatu and the Solomon Islands. European settlers – inspired by what they considered the success of slavery on other continents (and, in some cases, from personal experience in places such as the West Indies) – had recruited the men as cheap labour since the mid-nineteenth century. While some came voluntarily, others were subject to the shameful practice of blackbirding: making Pacific Islanders work for a pittance through kidnapping, force or trickery. Shortly after the turn of the century, hiring foreign labour was outlawed and most Islanders were deported. But the vile attitude that allowed the practice in the first place endured. Settlers started calling Italians 'blacks', because they continued to do the work that white people wouldn't.

By 1924, about 44 per cent of all sugarcane plantations in the Herbert River area were owned by Italians. They had broken their backs to go from cane cutters to owning their own farms. But it had earned them contempt, not respect. According to Dewhirst, the *Worker*, among other newspapers, complained that the federal government was allowing 'Mediterranean scum' to invade the sugar plantations.

There were, however, genuine reasons for those in Ingham to be wary of some Italians who had settled there. By the 1930s, the town had become a plaything of senior figures within the Calabrian Mafia, or 'Ndrangheta. Families linked to the original five clans that founded the organisation started arriving in Australia in the previous decade. Some found their first jobs in their new country on the sugarcane fields of North Queensland. One of these figures was Vincenzo D'Agostino, who hailed from Palmi, on the Calabrian west coast. He arrived in Brisbane on the *Citta di Genoa* on 11 October 1924, before making his way to Ingham, where he worked as a farmhand and baker. According to writer Adam Grossetti, who was raised in North Queensland and researched D'Agostino, the Calabrian soon started taking advantage of his countrymen through an extortion gang. The gang was called La Mano Nera – the Black Hand. And its fingers reached across North Queensland.

The gang was linked to murder, kidnapping, poisoning, arson and vicious crimes of mutilation, including using a razor to hack off the ears of those who refused to pay up. D'Agostino was interviewed by police in connection with the delivery of extortion letters, being armed in public, threats of intimidation and his involvement in procuring sex workers from Sydney, some of whom would be murdered.

In 1935, a prominent sugarcane farmer, Domenico Scarcella, who had refused to pay the Black Hand, was gunned down in Ingham. Three years later, someone came for D'Agostino. A bomb blast tore through the flour room of the bakery in which he slept, and the gang leader died in hospital the next day. His killer was never found.

As terrifying as the influence of the Black Hand in Ingham had been, events in Europe were having a far greater impact on the town's Italian community during the 1930s. As Mussolini clenched his fists, Italians in Ingham splintered into three groups: Fascist, anti-Fascist or unaligned. Some say the divisions in North Queensland remain to this day. Eventually, when war took hold, hundreds would be thrown into internment camps – more Italians were interned in Queensland than in any other state, Dewhirst says – leading to labour shortages on the cane farms. And by 1954, the year Pietro and Egidia arrived, those Australians in Ingham who still supported Italians – despite the war, despite the Black Hand, and despite their unfathomable embracement of jobs meant for blacks – were being called 'white dagos'.

The Stoccos' first child, Mario, was born that year. Gino was born three years later, spending the first four weeks of his life in intensive care. He later said he was not sure what had ailed him, but did not believe it had a significant impact on his development. Two other children, Eddie and Maryann, followed.

Their parents spoke Italian. Pietro, who was known as Peter, worked as a cane cutter and then at a sugar mill. Egidia looked after the house while her children were young and, later, had a casual job as a cleaner.

Gino remembered his childhood fondly. The family had no significant money trouble and was, in his words, 'quite functional'. He did not feel ostracised or struggle with his identity, despite the history of Italians in Ingham, and did not share the negative experiences of many other children who were the first generation born in Australia to migrant parents. Gino said he enjoyed school, made friends and fitted in well, and had no learning problems or serious issues with misbehaviour. But he would never do his homework and, while he accepted most school rules, was only '98 per cent behaved'.

Perhaps the entire two per cent of his misbehaviour can be attributed to one crude prank Gino played while he was a boy.

He urinated in the teacher's inkwell, leaving it there to be found mid-lesson. Egidia laughed when she was told what Gino had done, but, according to a Fairfax Media report from 2015, Peter said he walloped the boy so hard he bolted for the hills and didn't come back for hours.

But his misbehaviour, Gino said, never related to fighting, truancy, damaging property, lighting fires, or cruelty to animals – all questions asked by a psychiatrist later to glean whether he had long held a predisposition to any particular form of offending. He played cricket and attended Gilroy College, an all-boys school run by the Christian Brothers and named after Norman Gilroy, the archbishop of Sydney. There was an all-girls school in Ingham, Santa Maria College, and a state school. Gilroy boys and Santa Maria girls spent most of their time outside of school courting one another.

During his childhood and into his teenage years, Gino travelled with his family to see relatives in Werribee, which was then a small farming town west of Melbourne. They made this trip during summer, when North Queensland became unbearable. They often worked on farms in the region while they stayed.

Gino left school at fifteen, having completed Year Ten. Gilroy and Santa Maria merged the following year – a joyous day for Gino's sixteen-year-old former classmates, who were no longer limited to courting outside school. Gino had been picking tobacco in his school holidays, and once he left school he worked various trades. He became a fairly accomplished bricklayer, electrician and carpenter, but never started an apprenticeship or gained formal qualifications.

*

Giuseppe Fragapane left Italy during Mussolini's reign, but before the outbreak of the Second World War, in 1937. Two years earlier, Italy had invaded Ethiopia, and Germany had been the only European nation that did not oppose the action. Italy, in return, withdrew its opposition to Germany absorbing Austria. Europe was on the brink of war, and it seemed there were few more stable places to escape to than Australia.

Giuseppe left Sicily and moved to Werribee South, where vegetable farms had been established in the small settlement to service Melbourne, about 30 kilometres to the east. The name Werribee was derived from an Aboriginal word for spine or backbone, which had probably been used to describe the river that flowed from the Macedon Ranges into Port Phillip Bay and was a boundary between different Aboriginal clans before European settlement.

Giuseppe had a small plot of less than four hectares, and grew artichokes, beans, cauliflower, peas and tomatoes. He supplied the Queen Victoria Market, which was the only wholesale market in Victoria at the time. He and his wife, Anna, wanted to start a family there, and in April 1959 their daughter Concetta was born. Concetta went by the name Connie. She went to school in nearby Werribee, and spent much of her childhood with cousins.

Giuseppe and Anna's business rapidly expanded while Connie grew up, and would eventually grow to occupy hundreds of hectares of prime farming land either side of Duncans Road.

Connie was seventeen when she started seeing her first boyfriend. He was nineteen, tanned and had dark features, short, but with a body honed by the hard work he had done since his mid-teens. He regularly travelled to Werribee South from Ingham during summer, and, as he got older, he helped relatives on nearby farms. One summer, he met Connie. He was not merely a solid labourer with a renowned work ethic; he was also skilful at mending things, had an eye for detail, and was intelligent, despite having left school at fifteen. He was quiet, with watchful eyes, but, when you got him talking, he didn't mind big-noting himself and had a touch of the larrikin. He was from another Catholic Italian family who had also forged a life for themselves on the land, albeit more than 2700 kilometres away.

The young man was Gino Stocco.

Gino brought Connie back to Ingham with him. They were married soon after in her new home town. A wedding photo of the couple appears to show them standing in Rotary Park, which is bordered by Herbert Street in the middle of town. They are squinting into the afternoon sunshine, the long train of Connie's dress stretched out to her left, her veil back and covering her shoulders, dark hair and eyes sharply contrasted with the cascading white. Gino stands to her right and slightly behind her, clad in a slate suit, his pants pleated and hemmed below the ankle, a white shirt with dark trim along either side of the buttons, and a black bow tie. They are both beaming.

Another photo taken later in the day shows them during their reception in a brown-brick building, leaning into each other, Gino better prepared for the camera than Connie, who appears stuck in a half smile. A necklace hangs on her neck, framed by the lace on her neckline. Her bouquet is on the table, next to a glass of red wine. Closer still to the photographer is a three-tiered wedding cake, topped with figurines of a bride and groom standing in front of a marzipan house.

Before her twentieth birthday, Connie fell pregnant. In October 1979, she gave birth at Ingham Hospital to the couple's first child: Mark. A daughter, Christina, arrived soon after. By twenty-two, Connie was a married mother of two, trying to make a home, thousands of kilometres from the only home she had ever known.

In 1976, about the time Gino was in the throes of his first teenage love affair, he started his cane-cutting business with his father, Peter. Cane was increasingly being cut by machine, with the first mechanical cane harvester developed in the early 1960s. Harvesters were commonplace by the 1970s, so the employment of cane cutters shrank, while profits increased.

By 1974, the price of sugar spiked; it was sixty-five times what it had been when it hit record lows in 1967. But the price dropped again by the late 1970s and, despite a rally in the early 1980s, never regained what it had been when the Stoccos started the business and forked out a considerable sum for a harvester.

By 1984, the business was starting to fail. With two children under five, it was a stressful time for Gino and Connie, but Gino thought it would help if he swapped properties with his father. Peter moved to a house Gino had built in Toobanna, just outside Ingham, and the young Stocco family moved further south to Bambaroo, a scatter of farms strung together with a school and a Catholic church, near the edge of the Paluma State Forest. In August, Gino, twenty-six, received his first criminal conviction: he was fined $80 for stealing, but no further details about what he stole, or from where, are available.

After Gino sold the cane-cutting business and moved into his father's house, he set about building another house on the vacant block next door. There was a hill on the block, meaning he could build higher than the level of the Bruce Highway and gain a better view of the Paluma Range, to the west. He was doing other odds and ends at the time, including working further south at plantations near Crystal Creek and other properties in Bambaroo. And he continued to visit Werribee South and work there in the summer.

The new house slowly took shape. It was a brown-brick veneer, with an undercover front patio ringed with open archways, looking out over palms to the sugar plantations and the mountains. It was as grand as a property got along the highway in Bambaroo. When it was finished, Gino planned to move in with his family and open a service station in his father's old property, where they were currently living. His children were both high-school age, and he needed a more regular income to support them. In 1993, he opened the service station. It was the same year Gino and Connie started to fight.

The Bruce Highway between Townsville and Cairns was thick with industrial and tourist traffic, and the Stoccos hoped to ensnare some of the latter with a particularly kitsch attraction: a giant slice of watermelon, a three-tonne concrete green and pink triangle that you could walk inside. Writer Bill Bryson once described these Australian novelties as 'like leftover props from a 1950s' horror movie', typically set along a dull stretch of highway. Gino and Peter built the sculpture, which was not quite as impressive as other big fruits of the day, like the Big Pineapple or Big Banana, and dubbed the service station the Big Melon. Whether it was part of their plan when they started the business, or a desperate bid to right the ship, the melon did not bring in the flocks of customers they'd hoped for. The service station struggled, putting further strain on Gino and Connie's marriage.

Connie worked hard to make a life for herself in Ingham. She fitted in quickly, always smiling and welcoming, and made close friends, including some she would remain in contact with for almost four decades. She did not just stop for chats when she bumped into you down the street, one local woman said; she would actually call out after you and come striding over. 'You wouldn't meet a nicer person. She was just lovely, Connie. Everybody liked her. I can't speak highly enough of her.'

There was, however, one thing the woman did not understand about Connie: 'How the fuck did she even end up with two kids to this bloke Gino?'

The kids, thankfully, appeared to be safely lodged under their mother's wing. Mark and Christina were always well kept, and are remembered for their impeccable manners. From the outside, Connie Stocco appeared a happy and accomplished mother, making the best of life with her slightly strange and light-fingered husband. But all was not well behind closed doors.

Ingham locals who knew the couple believed Gino was controlling. He needed to know where Connie was and what she was doing. He only gave her enough money to buy what the household needed when she went shopping, no more. Now, that stifling restraint of a spouse is considered a form of family violence. But in the 1980s and 1990s in Ingham, people just took pity on Connie: a bright and attractive young woman tethered to her husband.

Perhaps Gino thought his wife was frivolous, and providing her with a stipend was the only way to manage their meagre finances. But it is far more likely, given a pattern of behaviour that we now know existed throughout his life, that Gino simply wanted to be in control.

Eventually, when Connie reached her thirties, she started to imagine a life without Gino.

One of Connie's closest friends was Joanne Zatta. She lived with her husband, Remo, and their children at a house to the north of the highway in Bambaroo, on the other side of a railway line used by cane trains after harvesting. Remo and his brothers owned one of the larger sugarcane plantations in the region.

Connie bonded with Joanne, a woman of a similar age with children of a similar age who had married a similar man: the son of Italians who migrated to Ingham. She did not know it when the pair became friends, but Joanne would be Connie's ticket out of Ingham.

3

It would be easy to paint Gino as an unlucky battler, a bloke trying to make the best of his lot in a town surrounded by other battlers. Perhaps that's how he thought of himself. He was as good a builder, plumber and electrician as anyone with formal qualifications. But that didn't count for much. And now, after watching his first business go down the drain – the cane-cutting business he ran with his father – another was going with it.

It was not that straightforward, however. Ingham in the late 1980s and early 1990s was a town that easily forgave a scoundrel. Not everyone living there was a cleanskin. It was okay to pinch a plant from the bush for your backyard, or to defraud the government of tax or benefits, or to turn a blind eye to that neighbour who grew some dope. It was staggeringly common, police say, for a property that had been on the market for months to be burnt to the ground in the dead of night, and for an insurance claim to be lodged a few days later. Local scuttlebutt goes that Peter Stocco may have even done that himself once, when he could not sell a property. A bit of graft was normal in Ingham, as was a distrust of authority – an identity forged not long after the town was founded that endures today.

But there was a bit of graft and then there was Gino Stocco.

Small businesses are only as strong as their owners. Gino's never really stood a chance. He was too untrustworthy. He would steal farming equipment from properties while employed to cut cane. In fact, he would steal from most other businesses in town, yet be incredulous when he was not given their trade in return.

When Gino operated the service station, he asked some neighbours if he could pick mangoes from their overladen tree. They said they didn't mind, so Gino came back with Connie and the kids and loaded up. The mangoes were cut up, packaged into cups and sold from the service station. While the neighbours thought that was a bit cheeky, they were willing to overlook it. Until they realised that spinach and tomatoes from their vegie garden had been raided as well.

Gino bought an ice machine for the service station and ran a side business delivering ice around town. One of the premises he supplied was another service station down the road in Toobanna. Gino would deliver the ice in a van, backing up to the cool room if he could, unload it and leave, without having to bother the business owner. But the service station owner at Toobanna had been getting suspicious that Gino was taking as much as he was delivering. So one day, after he heard Gino arriving to make a delivery, he decided to see what he was up to.

Gino had unloaded the ice and was in the process of filling up his van with the contents of the cool room. When the owner caught him, Gino had already stocked it up with frozen chickens, pies and pasties. He was told to unload it and never come back. The servo owner then made it his business to tell every other proprietor in town what Gino was up to. If he saw Gino in a shop, like the supermarket, he would go and tell the manager to keep an eye on him. A lot of the time, they already were. Eventually Gino was banned from a lot of businesses.

'He was just a villain,' the service station owner said. 'He had balls though, didn't he?'

Not everybody knew who Gino was, however. And so when he went to a food distributor one day to pick up some goods for the service station and saw two loaded pallets ready to go, he bluffed the bloke in the storeroom into believing they were his. They loaded them into his van, and Gino drove off without signing the docket. When the trader who had actually ordered and paid for the goods arrived later that afternoon, he was told that a colleague had already come to collect them. It did not take them long to realise who the 'colleague' had been.

Some who knew Gino rued that he could not keep his thieving at bay. One friend who had known him since high school was adamant he could have been a millionaire, such was his brilliance at fixing things and his ingenuity with a tool in his hands.

But even if Gino had not alienated himself from others in Ingham, I suspect the business would have failed anyway. There were problems with the service station that were out of his hands, but perhaps could have been predicted. The servo was just after a bend while driving north, and also hard to see while driving south, given it was tucked off the highway. And it was close enough to Ingham that people would probably prefer to stop in the town itself and stretch their legs.

As the bills piled up, and the concrete slice of watermelon sat empty, Connie and Gino were increasingly at each other. According to Mark Stocco, their elder child, the arguments never became physical, but they did become more common. And for two children at a sensitive age, as Mark and Christina were, it was a confusing time.

Mark was a shy boy, but he had no trouble making friends. He was well behaved at school, was never suspended, and excelled at his studies. He would later tell police he had always easily retained numbers. 'Just, um, like when I was a kid I just had an obsession with numbers,' he said, 'and I was like really good at maths so I just, I don't know, I just always had a thing about numbers and I could always remember numbers and dates and phone numbers and all that sort of stuff, yeah.'

He described his childhood as exciting and privileged, and particularly enjoyed travelling between Ingham and Werribee South with his father during the summer. He got along well with both parents and his younger sister. Mark was thirteen when his parents opened the service station. The next four years were marked by arguments between Gino and Connie.

Mark did not know it, but a feeling had been building in his mother for years. She felt she had no choice but to leave. The sugar cane that surrounded her was like prison bars. Connie loved her children and wanted the best for them. She would have left years earlier if it wasn't for them. But she knew now that she had to go regardless. Gino would not hurt the kids; she was sure of that. And so she thought about how to flee, and spoke to Joanne. They made a plan: she would pack a bag one day while Gino was working, and leave it with Joanne. And then, in the dead of the night, Remo would drive her to safety, until she eventually made her way back to the farm at Werribee South.

One day, in 1997, she made her move. As Gino and the children slept, Connie lay in bed with her eyes closed, her mind a jungle of tangled fear and excitement. She slipped from her bed and moved stealthily through the house her husband built, out the back door and down the driveway, and into Remo's car.

Gino thought he would be able to win Connie back. She was confused, that was all. And he understood that. In a blink, she had gone from a teenager surrounded by everybody she had ever known to living thousands of kilometres away and raising two kids. Now, with the kids approaching the age she had been when she left Werribee, her head had stopped spinning and she didn't like what she saw in front of her: a life where the kids would soon leave, as she had done, and she would be stuck in Far North Queensland with Gino.

In a bid to get Connie to return, Gino tried to explain away his increasing dalliances with the law, but he had racked up another four convictions since 1984. He was found to have received and been in possession of stolen goods in 1986, and was put on eighteen months' probation. In 1995, he was hit with his first suspended sentence: a term of four months, suspended for two years. He was convicted for possessing stolen property later that year, but was shown leniency by a Townsville magistrate. Rather than sending him to prison, the magistrate sentenced him to eighteen months' probation and 200 hours of community service, and increased his suspended sentence by a year. Gino again caught a break in 1997, when an Ingham magistrate convicted him of breaching his probation but imposed no further penalty.

Gino never claimed to be the perfect man, but Connie's life was with him; he knew it. And he would make her see it again too – no matter how long it took.

He fought hard to 'try and win her back', as he described it later, even buying a property in Werribee, near where Connie had resettled. But 'it quickly didn't work out' as 'she just wasn't happy'. He sold the Melbourne property and bought another in Toowoomba. The relationship had become impossible. Three years after she left, Connie told Gino she would never be coming back. The man who could fix anything could not fix his own marriage.

When he returned to Queensland, Gino Stocco's mind started to close in on him. He had never felt so low and helpless. He was not suicidal, nor did he seek treatment for his poor mental health. But he was consumed by grief and loss. Underpinning it, however, was not sadness but rage. And as it burnt deep inside him, his mind filled with a lust for vengeance. If he could not win his wife back, he would get her back, for what she had done to him. He started down a path that would lead him to murder.

Locals who knew the couple have their own theories about why Gino found it so hard to deal with the separation. There were probably peripheral factors: the perceived shame of his parents, the wider Italian community and other Ingham locals, fears about what the separation would do to his finances, and the loss of control – something a controlling man cherishes above all else. The local man who had known Gino since high school says he thought the relationship always seemed quite 'touch and go'. He does not know exactly why Connie finally decided to end things but thinks it was probably because Gino could not stop committing crime.

If Connie had indeed hoped her husband would change, it was futile. 'I don't really know, but I'd say she would have gone because of all of the stuff he got up to, all the stealing. She was just jack of it. I'd known him all his life, and he had always done it.'

Gino told people for years that his wife had been unfaithful, and that her infidelities had caused him shame. There were no rumours of this in Ingham, however, which was a place where even a stray glance would be noted and shared among the locals. Connie was attractive, with a personality that matched, and knew how to 'flaunt' her looks, one local said. But there is no evidence she had ever had an affair. What is far more likely is that Gino manufactured his own truth, as he had done with countless other things in his life, and he either honestly believed it or was simply hell-bent on making others do so.

One local who knew Gino for thirty years is convinced she knows the most significant factor that caused him to implode after the break-up. It was not a conspiracy about his allegations of an unfaithful wife, or the shame of his parents, or the isolation and loneliness, or a sense of loss, or loss of control. 'Gino believed in the sanctity of marriage,' she said. 'He believed in death do us part.'

4

While 1997 marked the end for Connie and Gino Stocco's marriage, it heralded a new beginning for another couple with Italian heritage. On 29 January, the Immigration Review Tribunal of Australia ruled that Italian Giuseppa Fazio was in a de facto relationship with Rosario Cimone, and she was allowed to stay in Australia. Giuseppa and Rosario did not know the Stoccos. But, almost twenty years later, on the outer edge of Sydney, the two men would meet. And it would change their lives forever.

The tribunal decision marked the end of an incredible period of upheaval for Giuseppa, who had arrived in Australia with her three daughters, her husband and rudimentary English in 1992. Within three years, her husband had fled the country because of huge debts, she had become an illegal immigrant and she had started a new relationship with Rosario. But that was all behind her now. The tribunal had agreed that she and Rosario were a couple, and granted her and her children a visa on spousal grounds, overturning an earlier decision that had refused the application.

Giuseppa was six weeks older than Connie Stocco. In February 1992 – six days before her thirty-third birthday – she moved with her then husband and their three daughters to Western Sydney. She had no immediate family in Australia; her parents and two sisters stayed in Italy. But they lived near Liverpool, in the midst of one of the largest settlements of Italians in suburban Sydney, meaning they could shop and socialise largely in their own language.

One such business, which the couple frequently visited, was a butcher shop in Casula. It was run by Rosario Cimone, a 44-year-old father of three, who had moved from Italy to Western Sydney with his wife in 1968, and had been a butcher since the late 1970s. Rosario, who was born in Sicily and known as Ross, separated from his wife about two months before the Fazios moved to Australia. The relationship had deteriorated long before, but the couple agreed to live separately under the same roof for the sake of their children: Maria, Vincenza and Filippo. When Vincenza married and moved out, as Maria had already done, leaving only a teenage Filippo at home, the couple began arguing more frequently. In 1991, after a particularly heated row at Christmas, Rosario moved out. He started sleeping at the butcher's shop.

The Fazios became friends of Rosario, and, when they discovered he lived alone at the shop, they began regularly inviting him for dinner.

In June 1992, the Fazios gained an extension to their traveller visa, allowing them to stay until October. But all was not well with the couple. Giuseppa said her husband had become distant and temperamental. After receiving a phone call from Italy, his behaviour worsened. Then, within a week of the call, he left home. Giuseppa believed he abandoned her because he owed a 'quite substantial' amount of money to creditors in Italy. Confused and alone, she contacted Rosario.

'Giuseppa telephoned me and told me of her predicament,' he told the migration tribunal. 'She was depressed and had no money and nobody else to turn to. I offered her assistance and advice. I used to go to her place every night and asked if she needed anything and to enquire about her husband.'

Rosario paid for the final month of rent at the house Giuseppa and her daughters were living in, and then found them another house in Fairfield. He also supported her during an appointment at the Department of Immigration; before too long, Giuseppa and the girls would have to return to Italy. But she was developing feelings for Rosario. She changed her mind about returning to her country of birth, and, when their visas expired, in January 1993, they stayed in Australia. Giuseppa said that while Rosario was the main reason behind the decision to stay, the girls also enjoyed Australia and were making friends at school.

Rosario was visiting the house every day, but never stayed the night. In May, the Fazios moved to a new place in Liverpool. It was rented under Giuseppa's name, but Rosario also lived there, and paid the $250 a week rent. They started living as 'husband and wife', Giuseppa said.

The Immigration Department had contacted her earlier that year, after she had failed to leave Australia, and granted a bridging visa to her and the girls until December the next year. She applied for a spousal visa that month, but had her application denied, partially because she had no valid reason for not initially leaving Australia when she was supposed to. As part of the process to have the decision reviewed, Giuseppa and Rosario had to give evidence about their relationship.

Rosario told the tribunal that Giuseppa, who by this time was known as Josie, did all the domestic duties and worked two days a week at the butcher shop, meaning all the regular customers knew about their relationship. 'Giuseppa always gives me a massage every day when I arrive home from work,' he told the tribunal. 'I purchased a Ford Falcon for her use, and two years ago on her birthday I gave her a video camera as a present.' Rosario said Giuseppa's daughters listened to and respected him, and that he respected them in return. Giuseppa – who required an interpreter during the tribunal proceedings – said that although her girls did not call Rosario 'Dad', 'they say he is better to them than their father was'. The relationship was less popular with Rosario's daughters. 'They are not happy about it but they have accepted the relationship . . . they both know that there is no chance of me getting back together with my wife,' he said. Rosario had spoken to Giuseppa's mother on the phone during her frequent calls from Italy and told her he respected her daughter. The tribunal also heard from several witnesses, including Rosario's brother Angelo, who said the couple were 'very much suited to each other . . . relationship is genuine and they love each other very much'. Other witnesses spoke about regularly socialising with the couple at the Marconi Club, a popular venue associated with the soccer club of the same name.

The tribunal accepted that Giuseppa had demonstrated compelling circumstances, and it overturned the decision to not grant her a spousal visa. But it had not heard everything there was to know about Rosario Cimone; or, if it had, it did not make it public when it released the reasons for its decision. Rosario had links to the Calabrian Mafia. He had been jailed in the early 1980s, about a decade before the Fazios arrived, over the cultivation of a substantial marijuana crop, and later that same decade he was convicted for selling cannabis. His connections with organised crime were so substantial that when Rex Jackson, the minister in charge of New South Wales prisons, started a scheme to release prisoners early in exchange for bribes, Rosario was one of the first freed. He and two others were released from Broken Hill prison in 1983, after underworld figure Fayez Hakim brokered the deal. Hakim had been tasked with finding inmates who had the connections to pay, and in Rosario he found one. Hakim paid Jackson $12 000 for the three men to be released, money that Jackson subsequently used to pay gambling debts. Jackson resigned in disgrace and was sent to jail, and upon his release he ran a hot-dog van.

Rosario stayed involved in organised crime. All the while, he maintained the veneer of a suburban butcher. In 1997, he had again landed on his feet, with a partner who was twelve years younger and treated him like a king. But there was no escaping his roots. And, eventually, Rosario Cimone's links with the Calabrian Mafia would leave him in a shallow grave.

5

As Gino spent his days constantly thinking about his wife, whom he had separated from but would never divorce, and who he felt had betrayed him far worse than he had ever been betrayed before, the couple's son was excelling. Mark started a civil engineering degree at James Cook University in Townsville the year his parents separated. To gain entry to the course, he would have needed to achieve higher marks than about 70 per cent of other Queensland high-school students graduating in 1996.

Mark lived at a residential college at the university. It was a heady environment of sex and parties far removed from his life beside a highway in Bambaroo. Residents followed their late nights by seedily stumbling out the doors of their college the next day and hauling themselves across campus and into class, or not, as the case often was. Mark had never had a girlfriend. But in his second year of university, he met an attractive and career-orientated blonde and they became an item.

Mark was having no problem with his studies and had a close circle of friends. He had completed three years of his degree and was entering his final year of study. He had been seeing his girlfriend for more than two years. Then, in the second half of 2000, Gino arrived in Townsville and started building a house in Douglas, near the university. He had finally given up on his marriage.

Mark started helping his dad with the build. He had not seen as much of him since moving away for university. 'We drew really close back to each other,' he said later, reflecting on this period of his life. Mark appreciated for the first time how skilled his father was as a builder, and spent more and more time with him. His girlfriend 'did not like it at all'. It is unclear whether she was jealous about not being able to see Mark as often, concerned about his commitment to study, worried about the influence of Gino, or a combination of all three. She could not be contacted for this book.

Mark described what ensued as a 'tug of war' between his girlfriend and father as they vied for his time and attention. She started 'pulling away' from the relationship, he said, partly because she was focused on her career. But others say Gino also had a bigger influence than Mark may have acknowledged years later. 'He was saying to him, "Get rid of her. She's no good,"' a former family friend said.

When the relationship ended, Mark was down and sad, but he did not fall into depression. He was still working with Gino on the house. He said the break-up 'drew me to following Dad more, building works, simple things'. By April 2001, Mark stopped attending university. It was, he said, a 'big turning point' and the year 'all hell broke loose'.

After Gino and Connie reached a property settlement that year, father and son tried to open another service station. It failed, just like the Big Melon had. Mark and Gino were bitter about the settlement – they felt it favoured Connie. They were also bitter about the business failing. For Gino, this perceived unfairness only reinforced his view that the world was out to get him, and it helped Mark reach a similar conclusion.

Mark, who had never before been in trouble with the law, started to shoplift, and to pilfer from building sites. He rented a surfboard one day and did not return it. Within months, he had gone from a successful engineering student to a petty criminal. Mark did not feel he had been pulled into Gino's orbit. He was closer to his father, but later claimed he never felt pressured to think or act the same way Gino did, nor felt pressured to commit crime. He was no longer speaking to his mother, and had reduced contact with his sister. Given Gino was similarly isolated, it was inevitable that the two would become increasingly in sync. But why was Mark so entranced by the ways of his father?

Mark had been a shy boy, with a strange obsession with numbers that may, had he been at a larger school a decade or so later, resulted in a diagnosis as being on the autism spectrum, according to some who knew him. He was a follower, intelligent but not endowed with the confidence to talk about what he knew. He did not fit in with the loud and imposing men common to North Queensland, who enjoyed rum and rugby, nor with the shady set, who revelled in their indifference to authority. A family friend said that at one point Mark even joined the army, and spent a few months at the nation's largest base, Lavarack Barracks, in Townsville, before he realised he was not cut out for that either.

It is impossible to untangle Mark's reasoning in joining Gino in his madness without thinking about the complex relationships that exist between a son and his father, particularly in the context of Italian migrant families and their unique form of patriarchy. For a long time, it had been understood that the children and grandchildren and even great-grandchildren of Italian migrants who had settled in Ingham would take over the family farm. This was particularly true for boys and men; cane farming was seen as men's work, after all. But this was no longer the norm. By the 1990s, it was becoming more common for the descendants of Ingham's first Italian settlers to move on, travelling south for better opportunities and leaving the farm to someone else.

For those who decided to stay and take over the business, there was the delicate matter of when this would actually happen. There was an unspoken tension in the region between those who felt it a betrayal for the farm to be abandoned and those who believed that chaining offspring to a property from birth was an even greater injustice. Some of the farms were worth millions, and had been built up by migrants who had arrived in North Queensland with not even the shirt on their backs, because it was too bloody hot to wear it. But what was the point of having something valuable you could never sell, or never enjoy?

North Queensland was becoming the home of some of Australia's most disenfranchised people, people who felt that the political party One Nation gave them a voice, such was their desperation about how hard it was to find a job, how worthless their homes were, and how the rest of the country did not care about them. Wrapped up in all this was the conflict between those who left and those who stayed, and those who felt they did not have a choice either way.

A tragic manifestation of this clash between the old world and the new, of how an Italian father treats his son and his inheritance of a cane plantation, and of the malaise of the noughties in the North, was the case of Paul Mallardi. In 2006, he was a forty-year-old married father of three teenage children who felt his parents, Vito, seventy-five, and Maria, sixty-eight, had constantly reneged on selling him their $3 million farm at Mutarnee. He had worked at the farm, just down the Bruce Highway from Bambaroo, since he was seven, and feared his parents would never hand it over to him. So he blew them both away with a shotgun. 'My thoughts kept going around in circles, thinking only of my children and the trust I had placed in my parents, and them not honouring my trust,' he said.

How much of this was whirring in Mark's mind when his father, devastated at his separation, arrived in Townsville? Was there an implicit understanding between them that Gino had nothing to offer Mark but his companionship? Was there an open discussion about how little Ingham had to offer either of them any more? And did the fact that Gino would get no inheritance from his own father, Peter, that was worthy of staying in Ingham or even behaving himself play a part? Did Mark fear what would happen to his father if he rejected him? Or did he just fear him? It could have been nothing more than the power a father has over his son, a power that may appear to wane each day from birth, as the son makes his way in the world, but that in some men, and in some fathers, remains absolute. A power that, when unleashed, makes the son a clone of his father. As Italians say, *tale padre, tale figlio*; like father, like son.

Mark described the crimes the pair committed during this period, when Gino swept into Townsville, as behaviour 'the system sees as stealing'. But he and his father felt entitled to steal because 'the financials were unjust'. He acknowledged the thefts were greedy but said they wanted to achieve something within an unfair system. They were attempting to lead a self-sufficient lifestyle, as Mark called it.

The pair were constantly on the move. They felt the law was restraining them. 'We didn't like the law,' Mark said. A safe place was Peter and Egidia's house in Toobanna, which had a vacant block behind it. They could park in the street nearby and climb the back fence without the police knowing they had been there, which would give them an easier getaway. Gino had thought like this all his life, always scheming and planning escape routes. But for Mark, this was a new way of life, and a seed had been planted in his mind.

Within two years, however, Gino and Mark felt trapped. Gino was already reasonably acquainted with Ingham and Townsville police, and Mark would soon have a similar reputation. Something needed to give. Despite having lived in North Queensland his entire life, Gino sold his remaining property in Ingham and the house near the university in Townsville. He had enough money after his settlement with Connie to buy more property, and he and Mark considered doing so. But eventually they decided on something else. Perhaps Gino's hatred of authority, which he felt had become so insidious it gnawed to his very core, spurred him on to his next move. Or, after the failure of a marriage and three businesses, perhaps he simply came to a realisation that it was time to cut ties with North Queensland. Maybe it was just a mid-life crisis. Regardless of the motivation, on 10 December 2003 Gino bought a yacht.

There is nothing to indicate that, before this point, he was particularly familiar with sailing or had an affinity with the ocean. Ingham is landlocked, and Werribee, while located on Port Phillip Bay, is hardly a sailing mecca. If there was any frolicking in Gino's childhood, it happened in cane fields, not the surf. And while it was a comfortable upbringing, it was not so comfortable that Peter and Egidia Stocco could afford to take their four kids on regular trips to visit the Great Barrier Reef, let alone to rent a yacht once they got there.

For most people of that era and background in Ingham, a holiday involved travelling somewhere cooler in the south for summer after cane cutting finished for the year, or going on shorter trips to beaches that were safe from stingers. It was not the kind of town where people retreated to beach houses on the weekends to go sailing. But it had been a transformative three years for Gino and Mark Stocco. Perhaps they felt so removed from their previous lives that buying a yacht didn't seem unusual.

With their new purchase, they headed south. True to form, they took with them something they had stolen.

Back in the 1990s, Gino and Connie had lived in Toowoomba, north of Brisbane in the Darling Downs. While they were there, they became friendly with another couple who lived across the street from them in Elvery Court. The couple – let's call them Michael and Debbie Parish – were younger than the Stoccos, and had two daughters. Michael was in the army, and was based at the nearby Borneo Barracks.

Gino, whom the couple knew as John, had been working as a builder at the time. He helped roof a pergola and build a shed for the Parishes, and the couples visited each other fairly regularly until the Stoccos left sometime in 2000. By August 2001, the younger couple had also separated. Michael kept living in the house for about four months with his daughters after Debbie moved out.

One afternoon in November, there was a knock on the door. It was Mark and Gino. They said they had come to see their old house and decided to pop in while they were across the road.

Parish found the visit odd. The Stoccos spent at least a couple of hours there, making small talk. There was a difference between being friendly with a neighbour and showing up on their doorstop months after moving out for a cuppa and a chat. And Mark appeared to be making a lot of trips to the bathroom.

Five years later, after tours with the army overseas and moving to Western Australia, Parish would discover why. In 2006, stowed in a yacht more than 1700 kilometres away from Toowoomba, on the Victorian coast, police would find a passport with his name and birthdate on it. But the photo on the passport was of Gino Stocco.

The *Kiwarrak* was a 14-metre-long yacht built in Taree, a small town on the Manning and Dawson rivers halfway between Port Macquarie and Newcastle. The builder was Brian Crouch, who launched the yacht, a Radford 47 Cutter, in April 2001. The name, Kiwarrak, is shared by a small locale and a state reserve, which were near his house. But about two years after building the yacht, Crouch had to sell it. He was battling leukaemia, and could no longer sail. He advertised the *Kiwarrak* for $265 000 online.

On 4 December 2003, two men came to inspect the yacht. The older man introduced himself as Michael Parish. He had also been going by another name, however: Patrick Brodnik. But his real name was Gino Stocco, and he and his son, Mark, were looking for a yacht.

Patrick Brodnik was an ordained Christian pastor from Toongabbie, a suburb in outer Western Sydney. He had met Mark and Gino earlier in 2003, and they lived with him for a week, explaining that they were travelling Christians who had long beards because of their religious beliefs. They spent most of their stay speaking with other Christians. The Stoccos were trying to convince people about an impending apocalypse. They spoke openly to Brodnik about how they would survive the chaos of the new world. Before the apocalypse, they would take land from people. When the world ended, and all people were forced into a survival of the fittest, they would be well placed, because of all their land.

Brodnik thought the beliefs were odd, but harmless, until later, after the Stoccos had left, when he was told by a friend that they had threatened her for refusing to open a post-office box in her name for them. Thinking back, he realised the Stoccos had been angry about other things, too. Gino had frequently railed against Connie, admitting to spying on her and threatening to stop her seeing a lover. And he was also harsh on others, regularly abusing those who frustrated him. Nevertheless, Brodnik thought little of the pair as time passed, until early in 2007 when he had a call from police. As with Parish, documents in his name had been found on a yacht hundreds of kilometres away.

Six days after inspecting the *Kiwarrak*, and negotiating a price of $100 000, the Stoccos took ownership of the yacht at Pittwater, on Sydney's northern beaches. Gino told Crouch he planned to sail to Tasmania and then out of the country. He said he wanted to get 'off the grid' after spending some time in prison.

There was just one problem: the pair did not know how to sail. A friend would say later that Gino told him he paid for some rudimentary sailing lessons, but that he still resorted to using a small outboard engine meant for the dinghy to power the yacht, because he had not mastered the use of a sail. Gino had told him that he sailed out between Sydney Heads using the outboard, holding on to it as they went – a hilarious tale that the friend regularly retold. But Gino also told him he sailed to Venice: an incredible boast that almost certainly did not happen.

What is most likely is that the Stoccos hired someone to teach them to sail. Regardless of where the truth lies, two things are clear: Gino and Mark had little or no sailing experience when they bought the *Kiwarrak*, but both men had an aptitude for quickly mastering practical tasks.

Based on accounts and timelines later given by the Stoccos, police and witnesses, it appears their first journey was to Tasmania. The 1100-kilometre voyage would have been far from simple. It is, of course, the same route taken by the Sydney to Hobart yacht race, and may have occurred at roughly the same time of year: late December. The fleet in 2003 did not experience violent seas, with variable but mostly light winds for the majority of the race, but the journey would still be a handful for first-time sailors. Four yachts did not complete the race that year.

It is more probable that Gino and Mark did not take their maiden voyage until the second half of 2004, or even early in 2005. They had business to take care of on land before taking to the high seas.

Early in 2003, about the same time that the Stoccos were deciding how to spend the financial settlement from Gino and Connie's separation, police in New South Wales were planning a drug raid. About 30 000 cannabis plants worth more than $60 million were being grown at isolated properties in Nimmitabel, Bombala, Braidwood and Dubbo. This was not the work of a few local stoners trying to turn a quid; they were sophisticated plantations, designed to be regularly harvested, and requiring significant manpower to maintain them. It looked like the work of the Calabrian Mafia.

In January, police raided the property in Nimmitabel and found 15 000 plants worth $30 million. Four men who were at the property were arrested, and the crop was destroyed. The next month, police used a helicopter to access the property at Bombala. It was empty, apart from the almost 13 000 plants growing in an irrigated plot of almost 5000 square metres. This haul, they estimated, was also worth about $30 million. Smaller crops were found at the other properties, including about 500 plants at Braidwood. But there were still only four people in custody. Police suspected these men were close to the bottom of the food chain. Who owned the properties and had helped bankroll the infrastructure needed to grow the crops? And who was taking the harvest back to the city for distribution? All roads pointed to Western Sydney.

One of the men arrested had been a butcher in the Liverpool area. His name was Rosario Cimone. Another was his younger brother, Angelo. The others were Salvatore Catalano and Mario Cataldo. All were aged in their fifties – old hands who, most likely, had been middle-men in similar drug operations before. For them, turning over a new leaf meant harvesting another crop.

By April, all four men had been charged. If two of them had decided to walk away at this point, leaving the marijuana harvesting to other green thumbs, they would probably still be alive today. Instead, Mario Cataldo was electrocuted when tinkering with a hydroponic marijuana crop in a shed in Bringelly, in outer Western Sydney, in 2014. He was dead for two days before his family called police, worried that they had not heard from him. His body was found near harvested cannabis plants. The mains electricity had been bypassed in order to power the hydroponic operation. Nobody else was ever charged in relation to the set-up. It was a sudden and lonely death, all for a marijuana crop. Much like the fate that, almost exactly a year later, would befall his old friend Rosario Cimone.

6

Connie Fragapane had been living on and off in Victoria since around 1997, mostly near her family in the Werribee region, west of Melbourne. It had taken about four years of Gino trying to patch up their marriage before he accepted it was really over. By 2003, Connie was in her mid-forties, working at a nearby hospital and living with her de facto partner, Lee, in a simple house in a cul-de-sac. She had a close relationship with her siblings and extended family, most of whom were in some way involved in farming, but who also operated their own businesses, including a local motor inn. Occasionally, the family hosted relatives from Italy.

It was a simpler and more family-orientated life than what she had in Ingham, where she had been a mother by her early twenties, was heavily reliant on Gino's parents, and was condemned by her husband's reputation as a ne'er-do-well with a deep indifference to the law. She had been married to Gino more than half her life, and, despite having separated from him, he still cast a shadow. Gino had not only struggled to accept the separation but had also insisted on tormenting her. And, since 2001, he'd had an accomplice: Mark.

In 2003, after the Stoccos cut permanent ties with North Queensland, but before they bought the *Kiwarrak*, Mark and Gino travelled to Victoria. In April the previous year, Gino had been sentenced in the Townsville District Court for a string of fraud and property offences between 1998 and July 2001, and for breaching a suspended sentence. He was sentenced to two months' prison time, and would also have a suspended sentence of eight months imposed that would not expire for the next two years. This may have been a factor in Gino and Mark deciding to leave Queensland.

It is unclear whether a perceived slight by Connie had motivated this journey, or whether they merely felt liberated by their recent embrace of a nomadic lifestyle. But Connie was about to be subjected to a nine-month campaign of terror.

Between October and December, Connie's family and friends started receiving letters. Their content was vulgar and offensive, describing Connie as an adulterer who had abandoned her husband and children. During this period, her house was also broken into by the Stoccos, who destroyed property before leaving.

In January 2004, the Stoccos were arrested in Wodonga, and charged with stalking, criminal damage and making false documents. They faced the Sunshine Magistrates' Court on 8 January, where Gino received a four-month sentence, suspended for twelve months, and Mark was fined. Indefinite intervention orders preventing the pair from contacting or approaching Connie were granted.

The intervention orders did not work. Connie was convinced that prank calls to her house in early 2004 were made by Mark and Gino, but she was told the pair were on their way back to Queensland.

Less than five months after the Sunshine court appearance, Connie was shopping at Sims Supermarket, on the corner of Shaws and Tarneit roads in Werribee. She had finished her shopping when Mark approached. He hugged her and told her he loved her, saying he wanted the family to be back together and happy again. He was frightfully skinny, bearded and possessing the stench of a vagrant. But he was also her boy – a 24-year-old who seemed to genuinely want and need his mum. He disappeared again after little more than a minute, and Connie was left struggling to make sense of it.

Ten days after the bizarre supermarket encounter, Lee answered the phone at the house he shared with Connie. A person with a strange accent asked for Mr Flat Bean. Lee hung up.

On 25 June, Connie found two A4 pieces of paper stuck to the front of her house. On one piece, in bold type, were the words, 'Connie a mother of two children fucks Lee in this house provided for by her past family.' The other page had seven family photos on it: photos of Gino and Connie with Christina and Mark. The photos were of them as a young family in Ingham, of family pets, of birthday parties, of the kids playing. Of the happy family Mark had told his mother earlier that month at the supermarket that he desperately missed.

Connie soon received a call from her brother, who told her their mother also had pages stuck to her house. They were fixed to her kitchen window, along with a note that read, 'Anna Fragapane is a bitch like your daughter.' Connie's uncle's motor inn was also targeted. Connie's sister-in-law later showed her two letters that her sister and mother, who both lived in Werribee, had received.

About 2.45 pm on the day the notices were posted, the phone rang at Connie and Lee's house. Lee picked up but there was no answer. It rang again. Lee answered, and there was no response. The third time the phone rang, Connie picked up. A voice she knew to be Mark's said, 'We're coming to get you and nothing is going to stop us.'

Connie spoke to Christina, her daughter, a few days later. Christina told her Gino had been asking questions about Connie and Lee. Christina told Connie to move house, and to get a new car. Connie and Lee stayed with a relative for almost a fortnight and, later that year, sold the house, which had been on the market even before Mark and Gino started terrorising them.

There was something not quite right about Thomas Anderson. He had stopped at a panelbeater in Guyra, a town of about 2000 people between Armidale and Glen Innes in the New South Wales Northern Tablelands, in a 1997 white Toyota Corolla with Victorian numberplates, and wanted some work done.

Anderson told the panelbeater he wanted the car repainted metallic blue, as his wife did not like white any more. After he pulled into the shop, he was joined by a younger man, who had been driving a Holden ute with Queensland numberplates. The pair set about swapping the mag wheels on the Corolla for normal rims. They also removed the Corolla's numberplates.

The panelbeater told them the paint job should be finished in a couple of days, and he would let them know when it was ready. After they left, he called Guyra Police. He told them about the encounter, and detailed the car, the numberplate, and the two men: both bearded, an older, shorter bloke and a skinnier younger one, both with dark features. Guyra Police called Victoria Police and told them about Anderson and the Corolla and passed on the numberplate details. Five days later, on 19 July 2004, the men collected the Corolla, and Mark and Gino Stocco started driving south.

Connie started work most days at 6.30 am. It was no different on the morning of 22 July. She finished at the hospital about 3 pm and went straight to her aunt and uncle's house, which was a short drive away on Old Geelong Road, Hoppers Crossing. Relatives from overseas were visiting, and her cousin, Sandra, would also be there, visiting her parents. Sandra had three children under three, including a two-and-a-half-month-old.

About two hours after Connie arrived, the children woke from an afternoon nap. Sandra had to go to the butcher at the shopping centre down the road, and Connie had to go to the supermarket, so they decided to go together; Connie could watch the kids in the car while Sandra went to the butcher – much quicker without the kids in tow – and then Connie could do her shopping. They drove down Old Geelong Road to the shopping centre, Connie leading the way. She parked in the car park in front of the Safeway, and Sandra did a loop of the parking lot before parking her four-wheel drive parallel to the entrance, close to the butcher.

Connie waited on the footpath near a chemist, and when she saw Sandra park, she started walking towards her. They met at the driver's side door. Sandra got out and started to walk around the back of the car, with Connie following. As Sandra reached the footpath, she realised Connie had turned back towards the four-wheel drive. Then she heard her screaming.

A metallic blue Toyota Corolla was double-parked near the four-wheel drive. A man got out of the car and charged towards

Connie, pushing her to the ground with two hands. She landed on her behind near the gutter. The man was grabbing at her handbag, which had been on her right shoulder, while Connie screamed at him not to take it, not to let him take it. He yelled, 'Give me the bag,' and stood over her, pulling at it.

There was no way Connie could stop him, Sandra thought, but she held tight. Sandra then recognised the man: he was Mark Stocco. He had a long beard and hair past his shoulders. His face was barely visible. Mark grabbed the handbag and jumped in the passenger seat of the Toyota, which then sped off. The whole thing had taken no more than 15 seconds.

Connie was hysterical, screaming about the contents of her bag: purse, mobile phone, car keys, garage remote. They called the police from the shopping centre, and when Sandra gave Connie a lift home, they had already arrived. Connie told them later that she had turned to face the Toyota in the car park when she noticed it was following her very slowly. She started screaming when she realised her son and husband were inside.

A Victoria Police warrant was issued for Mark and Gino Stocco the next day.

The pair would be on the run for less than a month. On 20 August, police in Townsville noticed a Nissan Patrol that had been driven by the Stoccos at a local Bob Jane T-Marts. When they spoke to the driver, he presented a passport with the name Michael Parish. He told police he was staying in the Coral Coast caravan park, just north of Townsville, and that they had the wrong bloke. They apologised for bothering him and said he was free to go. But another officer told those who had spoken to the driver that he must be using fake identification: he was definitely their man, Gino Stocco. He was tracked down at another tyre shop and arrested later that day for outstanding offences in Queensland.

Gino spent almost three months in the Townsville Correctional Centre. When he was released, on 11 November, he was slapped with the Victorian warrant containing charges relating to the robbery of Connie, stalking offences, and breaching the intervention order that had been issued earlier in the year. The warrant was still active for Mark, who had not been tracked down, despite his father being in prison.

Gino appeared in the Townsville Magistrates' Court and was remanded to appear in the Melbourne Magistrates' Court four days later. He told Victorian police that the flyers posted on Connie and her family's properties, and mailed to other relatives, were Mark's idea. He said he did not know about the threatening phone call Mark made, when he said 'nothing is going to stop us'. Of the robbery, Gino said it was simply a 'chance meeting' that had gone badly wrong – all they had hoped to do was speak to Connie.

On 15 November, he was sentenced to three months' prison in Victoria, suspended for twelve months, and with four days served, for stalking, breaching an intervention order twice, robbery, failure to answer bail, and shoplifting. A magistrate also ordered that he serve the four-month suspended sentence imposed in January. In December, it was also found he had defaulted on a $1000 fine imposed during the January appearance, and he was sentenced to another eleven days in prison.

7

Much of the year since the purchase of the *Kiwarrak* in December 2003 had been spent terrorising Connie and with Gino subsequently in prison. So what better way to celebrate Gino's release in March 2005 than with a yacht trip?

It is unclear where the yacht had been moored between December 2003 and their first yacht trip: the Stoccos obviously had access to a car, and links to towns across the country, but there is no evidence they were using the boat during this time. It is also unclear where Mark was during Gino's prison stint (he had been the first Stocco to rack up a Victorian conviction, pleading guilty to two driving charges and fined $700 in July 2003 – a fine he still had not paid almost four years later). There is no evidence they had stable accommodation, or even a base; aside from the yacht in New South Wales, Gino had been registered as living since 2001 in Wodonga and Townsville. In 2004, his registered address, according to property records, was the Fragapane family's farm in Duncans Road, Werribee South.

The yacht probably stayed moored near Taree, or Pittwater, where the sale was brokered. It is unlikely it was moored anywhere in Victoria. It may also have been moored in Coffs Harbour. That is within striking distance of Guyra, and would loosely fit a timeline Mark gave about the expedition after his arrest in 2015.

Mark said that after hiring a skipper to teach them how to sail, they firstly went to Tasmania, and then to Coffs Harbour. While they were there, they worked on local farms. The Stoccos spent most of their two years on the *Kiwarrak* sailing between Coffs Harbour, Tasmania and as far west as Adelaide. Mark said the trip taught him about sailing and fishing, but also construction, and that it was a 'very adventurous' and 'very exciting' time, and that he 'enjoyed it immensely'.

When police later tried to piece together exactly where they had travelled, they were left frustrated by the low standard of the navigational equipment in the *Kiwarrak*, which only kept records lasting a few days, and the lack of regulatory requirements regarding the mooring of a boat. Police were staggered that there was no need for the registration details of a boat to be logged if it was moored in a particular harbour. Combined with the fact that, as Mark admitted, they had tried to avoid mooring fees, and eventually stopped paying them, it was impossible to determine exactly where the Stoccos had been at a given time. It also meant it became far more difficult to link them to any unsolved crimes.

Mark said that after the first trip, down to Tasmania and then back to Coffs Harbour, they returned to Tasmania and sailed up the Tamar River. The Tamar links Launceston, about 60 kilometres inland, with the sea. After their trip to Tasmania, according to Mark, they sailed for Adelaide, where they arrived in April or May 2005, and stayed until November.

There is no record of what they did during this time in South Australia. Police speculated that they may have worked at vineyards in the area, but could not confirm this. There have also been discussions of them having spent time on Kangaroo Island. There is no record of them falling foul of the law during this time, and South Australia Police say that the pair are not suspected of having committed any offences in the state. So how did they pass seven months there? It is possible they found one solid job or property – as they had done in the past – and stayed there. Either they left without stealing or destroying anything, or their crimes were not linked to them because whoever they were working for did not know their identities. One thing is certain: it would be one of the longest periods for a decade in which neither man was suspected of committing a crime.

By March 2006, they were back on the Tamar. A fellow sailor who spoke to the Stoccos, and, months later, would report the exchange to police, said that they told him they were doing the same trip he was: sailing from Tasmania to Adelaide. The sailor was moored on the Tamar, about 15 kilometres from Beauty Point, which is surrounded by vineyards, cattle and sheep farms, and is at a wide point in the river, which allowed the creation of a deep-water port. He met the Stoccos at the yacht club in the town.

The sailor said that Mark and Gino – with Gino doing most of the talking – told him they had been in the town a couple of weeks and were looking for building work. They had been able to use the bathroom at the yacht club, as they had been given keys. The man described Gino as angry and bitter, with a 'huge chip on his shoulder' about his separation. He said Mark told him he had dropped out of university to follow Gino around and appeared 'brainwashed' by his father's anger.

A few days later, the sailor bumped into the pair at Devonport, a town on Bass Strait, about 60 kilometres west of the mouth of the Tamar. When he sailed to King Island, about 250 kilometres north-west, he again saw them. But that was the last he saw of them: after he left for Adelaide, he never again saw the Stoccos or the *Kiwarrak*.

There are several time periods, usually not longer than a few months, in which it has been difficult to track exactly where the Stoccos were. The winter and spring of 2006 is one such period. Less than a year after this, police called ports across Tasmania, Victoria, New South Wales and South Australia, asking them to check for records of the pair or the *Kiwarrak*, but they had no luck. They had similar results when asking local police at coastal stations from Byron Bay all the way to Kangaroo Island whether there had been any thefts reported that could be linked to the Stoccos.

It is unclear exactly when the sailor saw them on King Island, as he only told police that his first encounter with them in Beauty Point had occurred in March. It is likely they took days, if not weeks, to get from Beauty Point to King Island. If they had stayed for any length of time there, on an island with a permanent population of less than 2000, it is highly likely that someone would have remembered them when police asked less than a year later. Perhaps they sailed north, given it was autumn, and planned to spend the cooler months along the coast of New South Wales, or perhaps even back in Queensland. There is no record of them ever spending time further north than Cairns, or in Western Australia.

There remains the distinct possibility that they travelled to Italy, with friends and family both saying they believed the pair had been there. But they were vague as to whether this occurred during 2006 or later. Regardless of where they had been, in November 2006 Gino did what he had done regularly for the past thirty years: he travelled to Victoria for summer.

On 10 December 2006, the *Kiwarrak* sailed past the red dome of the Port Fairy lighthouse and glided down the Moyne River, leaving Bass Strait behind her.

The lighthouse is perched on Griffiths Island, a shearwater colony. Also known as mutton birds, because of their fatty meat used for food and oil, the shearwaters had recently returned to their burrows after spending the second half of November at sea. Shearwaters return to colonies near Port Fairy after a 15 000-kilometre journey from their wintering grounds in the far-north Pacific Ocean, near the Aleutian Islands. After mating, they depart again to spend a fortnight at sea but then return to lay their eggs. In mid-April, they make for the north Pacific, flying past the west coast of New Zealand, and then along the east coast of Japan and Siberia, before crossing the Bering Sea. The young are left in Port Fairy, but two or three weeks later they also head north. Half never make it. Those that do and then come back to Port Fairy create a new burrow; it will be the same home they return to, year after year.

On the starboard side of the *Kiwarrak*, the opposite side to the shearwater colony, a white strip of beach stretches around the bay. Norfolk pines line the river, dark green spires piercing the sky. The previous day, a Saturday, it had been oppressively warm for the first fortnight of a Victorian summer, with the temperature nudging 40 degrees. But as the Stoccos eased down the river and moored on the western side, it was in the low twenties. A day so calm it was hard to imagine this stretch of coastline was renowned for seas of terrible violence. Dozens of ships and hundreds of lives were lost as the area was settled in the mid-eighteenth century. It is now known as the Shipwreck Coast.

Port Fairy, settled in 1843, was a whaling, sealing and farming town. The Norfolk pines were planted as windbreaks in the 1860s when settlers realised stripping the land of all vegetation had made it fairly unbearable when the prevailing south-westerlies whipped up. Tourism sustains the town now, and, on Boxing Day, little more than two weeks after the Stoccos dropped anchor, an annual pilgrimage would start, mostly from Melbourne, for the summer.

Moored on the same side of the river as the *Kiwarrak* was the remains of the local fishing fleet, about half a dozen boats, mainly chasing gummy shark, crayfish or squid. Some of that shark ended up in the fryer at a fish 'n' chip shop only metres away from the wharf. But most of the catch went in the opposite direction to the tourists, back along the Princes Highway to Melbourne.

A normal tourist to Port Fairy would probably spend their days moving idly between the beach and the town's cafes, before perhaps extending themselves with a spot of golf or a stroll around Griffiths Island, and heading to a pub or restaurant at night. But who knows what Mark and Gino planned to do there. Perhaps they fished from the deck of the *Kiwarrak*, or at another spot along the river. Maybe they looked at maps, planning their next trip. Maybe they made phone calls about possible work. Almost certainly, they stole something from somewhere.

Soon after they arrived, the harbourmaster told Mark and Gino that mooring fees were $15 a day. He also said that the yacht club, on the opposite side of the river, had in the past provided shower access to sailors, but that they would have to enquire at the club if they wanted to use the facilities there. Evidently the Stoccos did, because the pair were given a key to the showers. To get to the club, they walked along the wharf, crossed the river on a footbridge and turned back the way they'd come, but on the opposite bank. They stayed for a week.

The night before the Stoccos left Port Fairy, the yacht club hosted a Christmas party. It was not as warm as the previous Saturday, but there were still people on the lawn in front of the club, looking out over the river and towards the *Kiwarrak* on the opposite bank.

That night or early the next morning, Mark and Gino left their boat, walked along the wharf to the footbridge, crossed the river and made for the yacht club. Once they got closer, they slipped blue socks over their hands. One of them smashed a small corner from a sliding window, unfastened the lock and went inside. The padlock to the cool room was forced open, probably with a butter knife found later at the scene, but the alcohol inside was untouched.

The Stoccos had come for the bar profits, which were swelled from the party the previous night. They left $200 in coins but took the $500 float from a till and $700 from a cash tin. They also took some tea towels, removed the socks from their hands and left them at the club, and then went back to the *Kiwarrak*. Mark and Gino sailed out of Port Fairy about 6.30 pm the next day.

On the afternoon of 18 December – two days after the Christmas party, and the day after the Stoccos left town – the burglary at the yacht club was discovered. It was an uncommon crime in Port Fairy: there were, for example, only nine burglaries in the entire postcode during 2015. And it was even rarer for a community organisation or club to be targeted. So it did not take long for authorities to look at who had been moored on the wharf in the past few days.

The harbourmaster only had one boat during that time with shady occupants, who, as it turned out, had also failed to pay the $105 in mooring fees they owed: the two bearded blokes on the *Kiwarrak*.

8

At a quarry on the western edge of Port Fairy, bluestone is dug up. Much of it is cut and polished and ends up in Melbourne, featured in high-end buildings such as the Crown Casino, paving Collins Street or lining a road edge in East Melbourne. The stone also looks like it could have been used to assemble Sergeant Mick Wolfe, a local copper, whose head is like a big, unpolished hunk of bluestone, sitting atop an even larger hunk. His hands are boulders. But he is not a copper who only got accepted at the Academy because police recruiters realised his noggin had the potential to break down doors. He simply wanted to do as the Victoria Police motto stated: uphold the right.

Wolfe was one of the busiest coppers in Victoria, despite the town's minuscule crime rate. At one stage, he was the sergeant, a local government councillor and the president of the Port Fairy football–netball club, the Seagulls. It meant, theoretically, that if the footy club was set alight, he would have been the one reporting it, investigating it and handing out funding for a rebuild.

When the harbourmaster told Wolfe about the *Kiwarrak*, he knew it could be the key to the yacht club break-in. But he had little to go on, other than a loose description of the men and their boat, the boat's name and its registration, which, he soon learnt, had expired. Wolfe set about calling places within a day or two's sailing from Port Fairy: east along the Great Ocean Road, west to Portland, and South Australia, and south to Tasmania. He gave the investigation the name Operation Kiwarrak.

Eventually, the harbourmaster in Apollo Bay confirmed that a boat by that name, which had two similarly described men on board, was moored there. Wolfe assembled a team of police from several local stations and planned to raid the *Kiwarrak* on the afternoon of 20 December. A warrant was granted, and the police mustered in Apollo Bay, about 180 kilometres east of Port Fairy. The yacht was raided about 3.30 pm. The two men on board did not resist, and they told police they were Michael and Mark Parish.

The yacht was a mess. 'There was shit everywhere,' Wolfe told me. Food was scattered around the cabin. Clothes were piled on a bunk bed. 'There was no pride in it.' In the cabin of the yacht, police found a wicker sewing basket that contained a plastic bag holding $3600 in $100 notes. There was also a Tupperware container on a shelf nearby containing a trove of documents. These included a passport, birth certificate, Australian Army certificate, and telecommunications and cabling certificates in the name of Michael Parish, and a certificate of ordination, Australian Taxation Office refund notice, and exam results in the name of Patrick Brodnik. There was also an expired Victorian driver's licence in Gino's name with the address of the Fragapane family farm in Duncans Road, Werribee South.

Wolfe and the other officers were perplexed. They had no idea who the men were, what they were doing and how long they had been doing it for, but they got the impression that they were religious. Because of their beards, the police thought they were Muslim. Wolfe and the other police soon called them the pirates. Wolfe was sure the pair and the boat were suspicious. So much so that he requested that police squads from Melbourne, who handled dogs trained to detect drugs and explosives, come to inspect the *Kiwarrak*.

Wolfe and his colleagues split the pair up and interviewed them. Both soon admitted to the identity theft and gave their real names. But Wolfe still wasn't sure who he was dealing with, or why they had been found with a significant amount of cash and false documents on board an unregistered yacht. 'Something wasn't right. We were just thinking, "What are these pricks up to?"' They wouldn't give any information about where they had been, or where they intended to go. The navigational equipment on the boat, he soon found, was no help either.

The Stoccos did not really want to engage with Wolfe at all. They were not rude about it, like a lot of crooks can be, Wolfe later said. But it was clear they did not want to be there, and were not going to make it easy for police. 'Some [crooks] are "Get fucked, no comment,"' Wolfe said. 'They were just selective. They would think about everything. They were assessing us as much as we were assessing them.' It made for an interesting mental battle, Wolfe says, describing the interviews. 'Their heads are spinning about what we know about them, and our heads are spinning about whether we even had the right names for them, what they had been up to, where they had been. It was one of the most engaging interviews because you're just looking for anything that will tell you more about them. But mostly they were just interested in each other, and how the other was doing.'

There was one thing the Stoccos were happy to talk about: they had nothing to do with robbing the yacht club. They admitted not paying mooring fees, saying that nobody had ever seemed to really mind before, but were steadfast in denying the burglary. They were so vehement that some of the officers started to question whether they had the right men. Gino claimed that the yacht club and the harbourmaster were in cahoots. He said the harbourmaster knew police would not chase down $105 in lost mooring fees, so he concocted the break-in with the help of the yacht club, knowing a more serious crime would demand investigation.

This conspiracy theory revealed either the extent of Gino's belief that the world was out to get him or the shamelessness of his dishonesty. Whichever is true, it says something about how emphatic his denials were that even the police began to entertain this fanciful scenario. But there were a number of things linking the Stoccos to the crime, not least of all the tea towels, which were also found on the *Kiwarrak*, the unexplained cash, and the timeline of their arrival and departure in Port Fairy.

Gino described using the false identification as an opportunity, and was found to have also been using the aliases Brian Crouch, Mario Stocco and John Anda. Mark showed no remorse and was deceitful to police, perhaps because he was still subject to the warrant issued after robbing Connie.

Police made contact with Brodnik and Parish. Brodnik was overseas, but he responded by email telling the police everything he knew about the Stoccos, and saying they had probably stolen the documents when they had stayed with him. For Parish, the phone call from police helped clear up a mystery that had dogged him for more than three years: who had stolen his identity?

Soon after Parish had moved to Perth in 2003, Western Australia Police had served him with documents relating to a traffic infringement for which he had failed to show in court in Townsville. He had been on a military operation at the time of the infringement so was able to prove it wasn't him. Around the same time, Westpac contacted him to let him know there had been two unsuccessful credit card applications made in his name. He was told one of the cards was to be collected by a Debbie Parish, so he suspected his ex-wife and her new partner of fraud and informed the bank, who said not much could be done. Early the next year, a debt collector had contacted him about a Commonwealth Bank credit card that had reached its $10 000 limit. The bank accepted it wasn't him after his protestations.

Parish got a credit report and found there had been other credit applications made in his name. He told Western Australia Police, who informed him that the New South Wales police had a warrant out for him. Western Australia Police said it was likely there was another Michael Parish with the same date of birth who was causing the issue, and that he should closely watch his credit file to make sure no more applications were made. He would soon find out other information: a credit card had been sent to an address in Townsville, where he had never lived. An application was made for a phone from Vodafone in Mulgrave, east of Melbourne, in April 2003 – he had been serving in Iraq at the time. An application had also been made for an American Express term account, and a $4000 Bank of Queensland continuing credit account.

This new information helped put the pieces together. Parish suspected that Mark had stolen his identity documents during the Stoccos' bizarre visit to his house in Toowoomba. When Mark made those repeated trips to the bathroom, he was actually rifling through a filing cabinet in the bedroom nearby. Police later established that Parish had probably been defrauded of more than $50 000 in total by Mark and Gino.

The Stoccos faced court in Warrnambool on 2 February 2007. They would continue to claim for years afterwards that they had not robbed the yacht club, with Gino adamant that $105 in unpaid mooring fees was the only reason for their predicament. They claimed they only pleaded guilty to the robbery on their lawyer's advice, as she said it would mean avoiding time on remand that would likely have eclipsed their sentence. Gino pleaded guilty to ten charges, including burglary, theft, obtaining financial advantage by deception, making false passport statements and criminal damage. He was sentenced to four months and one week in jail and was fined $2400. Mark faced three charges, including robbing his mother in a Melbourne car park the year after she had reached a settlement with Gino. He was sentenced to two months' jail and fined $600.

Warrnambool magistrate Michael Stone said, 'It is quite apparent that you were just drifting around the coast of Australia taking advantage of whoever you could take advantage of.' Both the Stoccos had served forty-five days in custody, so Mark would be released before the end of the month, and Gino in April.

Almost a decade after Operation Kiwarrak, Wolfe is having a coffee with me on the intersection of Bank and Sackville streets, the busiest corner in Port Fairy. Most people who pass him say hello. Some thank him for various things, usually council related, such as cutting down an overhanging tree. 'I don't bang my head when I go by now,' an elderly bloke says.

The occasional interjections don't distract Wolfe from the subject at hand: the two crooks he nicked who, as coppers say, 'went on to bigger and better things'. He says there is no doubt they were capable sailors, given they, at the very least, negotiated probably the most treacherous part of the Shipwreck Coast, from Port Fairy to Apollo Bay, let alone completed two trips to Tasmania. He also says he has no doubt that they committed other offences in the area, dating back to November 2006.

There were six burglaries around Portland between 26 November and 7 December – just before the Stoccos arrived in Port Fairy. Wolfe has evidence the Stoccos were moored in Portland at that time. Strange items were taken: towels and face washers from one house, chocolate ice cream and a chocolate hamper from another, and mobile and cordless phones from other properties. The burglars had, in at least one instance, used socks to cover their hands, which were then found at the scene.

Wolfe has also thought about the nomadic lifestyle the Stoccos committed to. 'They just didn't want to conform with society and its necessary rules,' he says. 'They didn't want to comply with an employer. They wanted to have their own lifestyle, and didn't want to be controlled, and so to do that they had to commit crime [and] if anyone challenged or questioned that, it threatened them. And I understand that. You do get people who buy 50 acres of land in the bush and grow their own vegies and things because they want to live their own lives.' Wolfe is in no doubt that Gino was the driver of this mindset, but does not think that means Mark was unintelligent, or a sheep, looking for someone to follow. He was just utterly committed to his father. 'I reckon Gino could have talked Mark, if he was a Collingwood supporter, into barracking for Carlton.'

It is not just Wolfe who still thinks about that bust in Apollo Bay. A decade later, Mark was asked about it, and he spoke of how much he had enjoyed his time on the *Kiwarrak*. He again denied the yacht club burglary, and lamented their capture – not just because they had to serve time, or because it was the end of their magical run on the yacht. It was because, as he saw it, the storming of the *Kiwarrak* that December afternoon in Apollo Bay set off a 'spiral of events'.

9

When Mark was released from prison that February, 2007, it was one of the only times he had been freed from the influence of his father in more than six years. He was a 27-year-old man who had never had a full-time job, had only had one girlfriend and had no friends or contact with family other than Gino. It could have been the chance he needed to find clear air, to assess what his life had become, and to do what he could to change it. He could have found a job and settled somewhere else, leaving his father to fend for himself. Or he could have tried to find work that would keep both of them out of trouble once Gino was released, such as on a farm or labouring somewhere. Perhaps his father would settle down if he was released and saw his son had made an effort to go straight. But Mark Stocco's first stint behind bars did not shake him from the path Gino had led him down. He waited dutifully for his father to be released two months later, and for Gino to decide what to do next.

On 17 January of that year, the first major newspaper article about the pair had been published. The *Sunday Herald Sun* described the pair as pirates and outlined their arrest in Apollo Bay. The story, which was also published online by other News Limited sites, featured interviews with Wolfe, Gino's brother Eddie, and an 'estranged family member'. The family member said that Gino Stocco had once misused elder brother Mario's driving licence, and called Gino 'the black sheep of the family'. Eddie said he had not seen Gino in several years. 'He split up with his wife and he went haywire after that,' he said. The article showed that even if Mark and Gino had seen the error of their ways inside, they were unlikely to be welcomed back with open arms in Ingham.

The *Kiwarrak* had stayed in Apollo Bay since their arrest, continuing to rack up mooring fees with the harbourmaster. Gino realised in custody that the yacht was a financial drain, so it was taken to Melbourne, stripped of everything of value, and then sold for $25 000, despite it being worth about ten times that, he said. It is likely the pair still had access to some other money left from Gino's settlement with Connie. Soon after their release, they used the money from the yacht, and some of this settlement, to buy a LandCruiser ute.

The pair planned to do what Gino had done most of his life: work on farms in North Queensland in winter and in southern New South Wales or Victoria during summer. Gino said he and his son had become 'very disillusioned with the whole system'. 'Mark and I decided we weren't going to pay for anything any more . . . we just went off radar.' There was plenty of work about, and many on the land were desperate; Australia was in the grips of the millennium drought, which devastated most of the south-east, the Murray–Darling basin and as far north as Central Queensland from 2001 to 2009. Many regions experienced the lowest rainfall on record. But in parts of North Queensland, and particularly in north-west Australia, rainfall was above average. The drought was influenced by an El Niño weather phenomenon but also climate change, as the Bureau of Meteorology would conclude.

Mark and Gino looked for work in the classifieds of *The Land*, *Stock and Land*, *Country Life*, the Organic Farming directory, and on Gumtree, the online classifieds site. The idea, Mark would explain later, was that the pair 'just kept going, kept working, kept moving around'. They planned to become itinerant workers, part of an enormous and somewhat shadowy workforce that many Australian industries relied on. There were jobs picking fruit and vegetables, or harvesting grains and other food, all across the country, during every time of year; from grapes in Margaret River between January and March, to hops near Devonport from March to April, to cotton picking in northern New South Wales until June, and then harvesting sugar cane in North Queensland until the end of the year.

Then there were those on farms who needed people for only a few weeks at busy times of year, such as grain harvesting, lambing or shearing. Many farms, particularly in isolated parts of the country, had unused cottages or houses on them, which they would offer to workers as free lodging and then pay them a small amount for work, or not pay at all. One farmer said a lot of those who hired itinerant workers were lazy; they would rather pay someone $15 or $20 an hour for work they could not be bothered to do for free. But he also acknowledged there were certain periods of high demand that could not necessarily be planned for, and there were few people available for hire as farmhands in certain parts of rural Australia on a casual basis; if you lived in central or western New South

Wales, or further north in the tablelands, or even further north still, around St George, you were not doing so to work as a casual farmhand. And if you were a kid in school looking for work, you probably had your own family farm to help out on, and were not in a position to take up with a neighbour during a crunch period.

The work on these farms was mostly cash based, largely unregulated, and filled with everyone from backpackers to crooks like Mark and Gino who had no other legitimate prospects. Men like the Stoccos were, in many ways, similar to swagmen who wandered Australia from the mid-1800s until the mid-1900s. Swagmen were particularly prominent during economic depressions, as they moved from farm to farm seeking work; hard-doers with their lives strapped on their backs. They were such a feature of the first hundred-odd years since European settlement that they were immortalised in the song 'Waltzing Matilda'.

They may have had the same air of scoundrel, and limited prospects, as swagmen, but Mark and Gino were in a ute, not on foot. And it was not only jolly jumbucks they planned to shove into their tuckerbags.

Mark and Gino Stocco travelled up and down the eastern states for the next eight years, working at more than twenty properties. At some, they stayed for only a few weeks; at others, they stayed for eighteen months. They went north of Cairns, and as far south as Portland in south-west Victoria, past the Great Ocean Road, and Apollo Bay, the town where they had been arrested on the *Kiwarrak*.

One of the first properties they worked on was in Glenburn, in the hinterland of the Yarra Ranges north-east of Melbourne. This part of the state was ravaged more than any by the Black Saturday bushfires in 2009, which killed 173 people. Huge sections of the region, particularly near Flowerdale, Marysville and Murrundindi, were blackened wasteland when the Stoccos arrived. The only thing darker than the obliterated tree trunks was the minds of those who had been there, hearing the screams of those who died, or uncovering their corpses in levelled houses, which smouldered while the neighbouring property stood untouched. The capriciousness of the fire stayed with them, the injustice of it all. Why did it not take them all, rather than leaving some to ponder why they had survived?

Rick and Sandra Zipsin felt almost guilty at their luck, with their farm surviving, other than a few burnt paddocks and destroyed fences, and no harm done to them or their two young children. They had long hosted workers at their cattle farm in Glenburn and enjoyed the company of those who contacted them via a listing on the online Organic Farmers directory. People who travelled around working on farms were inevitably interesting. They had stories of the other properties they had been on and of life on the road; often, they were people on working holidays, keen for advice on where to head next. After the fires, the Zipsins needed a hand replacing fences that had been destroyed. They were grateful when a bloke called John, who was travelling with his nephew Mark, made contact.

The Zipsins couldn't fault the Stoccos' work. And, unlike others who had stayed, carrying their lives around with them, the pair were unfailingly neat, almost obsessively so. Gino would repeatedly sweep a small patch in front of the flat he was staying in. The pair regularly ate with the Zipsins and their young children in the house, and told the Zipsins that they treated them better than their own family. They stayed only a few weeks, but promised to drop back in. The Zipsins said they would be welcome.

Mark and Gino Stocco seemed to get used to their new life on the road. They were covering thousands of kilometres, sometimes seemingly driving days without stopping. Perhaps one slept while the other drove, or they listened to music or to the ABC to stay alert. Perhaps they picked up hitchhikers or simply talked to each other. Perhaps they just sat silently, eastern Australia a smudge of greens and browns beside them, and a wide stripe of grey in front of them, cutting straight through the horizon.

They helped to stretch the relatively meagre income they received from working as farmhands by shoplifting and committing other crude thefts. One of their schemes was drilling into anything that collected coins, particularly the washing machines and dryers in caravan parks or laundromats, or parking meters, to claim the loot inside. They had been wily enough to stay out of the grips of police for much of the first three years since their release, but they were not being pursued particularly vigorously. Nevertheless, there were warrants for their arrest in at least Queensland and New South Wales, albeit for fairly minor offending. In their home state, they were wanted for stealing in 2009 at Mundubbera (the home of the Big Mandarin) north-west of Brisbane.

Having outstanding warrants could be troublesome when you spent so much time on the road, as all it would take was a police officer running your details through the system for your travels to be over. But the Stoccos tried to avoid that likelihood by driving at night and keeping a low profile during the day. It worked fairly well for them, until October 2010, when they were camping at a caravan park in Dunedoo, a tiny town near Dubbo in central New South Wales.

One afternoon, a middle-aged couple from Victoria pulled into a site next to Mark and Gino at the park. The Stoccos had a Jayco Expander caravan, and a LandCruiser parked nearby. They were both almost new. As the couple set up camp, Mark and Gino came wandering over and introduced themselves. They started to chat. Mark asked where they were from. 'Port Fairy,' the woman answered.

Mark seemed to brace a bit, and then responded, 'Port Fairy. I'm familiar with Port Fairy.' Gino, by this stage, had walked into the couple's van and was checking it out. The husband asked him to give them a minute, as they had just pulled up, but they would have a beer with them later.

What Mark and Gino did not know is that the man knew exactly who they were, because he had been there in Apollo Bay, almost four years earlier, when the pair were arrested on the *Kiwarrak*. He was an off-duty police officer. The Stoccos did not recognise him, because he'd had a beard the last time they had seen him. The officer was gesturing to his wife, when the Stoccos weren't looking, to make herself scarce. As soon as it appeared they had spent enough time setting up the van, he intended to drive into town and make some calls to work out what the pair were up to. He was bordering on incredulous that, within three and a half years of being released, the Stoccos had managed to flog a four-wheel drive and caravan worth almost $100 000. Even if they weren't stolen, he was fairly sure that neither of them had a driver's licence.

Sure enough, he found there were outstanding warrants for the pair in multiple states, so he went to Dunedoo Police. But they could not do anything; the local cop was gravely ill, suffering from cancer. He was referred to Mudgee Police, about 100 kilometres south, who said they would send a car. In the meantime, they told him, he should go back to the caravan park and wait.

He pulled up in the caravan park, and saw that Mark and Gino had hooked their van onto the LandCruiser. They were looking right at him. The Stoccos hauled in an extension cord, grabbed their dripping washing from an outside clothes line, and spun the wheels as they flew out of the caravan park. The officer would never see them again.

It was not, however, the last time the Stoccos would be associated with Dunedoo. The officer was dumbfounded – and not a little bit angry – that the Stoccos had escaped. 'What are the chances, that of only a few coppers in the country who even know what they look like, I should pull in next to them at a camping ground in the middle of New South Wales?' he said. 'Infinitesimal. Absolutely infinitesimal.' He reckons that they probably twigged who he was after he left. But he also thinks there is another possibility: that the Stoccos were monitoring police radio with a scanner, and, when the call was put through for a unit to attend the Dunedoo caravan park because there had been a sighting of the Stoccos, they bolted. He'd already known the Stoccos were lucky, given they survived two round-trips across Bass Strait in a yacht with little experience and shonky navigational equipment. Now, he thought they were blessed.

After their good fortune in Dunedoo, Mark and Gino probably headed south; it was almost summer. But, within four months, they were back in Queensland. In February 2011, while working at Drillham, a town in the Darling Downs, they were suspected of an offence of 'steal as servant', a somewhat medieval-sounding charge meaning to steal from an employer. Five months later, they were suspected of stealing from Garbutt, a suburb of Townsville.

About the same time – and possibly even when they committed the theft – the Stoccos were working on a sugarcane plantation in Euramo. The town has two shops – a combined post office, supermarket and newsagent, and a pub – and is just west of the Bruce Highway, about 90 kilometres north of Ingham, on the Tully River. The Stoccos were employed during planting season, which runs from May to September. They lived in their caravan, which they were able to park on cleared land at the plantation where they worked. There was little manual labour involved, but the days were long, as both men worked on machines harvesting and planting.

The pair may have committed the odd petty crime, particularly theft, but, for the most part, their first four years after being released from prison had been without incident. They had not yet committed any acts of violent retaliation against those who employed them, the crimes that Gino called vengeful acts. They appeared to be building a solid network of properties that could host the pair, ideally at short notice. They had boltholes at farms across the country, not necessarily for taking refuge should authorities be hunting them but more as an insurance policy should they run out of work. One of these was the Zipsins' place, down at Glenburn, but there were others in Victoria, and in New South Wales and Queensland, where they had also taken caretaker or farmhand jobs, such as the position at Euramo.

They also kept travelling to Ingham. Gino would still tell anyone who asked, and plenty who didn't, how wronged he had been by his unfaithful wife, but he no longer seemed fixated on ruining her life. It had been more than a decade since she had left, after all. And Mark was all he needed. He knew that now.

10

In hindsight, there were two distinct four-year periods after the Stoccos were released from prison in 2007: the years until October 2011, when they committed few offences, largely stayed on the good side of the owners of properties where they were employed, and travelled around Australia almost without incident; and the four years from 2011 to 2015, a period of such profoundly disturbing behaviour that the Stoccos became some of the most notorious criminals in the country.

Mark and Gino Stocco had spent the first four years since their release from prison doing exactly what they had planned: living outside the system. It had strengthened their minds against those who were blissfully ignorant of the worthlessness of their existence. How were people satisfied with their toil on a farm or in an office, coming home to the same house, sleeping in the same bed, and then doing the same thing the next day and the next, until they were too old, and all they could do was sit and think about how they should have spent the past sixty years more wisely. That was, of course, if their brains had not turned to mush by that point, and they were even capable of thought. They were slaves to the system, surrounded by a cage they could not even see.

Mark and Gino could see it, and they avoided being stuck inside it by cunning and will and graft. But if the cage had seemed little more than a dull grey box from 2007 until 2011, it started to sharpen in the Stoccos' minds now. They were only suspected of three crimes in Queensland from 2007 to 2011; but they were suspected of ten in 2012 alone. These were committed across most of Queensland, but essentially in two clusters: around Atherton, north of Ingham; and at Yuleba, Taroom and Glenmorgan, in Queensland's south-west.

It appears that at the same time the Stoccos believed more than ever that their way was right, and that they were overcoming the system. The system conspired against them; and it forced them to strike back.

The event that, many years later, could be seen as a marker for their impending violence appeared insignificant at first. It came not in the form of a crime they committed but merely through a phone call, with not even a voice raised. There is little doubt, though, that it fed into what would become the Stoccos' prevailing mindset: that the system was closing in on them.

'Plenty' was an apt name for Peter Farley's farm. The 315-hectare property near Canowindra, in the central west of New South Wales, backed on to the Lachlan River. It was irrigated, and it had cattle and sheep yards, machinery and hay sheds, and grain silos. Not only was it an enviable farm but it also had a fine five-bedroomed homestead, complete with a pool and a tennis court, and a separate three-bedroomed workers' cottage. It was a mixed farm, on which Farley grew grain and ran sheep. Often, he hosted caretakers in the cottage, which was to the south of the homestead. Between the cottage and the homestead was a driveway, looping from the front gate around the homestead, the machinery and hay sheds, and the diesel pump and back out again.

In November 2011, Farley placed an advertisement in *The Land* newspaper for a caretaker. A bloke called John made contact with him a few weeks later. 'I had been hoping for an older couple, some grey nomads or something in their sixties or seventies, but this bloke said he was travelling around with his nephew. I thought that was a bit odd,' Farley said. But, nevertheless, John was keen, and he could start almost straight away. He was so keen, in fact, that he suggested he and his nephew come on Christmas Eve to check the place out. Farley said that wasn't necessary, and again he felt that his new caretaker was a bit strange to suggest such a thing, but he told them he would see them after Christmas. They said they would spend the holiday in Victoria and then drive north to meet him after that.

When they arrived, Farley was taken by two things almost immediately: how had two blokes who were working for free just so they could stay on his farm come into possession of an almost new LandCruiser ute? And why weren't John, a bloke of a similar age to himself, who was obviously capable and fit, and his nephew, who was younger and just as able, working full-time somewhere to earn a living, rather than caretaking for nothing on farms? He found both questions difficult to answer, and, when combined with his misgivings about the pair before they even arrived, he started to feel somewhat uneasy.

Farley had been hiring people to work for him for more than thirty years. He knew what to look for, and what he wanted. He knew when workers were putting in, and when they were slacking. And he knew when eccentricities were merely that, and not something to be worried about. Eventually he put his new caretakers into that category: 'oddbods', he reckoned, but probably harmless.

John and Mark dutifully got to work on the farm. They were fanatical about keeping it tidy, not only looking after machinery but also tending to trees on the property and mowing the lawns. Farley asked them to build a dog kennel; the result was far better than he expected. 'In a sense they were too good,' Farley said. 'It was embarrassing in a way. I said to them, "You're too good for the job, I should be paying you," but they didn't really say anything to that.'

The more they worked, the more amazed he was that they were willing to do so much for free, and the more unusual he realised the pair were. He thought the way John spoke to Mark bordered on belittling. 'If he was my uncle,' he thought, 'I wouldn't put up with being spoken to like that.' It was as if he was speaking to his son. 'He was bossy to him. Mark was under John's spell a bit.' The pair did not socialise. They never seemed to be laughing or joking. They worked so seriously it was as if they were in a trance. 'They didn't seem to be on the planet. They were just completely within themselves. You couldn't have a conversation with them, and, now I think about it, it was because they were completely tuned out from the rest of the world, and did not know what to say.'

Farley could not reconcile why the pair seemed so willing to work at an exceptional standard, and with an irrepressible energy, for nothing, and yet, when asked to do something a different way, or merely questioned about an element of their work, they were stand-offish. 'They always seemed to know better, even though they were doing more than you expected them to. It was like they wanted to be their own bosses.'

It was about 20 March 2012 when the pair told Farley they had to leave the property for a few days. They assured him they would not be gone long. He thought they may have been going to complete another job, or collect pay for some work they had done before they arrived at Plenty. It was not ideal; after all, Farley had hired John and Mark to be caretakers, allowing him to leave the farm when he needed, not the other way around. He could not really force them to stay, but was frustrated when John would not give him his mobile number, instead insisting he would let Farley know when they were coming back. They left some things in the cottage and took off.

Gino and Mark Stocco headed back to Queensland. In March and April, they committed the fraud, burglary and stealing offences around Atherton and Yuleba, before committing another fraud further south in Taroom.

After three weeks, Farley had not heard from the Stoccos. He decided that, when he did, he would tell them they had to take off. He had to line up another caretaker, and the longer he went without hearing from them, the harder it got. Eventually, John called. 'I said to him, "The time you were here you were good, you did a great job, but I need someone who can be here."' John seemed to understand, and certainly did not sound cross with Farley. He said they would come back to collect their belongings when they could.

The pair started an almost 1100-kilometre journey south. They probably took the Newell Highway, crossing into New South Wales at Goondiwindi and passing through Moree before returning to Plenty, only a few days after they had spoken to Farley.

Gino and Mark returned to the cottage at 3 am. They took their stuff but left all the lights on, the air conditioner running and the radio on full. They smashed a waterpipe nearby and took the keys from Farley's ute, which was parked in the drive. They filled their LandCruiser up with diesel from Farley's tank and left.

Farley did not know it, and the Stoccos didn't either, but they would return to Plenty, one winter's night more than two years later.

They headed back north. By May, they were working on the same cane plantation property at Euramo. But they did not have the caravan this time, so the plantation owner asked a neighbour whether he would rent the Stoccos his farmhouse. The neighbour, from a family so well known there's a road in the town named after them, said he wouldn't rent the place to two blokes he didn't know, but he would be happy to rent it to the plantation owner. And so the Stoccos moved in, and got to work on their second straight sugarcane planting season. That year, they also helped out on the neighbour's 245-hectare plantation.

The neighbour, whom we will call Carlo, soon found that his new workers were more than up to the task. He knew them as Mark and John, and did not know they were related. 'They were just model workers. Not only would they get the work done in the plantation, but they would keep the yard spotless. They would come around to our garden and do the weeding and mow the lawns. They said they didn't want to get paid, they just wanted to keep busy.'

He thought it strange that the men were so obsessed with tidiness and keen to be put to work even after a day of toiling in the plantation, but he certainly wasn't complaining. His wife, however, was less enamoured. 'I just didn't like them from the word go,' she said. She was convinced that volunteering to do gardening was a clever way of casing the house.

The Stoccos were not only hard workers but also capable ones. Gino usually commanded the harvester, and Mark the tipper bin. They worked in tandem with the property owners and their families, harvesting and planting. Both tasks would have to be finished by December, when the rains started and plantation owners had to do little more than watch their crops soak it up, and destroy the occasional weed.

Wet season was particularly wet around Euramo. Tully, the town kilometres north, is considered one of the wettest places in Australia, with an average annual rainfall of more than four metres. And there were, of course, occasional showers during the rest of the year, bringing to a halt the work on the fields, to ensure the machinery did not cut up the ground.

On one rainy day during the Stoccos' visit, Gino proclaimed he was going to fix the air conditioner in the harvester. It had been playing up for a few weeks, and he found it uncomfortable working in a stuffy cabin. He said he would go to a property in Burdekin, about 300 kilometres south, to get what he needed to fix it. Sure enough, he returned with the parts he needed, and he had the air conditioner up and running again by the next day. 'They were very capable,' Carlo told me later. 'Why they ever went off the rails, I can't understand it. Or, why they were already off the rails, I suppose I should say.'

Carlo and his neighbour, the man who had employed the Stoccos for the past two years, would soon find out a bit more about the pair they had been working the plantation with. And, as it happened, the reckoning would take place on another rainy day.

Mark and Gino had been working as normal in the cane fields one afternoon when it started to rain. They had been transporting cane from one field to another, but, as the rain fell, the property owner instructed them to pack up for the day. He told Mark and Gino to bring the machinery back to the shed. But, instead of using the track that bordered the plantation and wound back to the shed, Gino inexplicably drove the harvester straight across the wet field – risking exactly the sort of destruction to the ground that the property owner had been trying to avoid. He was incredulous.

'He said to Gino, "Well that was stupid, why did you bloody do that for?"' Carlo remembered. They got in an argument, and Mark and Gino were told to leave. The Stoccos packed up their LandCruiser, stealing some tools from the property owner, locked Carlo's farmhouse and took the key, and then left Euramo. It was mid-July 2012.

Carlo got a locksmith around to get into his farmhouse and replace the locks. Inside, he was perplexed to find the Stoccos had removed every cupboard door. They had also taken a few things of middling value, but the place was otherwise untouched.

On the evening of 21 August, Carlo pulled his 2010 dual-cab Nissan Navara into the driveway of his Euramo home. He usually parked in the shed, but it was more work to get inside the house from there when his back was crook, as it was that day. So he left the maroon ute in the drive, with the keys in the ignition and the doors unlocked, and hobbled to his front door. The next morning, the ute was gone. When he spoke to the police, they said it was probably a joyrider, and that he should check around the property. The ute would turn up soon, they said. But it didn't. Carlo became embroiled in a battle with the insurance company, who baulked at replacing a stolen ute that had been parked outside with the keys in it.

About a month later, he got a phone call from the police. He was asked to come and have a look at a few photos. It was to do with the ute. He looked down at the two blokes he knew as Mark and John, whom he had last seen leaving in a huff that July. 'I said, yeah, I know them.' He was told the two men were Mark and Gino Stocco, notorious thieves who had stolen everything from identities to guns going back more than a decade. And now they had stolen his ute. Carlo had not entertained the thought, up until that point, that the disgruntled workers could have been responsible, but the police were sure it was them. The Stoccos had been pulled up at a random breath-testing site in South East Queensland a few days earlier. But before an officer could reach the ute, they'd fled. Police gave chase, until Carlo's Nissan Navara reached speeds that were deemed too dangerous, and they let them go.

It was another escalation of their behaviour in 2012 – the year in which the Stoccos seemed to be losing control, and the veneer of trustworthiness and respectability they had used to get work across the country began to slip.

The crime that first marked the Stoccos' shift towards serious violence was not even linked to them until more than two years later. In one way, that was a blessing; had the victims known it was the Stoccos, they would have feared them coming back.

Rick and Sandra Zipsin, the couple who lived in the Yarra Ranges with their two children, were one of the first families to hire the Stoccos on their farm. And they had meant it when the pair finished a successful stint in 2009 and they had told them to come back whenever they wanted. They did not, however, envisage that would mean the men would come back every few months for the next two years. There was less work than there had been when they were hired, and the Zipsins were fairly strapped for cash and did not want to feel obligated to either pay them for work or feed them. They were, in fact, so tight with money they had decided against insuring their farm. A fire levy, introduced to mitigate the huge cost of Black Saturday, had been added to their policy, making it almost impossible for them to afford. So, when the Stoccos showed up again, one day in 2012, Rick told them to give them some space and maybe come back in a year or so.

Instead, that October, Mark and Gino crept on to the Zipsins' property and set their sheds alight. They came back again three months later, in January 2013, and lit another late-night blaze, this time targeting machinery. The damage bill was about $900 000. Almost four years later, the Zipsins – given they were uninsured – had not been able to remove the twisted wreckage of their sheds and equipment, let alone replace them.

In between the two attacks on the Zipsins, and to end a rather prolific 2012, the Stoccos were suspected of wilful damage and stealing at Golden Grove, a large farm in Glenmorgan, in the Darling Downs in Queensland. It was December, so they soon left Queensland, as they did every summer. Peter Stocco would later say that 2012 was the last time he ever saw his son and grandson.

It was clear that the Stoccos' mindset had changed. And if 2012 signalled the start of the transformation from petty crooks to violent and feared fugitives, then by the end of the following year it was complete. It seemed Mark and Gino were tired of merely getting by, keeping a low profile, not giving anyone an excuse to move them on from a farm, or to blacklist them with other farmers, or, worse still, to report them to police. They felt betrayed as they were increasingly booted from farms even when they believed they had done nothing wrong. And, like a shoot of sugar cane drinking the January rains in North Queensland, that feeling grew quickly. It became seared in their minds, exactly as Connie's supposed betrayal of Gino had. Slights that could not be forgotten, or forgiven.

Who knows why they turned. There was no spark, as there had been, in Gino's mind, when Connie left. But perhaps it had been a slow burn, rather than an explosion. Maybe, ever since they were released from prison, a flame had caught a trail of fuel. And it kept burning along the line, sucking up all before it but making little sound, causing little smoke. Until it snaked into a shed packed with more fuel than it would ever need and destroyed it all.

11

About fifteen months after Gino walked out of prison, was reunited with Mark and began the quest to live outside the system, a new detective started at Ingham. Dave Barron would have made a great country ruckman; he's tall and thin, but with broad shoulders and hands so big it looks as if he could clench an entire Sherrin in his fist. As it turns out, he can't even watch Australian footy, let alone play it. He finds it boring and too hard to get his head around; he prefers league.

It was August 2008 when Barron walked into Ingham's low-slung brick police station. Across the station driveway, only a handball away, was the courthouse. The double-storey brick building was adorned with four palm trees, two either side of the front entrance, and a plaque declaring it was opened in 1955 by Premier Vince Gair. Gair was one of the first in a long line of controversial Queensland politicians; he was expelled from the Labor Party two years after he opened Ingham court for being too close to the trade union movement, and was later involved in a scandal known as The Night of the Long Prawns.

Barron soon realised that the colourful antics of Queensland politicians from Gair to Bjelke-Petersen to Hanson to Joyce to Christensen were barely worthy of a raised eyebrow in a town like Ingham. It was a decidedly weird place. He found there was an obsession with money – having it, rather than spending it – and an antipathy towards authority. He found it difficult to gauge the influence the town's deep ties to Italian migrants had on this culture, but could make some guesses based on his early interactions with local crooks. 'You could pinch a 45-year-old fella here,' Barron remembers, 'who is not married or anything. And the next day his mother or his father or both would be in here, saying, "He a good boy, he a good boy."'

There was the local boy, the son of Italian migrants, who had done well enough to buy probably the stateliest property in Ingham, a huge modern home built by a local television presenter. But instead of living in the house, he stayed in a mouldy fibro shack with his parents. There was the natural death of an old Italian man, living in squalor with his wife, who was inside naked on a couch, and their adult son. Despite the state of the house, there were a brand new tractor and harvester – hundreds of thousands of dollars' worth of machinery – sparkling in the shed. And then there was the cash police would find everywhere when searching houses, stuffed in mattresses and curtain rods.

There was something else about Ingham that Barron soon realised would make his new posting tough. The phone didn't ring. Locals just didn't report anything. And it was not only a matter of failing to report the bloke across the road who hit the drink and then hit his woman; it was looking away from serious organised crime.

Barron learnt quickly that Ingham had deep ties to Griffith, the beating heart of the Calabrian Mafia in Australia. While farms down in the New South Wales Riverina had been used to grow marijuana for decades, the focus from police was fairly onerous; the 1977 death of anti-mafia campaigner Donald Mackay, among other things, had seen to that. But North Queensland had conditions even better than the Riverina for growing dope. And there was more land, and fewer police. Sure, there was the problem of moving it: it was harder to get to a major market for your gear when it was coming from Ingham, rather than Griffith. But if you've got more to move, then it's a problem worth having.

Barron, perhaps naively, thought he could count on those sitting in crop dusters, who flew low, and for hours, over the cane fields, to sling him the odd tip about a dope plantation hiding among the cane. But his phone never rang. What's more, if he did happen to bust a dealer or a grower, he could count on one thing: the phone would start ringing then. 'No one here gives you much. But you can bust someone with a heap of drugs and someone else will come up and they'll say, "He's a drug dealer." And I'll say, "Yeah, thanks for that. Would have been good to know that eight years ago."'

If Barron needed any evidence of how deep the ties between Ingham and Griffith went, he found it in plastic buckets in the bush bordering a sugarcane plantation not far from where the Stoccos had once had the Big Melon. Barron and other police had been searching the property for days, convinced the owners had something to hide. They were just about to leave when an officer noticed the buckets, partially buried. There was an 'A' and a 'C' written on top of them; as it happened, these were the first initials of the brothers who ran the property, and who also had close links to Griffith. The police opened them up and found $680 000 cash wrapped in plastic.

Despite the challenges of working in Ingham, Barron enjoyed pitting himself against the locals, the most humorous or cunning of whom he liked to call 'specials'. When he talks of the specials, his near constant smile pulls even tighter, shining through his silver-flecked brown stubble, and he slowly shakes his head.

Barron knew he could have it far worse than working in Ingham. Earlier in his career, he had been on Palm Island, an Indigenous settlement directly east from Ingham, over the cane and then the beach and then the Coral Sea. He left in early November 2004, two weeks before Cameron Doomadgee, a local man known as Mulrunji, died in custody. Chris Hurley, a hulking local copper Barron worked with, was charged with killing him. The island erupted into violence, as the locals sought retribution, and the police hunkered down, prisoners in their own station. Hurley was acquitted, but, when Barron started in Ingham, almost four years after the death, its impacts were still reverberating around Australia. Barron was grateful to have got out when he did. Even if, eventually, he had ended up in Ingham.

Barron was not long into his new posting when he was told to keep an eye out for a couple of former locals who were often still seen in the region: Gino and Mark Stocco. He looked them up and saw the rap sheets, Gino's far longer than Mark's, littered with petty offences stretching back almost three decades. He could see the crimes escalating from 2001 onwards, and that they had been in and out of prison. He read about the attack on Connie and the yacht trip. He saw that, since April 2007, they had both been out of jail.

While they were not wanted for any unsolved crimes in his patch, Barron was wary. Most of the businesses in town, and quite a few locals, his colleagues told him, suspected the pair had stolen something from them at some point. There was some certainty that the father and son were swinging back up to Ingham fairly regularly to visit their family. Who knows what else they got up to while they were here, Barron thought. If it was something illegal, he vowed to slot them. 'They were from here, so I took some ownership in getting them,' he says.

There was not much to go on. He did not even really know what they looked like. One day, a colleague told them he was adamant he had seen Gino Stocco in a local supermarket. Barron spent days trawling CCTV. He tracked the man all the way out of Ingham, along highways, to an airport, where he boarded a flight to New Zealand. They were also on to him when he got back; it was not Gino Stocco.

There was, however, starting to be more information lobbing on to the Queensland Police system about the pair. They were back to their old tricks: wanted for offences north of Ingham, and way down south, around the Darling Downs. And then, in 2012, things really took off: there was the farmer who had his Navara pinched at Euramo, and the other one who got hit down at Glenmorgan.

Barron kept studying the old photos they had of them, trying to commit the faces to memory. He knew they must float in and out through Ingham, like the steam that belched from stacks at the sugarcane mills. He just hoped they would be easier than steam to catch.

*

In a house in Bambaroo, not far from where the Big Melon once adorned the roadside, live a couple who have known Gino since he was a young man, and Mark his whole life. They are cagey, like a lot of other people in Ingham, when it comes to speaking about the Stoccos. It is out of a respect for Connie, and those who are still close with her around the region, and the possibility that they will bump into Gino's younger brother, Eddie, or his wife, who works in a cafe near the supermarket. There's also the fact that Peter, and Egidia especially, were regarded by most in Ingham as good parents, who did not deserve the attention their wayward second son brought upon them. But mostly it's because – as Dave Barron, the new copper in town, found – people in Ingham like to stick to their own business. Or, at the very least, be seen to do so.

There is, however, another reason locals don't want to talk. They cannot completely let go of the fear that Mark and Gino could return to Ingham one day.

The couple from Bambaroo, whom we will call Tony and Julie, had a fairly typical neighbourly relationship with the Stoccos before Gino and Connie split. After that point, visits from Gino and Mark became fairly sporadic. But they were always memorable. They gave Julie an insight into why Connie had to leave, and made Tony realise the hatred many in Ingham felt for Gino. Had Dave Barron knocked on the couple's door during that fitful first few years on the job, wondering where the Stoccos were, they would have played coy. But eventually they would speak to the local detective, and ask for his help.

Mostly, the Stoccos' visits were about little other than a drink and a chat, and the chance for some food and maybe a bed. Having people like Tony and Julie to rely on, even near Ingham, where the Stoccos had family, was important; they were ostracised largely from Eddie since the attacks on Connie, and, while Peter was sympathetic, it was best to stay at arm's length when they were back in their home town. And so the pair would arrive unannounced at Tony and Julie's.

Sometimes, Gino would have with him an expensive bottle of wine. 'He would say, "Why steal the $6 one when you can steal the $80 one?"' Tony says during an interview at his house. 'Sometimes he would have cheese he would steal too.' There was nothing Gino had not, at some point, stolen, or tried to steal – most nights, Tony believed, Gino would go and steal diesel from a pump on a farm somewhere. And he was renowned for heading inside while a party raged in the yard to flog some things from the hosts. But there were three utterly audacious nicks that, even in Gino's extensive back catalogue, really stood out to Tony.

One day, Gino was sitting in the yard at Tony and Julie's, staring at the back of his ute. In the tray was a portable fridge-freezer. He turned to Mark and said, 'Our fridge is a bit fucked I reckon, that Waeco. Mark, we'll go down and see if we can get another one.' The pair got up, and Gino said with a smirk to Tony and Julie, 'We're going shopping.' The Stoccos drove to the local Anaconda camping store. Gino walked in, clutching a piece of paper. He hoped it would look like a receipt. He put a new Engel fridge, which can sell for as much as $2000, into a trolley, and made for the exit. When he noticed the front cashier was busy serving, he wheeled it straight past her and out to the car park, where Mark was waiting with the ute. He unloaded it into the tray, and then kicked the trolley away and drove off. Gino told all this to Tony when he returned to the house later that afternoon.

On another occasion, at an IGA supermarket in Garbutt, an off-duty police officer spotted Mark stuffing a packet of biscuits down the front of his pants. He took off after them, and Mark and Gino bolted. They got away and changed the numberplates of the ute, eventually winding up back at Tony and Julie's. But the police knew who they were dealing with, and Gino's mobile phone soon rang. 'I just heard him say, "I don't talk to coppers. Get fucked,"' Tony says. 'And he took the battery out and changed the phone over.'

The final theft, so outrageous it cast a shadow over the rest, was Gino's way of getting new wheels for his ute. He booked in at a local tyre centre for a full set of wheels fitted with top of the range tyres, and organised to pick the ute up later. He knew the tyre company figured that they were safe to fit the wheels before people paid because they would have to come and pick up their vehicle. Gino reckoned he could give them the slip by using his spare key to take the ute when they weren't looking. And so he did, slipping into the tyre centre and driving the ute away, seemingly with them none the wiser. But the dealer – perhaps well aware of who their customer was – had taken down the registration. When someone spotted the ute later that day, parked just outside town with four sparkling wheels fitted, they called the tyre shop. A posse showed up to the property where the Stoccos had parked, tyre jacks in hand. Some men might have taken the jacks to Gino, but they simply took the wheels off and left the ute sitting on its axles.

Tony describes Gino as a kleptomaniac, but there appears to be little he stole that he did not have some use for. He and Mark, for example, once arrived at Tony and Julie's on stolen bikes. But even if they were used for only that trip, there was still some use for them.

The constant stealing may have been Gino's most memorable trait, but there were others. He hated the cold, and would often be overly dressed against it, or complaining about it. On those trips south to Victoria in the summer, he left before the hint of an autumn chill arrived. He spoke to Tony and Julie regularly about the 'system'. He and Mark appeared to share everything, and only be apart when one went to the toilet. Gino would constantly be trying to sell them things they didn't need, like a new microwave, which he had stolen from somewhere. He always carried his knapsack, where he kept what little cash the pair had. It was never out of his sight. And the pair always hoovered up whatever food they were offered; once, when Tony gave Gino a bag of tomatoes, he ate them all in front of him.

Julie says she felt that Gino had a special talent for demeaning women. He left her in no doubt that he felt she was inferior to him, despite the irrefutable facts that he was a widely hated petty thief, who had been abandoned by the only woman he ever loved, and who had few friends other than Tony and Julie, and his son. He would do it subtly, with comments that may have seemed innocent if taken in isolation. Like when she baked a cake, and he would simply stroll up behind her quietly and ask, 'Coffee going with that?' 'You would be in the kitchen with him, and you could just understand how Connie must have felt,' Julie says.

Such was the depth of Gino's hatred for Connie, and obsession with the separation, that the couple often found themselves trying to talk sense into him. 'I told him once, "When it's over, it's over,"' Tony says. But nothing got through. And, given the grip Gino had over Mark, Tony and Julie came to a troubling conclusion sometime after the Stoccos' final visit: that Mark and Gino would be capable of murdering Connie. 'It's a wonder they didn't kill her,' Tony says.

Julie and Tony once lived in a house surrounded by a sugarcane plantation south of Bambaroo, at Crystal Creek. Next door to the main house was a simpler structure, little more than a shed, made of sheet iron. For electricity, an extension cord had to be threaded from a window of the main property. In 2013, when Mark and Gino showed up, the couple told them they could stay there. For all the Stoccos' faults – most of them Gino's – Julie and Tony still pitied them. They felt truly sorry for Mark, the strange man-child being pushed around by his father, who seemed incapable of independent thought. They ignored those in town who were wondering why they were giving a hand to the two bearded scoundrels, whom some had taken to calling the bin Ladens.

And the Stoccos obviously trusted them: they confided in them about the estrangement from the family, including an incident at Christina's house a few years earlier. They had visited the youngest Stocco unannounced, but she had welcomed them inside. Her husband, Gino told Julie and Tony, was less accommodating. He was furious when he found them in his home. The son-in-law, with a body honed from his years in the army, overturned the table they were sitting at and ordered them to leave, snapping that, even if they needed help, 'they're not our kids'.

Gino and Mark settled into Tony and Julie's spare building, and had regular catch-ups with them over drinks in the backyard. They appeared to be finding some work nearby; another local said that, around this time, he hired Mark and Gino to build a back deck for him at his house in Bambaroo. But, as was their way, the Stoccos eventually got too comfortable at Crystal Creek. Tony noticed that they were making their own improvements to the simple shack they were living in, installing plumbing and electrical plugs, and asking him to pay for it. This, of course, was not part of the deal.

He warned them first, but when the home improvements continued he asked them to leave. They did not appear terribly upset, but they did leave some of their stuff behind; 'their', of course, denoting possession, rather than ownership. But even though they had not left in a rage, Tony was wary. He knew Gino's temper. And he knew he had given him a reason to be angry.

12

If, for whatever reason, you should find yourself contemplating the archetypal Queensland farmer, the shape of his head and the colour of his skin, and the lines on his face and the clothes he wears, and the way that he speaks and what he says, you would probably imagine someone quite similar to Doug Redding. He owns a cattle station that, for the Darling Downs, is considered small. It is about 20 kilometres outside Cecil Plains, a blip of a town roughly an hour west of Toowoomba.

Redding was in the midst of a personal crisis, which he would prefer not to disclose to me, and approaching sixty when he decided he needed a caretaker for his farm. He placed an advertisement, and had a few applicants. But one bloke was particularly persistent. His name was John, and he told Redding he was a retired builder. Redding conceded, and they agreed John would start in April 2013, along with another man, Mark.

The pair would be on the property by themselves, as Redding

planned to work away, at a nearby mine. He was slightly uneasy about the prospect of them being alone on his property, and the feeling was not quelled once he met them. They spoke as if on the edge of insanity, Redding felt. They had bizarre conspiracy theories, about everything from the corruption of government and police to rugby league referees and the South Sydney Rabbitohs. But their work was good, and there appeared little they could not do; they were not the sort of caretakers he expected regular calls from asking how to fix something, or how to deal with a particular problem. He had some concerns with how they were looking after his workshop, but, along with the strange behaviour of the pair, he felt he had to ignore them, given he was in somewhat of a bind. He really needed help, and, given they were already there, it made little sense to move them on. Redding would be back on his days off to check up on the farm, but the day-to-day operation of moving and feeding cattle, keeping up water to them, and ensuring fences and other parts of the farm were properly maintained would fall to the caretakers.

Mark and Gino Stocco soon realised that the situation they found themselves in at Redding's farm was as close as it got to ideal. They had the run of the place. And they had notice when Redding would be back to check on things. It meant they could do as they pleased for days at a time, and then return before Redding did to maintain the impression everything was running smoothly. It also gave them perfect cover to go on night-time raids at other properties in the area, stealing what they could under cover of darkness and then going back to the farm. Nobody would suspect them, because nobody knew they were even there.

It was not just theft that they could commit when night fell, before returning to their new lair. They were also free to commit 'vengeful acts'. And so, in late June, a couple of months after arriving in Cecil Plains, they started plotting a trip north. It was almost 1400 kilometres to Crystal Creek – a sizeable journey for most people, but barely a day's work for the Stoccos. Mark and Gino could pass the time discussing all the things they would do once they got there.

Tony had noticed some stuff going missing since he had sent the Stoccos away from Crystal Creek. He would go looking for a pump, for example, and realise it was not there. He suspected it was them, but was not too bothered. They may have even taken it before they left. He wondered whether they had deliberately left things behind so that they had an excuse if he ever caught them hanging about. More likely, he figured, was that the Stoccos, knowing that Tony and Julie were boozers, and were up until 11 pm or midnight most nights, polishing off a couple of bottles of wine, would wait until the early hours. Then they would park on the road and wander in, roaming around the property, looking for things to steal.

The pump was almost certainly one of the items bouncing around in the Stoccos' ute somewhere. Where that was, however, was almost impossible to predict. Tony had never known where the Stoccos were, even when they were on speaking terms. Now, they could be camping in the field behind him, for all he knew. 'You just never knew where the fuck they were,' Tony says.

On 30 June 2013, hours after Tony let his wine-soaked head hit the pillow, Mark and Gino slunk down his driveway. They each had a Stanley knife, a glint in their eye and damage on their mind. Tony woke to loud bangs from outside. It was his tyres being punctured. He ran outside, but it was too late: the tyres on his Hilux, a Subaru and a boat trailer had been punctured. The windscreen of the Hilux was also smashed. He cursed loudly into the black, but nobody heard it. Mark and Gino were already on their way back to Cecil Plains. Tony called the police.

A couple of days later, a lanky detective knocked his huge fist against the front door. It was Dave Barron. Before too long, Barron realised that Tony was a bit 'of an old larrikin'. But he believed him when he said he thought the Stoccos were responsible for the damage.

For the first time, Barron had a crime linked to Mark and Gino to investigate for himself. He knew the pair were capable of lashing out, and believed Tony's explanation for why they targeted him. He was also investigating, although he did not know it, one of the first cases where Mark and Gino Stocco had methodically destroyed property owned by someone they felt had wronged them. Dozens more tyres would be slashed. Millions of dollars more in property would be damaged. Barron was inspecting the early maniacal strokes in a pattern that would stretch for almost 3000 kilometres and leave people in three states paralysed with fear that the wraiths responsible could return as soon as they closed their eyes.

While this pattern would not become clear for many months, Tony had told Barron a few things he did not already know about Mark and Gino. They were valuable drops in a fairly dry well. But it was not enough to steer him towards where they could be.

Cecil Plains was proving fertile ground for the Stoccos. On occasion, as during their trip north to Crystal Creek, they had ventured well away from the Darling Downs. But usually they stayed nearby, using their relative anonymity and the assurance of a place to hide to hit neighbouring farms and pilfer from local businesses. Mostly, it was painless. People in the bush took little precautions to safeguard against theft, and business owners, should they even bother reporting what was stolen from them, would contact local police who were usually a fair drive away and too overworked to proactively hunt a two-bit crook. Or two two-bit crooks, as the case may be.

There was, however, one 'shopping' experience that had been a troublingly close call. On 14 June 2013, during a trip to St George, Gino had to beat up a local copper to save Mark from being arrested. They'd had to flee across the border to New South Wales, and only snuck back over the border when they were sure the coast was clear. What a shock those coppers would get – let alone the big bastard Gino had belted – if they knew the blokes they were after were only three hours down the road; practically next door in outback Queensland distances.

As far as Doug Redding was concerned, everything was going smoothly. By September, the caretakers had been there for almost six months. The cattle were being kept well, the property had not fallen into disrepair, and John and Mark, while weird, certainly seemed to be holding up their end. Redding knew the older man was headstrong, and that his conspiratorial ramblings were not the only thing that showed how set he was in his ways. He also had firm opinions about how to run the property and, often, appeared unwilling to bend.

And so it was when, in September that year, the men had a dispute about pool chemicals. Redding did not think John needed to buy them. But the caretaker was so adamant that it took some stern words from Redding to set him straight. Redding thought that was the end of the matter. Until he returned to the cattle farm on 8 October and found that the world he lived in had been kicked irretrievably from its axis.

Redding knew something was wrong even before he reached the farmhouse. Cattle of his were wandering on surrounding roads. He found fences had been cut. And the cattle appeared in poor health. Their troughs, he discovered, had been destroyed. He went to his shed and found a drill had been taken to the tyres of almost every piece of machinery he owned. There were three guns missing from his gun safe. Other tools and equipment, including a generator, were gone.

Redding went to the house and was glad to see it had been spared. But there was something missing from here, too. The caretakers had ripped pages from a notebook that contained information about them, including their car registration. Redding's troubles, which had forced him to put on the caretakers in the first place, now appeared insurmountable. 'The good in people, they saw that as an opportunity to take advantage,' Redding says. 'That's the lowest of the low.'

Mark and Gino Stocco had done well out of Doug Redding. It had been a fairly restful six months, given the usual trials of life on the road. They had still driven a lot of kilometres, but it was far less hassle when you knew you had somewhere to return to, with food and a bed. Redding had forced their hand, the pair reckoned, when he got pushy with the pool chemicals. No matter: they had taught him a lesson, and they were able to load up on some things to trade, including the guns, and make for another property.

However, it had been a misstep making an enemy of Redding. He may have looked a typical Queensland farmer, but he was far tougher than most: as he would prove over the next two years.

About a month after leaving Cecil Plains, the Stoccos parked outside a familiar driveway: the one that led to Tony and Julie's place, in Crystal Creek. Tony was woken the same way he had been five months earlier. It was about 4 am when he heard the banging. The Subaru was parked in the garage, so it had been spared, but the tyres he had just replaced on his boat trailer, the tyres on the Hilux, and the tyres on another car that a friend had parked there were all punctured.

More troublingly, he found a full box of matches near his front gate a couple of days later. Tony thought the Stoccos planned to set the cars alight but either backed out or were spooked. All up, twenty-one tyres had been destroyed, and the damage bill was almost $4500. 'There's that many people in this town who have helped [Gino] and have done him a favour and he's fucked them over time after time,' Tony says. 'I have known some cunts in my life but they are the worst cunts I've ever known.'

When Barron was told about the second moonlight raid at Crystal Creek, it reinforced what he was already feeling: the Stoccos were toying with him. He couldn't get close to them, had no idea where they were and could barely even find anyone to talk to about them. He would find out later that only hours after the Stoccos were in Crystal Creek, they had damaged and stolen property at another small farming community, Silky Oak, and at Mareeba, which was more than 300 kilometres north.

Eventually, Barron thought paying a visit to Peter Stocco, down in Toobanna, could be worthwhile. He knew Peter was still paying for Gino's utc registration. And the Stoccos had to stay somewhere when they were in the region, and they had run out of friends to rely on. If they were camping in the open, he reckoned that by now they were so despised that even someone in Ingham would report them to police. Or they could take matters into their own hands, which was perhaps what the Stoccos most feared about holing up in the bush, so close to people they had wronged.

One way or another, they were relying on Peter. Egidia had moved into Bluehaven Lodge, an aged care facility in Ingham, by this point. Barron had heard that the Stoccos might be sneaking in on occasion to visit their dementia-stricken mother and grandmother. There was little he could do about these visits, save telling the staff to keep him in the loop. But maybe putting the blowtorch on Peter would be a good idea.

Barron pulled off the Bruce Highway into the service road where the house that Gino built stood. He parked, walked from the roadside across the front yard and up the front steps, across the patio tiles that Gino had laid, and knocked on the door. Peter answered, wearing a white shirt tucked into white pants and grey vinyl zip-up shoes. Barron introduced himself. It did not take long for him to realise it was a waste of time. 'He was just an old shyster. He was plainly lying.'

But Barron was relentless, and decided to play a long game. He vowed to keep stopping in on Peter whenever he could, which was fairly regularly, given his house was south of Toobanna, meaning he had to drive past Peter's to get to work each day. 'The garage door was always down. I knew [the Stoccos] were staying there on and off. But I just couldn't get the cheeky bastards.'

After several months, he realised that his regular trips to Peter's would not yield anything, unless Mark and Gino slipped up. 'I eventually took a hatred towards the old man, because he was just so dishonest.'

Barron heard from other police that the pair had been answering classified advertisements to be farmhands, so he considered setting a trap. He would place an ad in *Country Life*, or another publication, and hope to lure the Stoccos that way. But police never placed the ad – yet another example of the Stoccos' crimes being considered troubling but not serious enough to justify a more thorough investigation. Gnawing at Barron was the knowledge that somewhere, given the Stoccos had stolen so much property, was an 'Aladdin's cave'. But he couldn't find that either. He even found it difficult to track down Connie, who he hoped would give him more information about her son and estranged husband. Anything would be better than what he had.

Barron had felt he was closer than ever to catching Mark and Gino when he first visited Tony's in Crystal Creek, but now the trail had run cold. 'You just couldn't get a start on them,' he says. 'Not one single scrap of anything.'

The day after striking at Tony and Julie's, and at Silky Oak and Mareeba, the Stoccos found themselves back on the Darling Downs – more than sixteen hours' drive south. But they were not there to pay another visit to Redding. Instead, they were stopping in at the farm where Gino's little sister, Maryann, lived. Maryann Bender and her husband, Greg, owned a cotton farm near Chinchilla, about 120 kilometres north from Redding's property, where they lived with their two children. It was an 810-hectare property called Burradoo, where they farmed mostly cotton but also other crops, including chickpeas. Maryann had married into one of the most prominent families in the area: the Benders were so well known that locals said there was 'a Bender on every fence post'.

Less than two years after Mark and Gino visited, the Benders would reach a measure of national prominence. In October 2015,

George Bender – the uncle of Maryann's husband, Greg – committed suicide, under the weight of a near decade-long fight against the coal seam gas industry. The Benders had farmed in the region for five generations, since their ancestors arrived from Germany in the early 1900s.

Maryann was close to her other siblings, and their partners, but wanted nothing to do with Gino. She had even stayed in contact with Connie, mostly through social media. While Mario had settled down in Werribee South, where the Stoccos had spent summers, and Eddie was still in Ingham, Maryann had moved to her husband's country. But she still made regular trips north, to see her parents. She particularly wanted to make sure her father was okay, since Egidia had moved to the nursing home.

Maryann finds it difficult to understand why her brother became so evil. The only thing she is sure of is that it had nothing to do with their upbringing. She will not hear anything otherwise; her thick Queensland accent becomes broader, more forceful, should you merely suggest it. 'Why does any criminal become a criminal? I have no reflection on why he started doing what he was doing,' she tells me. 'But we don't believe he's become anything that he's become because of anything to do with us.'

You could 'flip around in your head ten times' trying to work out the descent of Gino and Mark Stocco, she says. The best explanation that Maryann can think of comes when she compares their acts to those of a local man caught duffing cattle. She could not work out why the man had done it, but she then concluded that he merely tried it once, got away with it and then could not help himself: he had to do it again. People take opportunities, is her logic. And if the opportunity keeps presenting itself, certain people will keep taking. And taking. It implies gluttony, of there never being enough, but that is not quite accurate. It is simply taking for taking's sake. 'Sometimes it just takes one sidestep that just becomes something you don't know. He was just like a kid going into a lolly store who takes something and gets away with it and so doesn't know where to stop.'

Gino and Mark stopped at Burradoo about five times between 2007 and 2012, says Maryann, but she did not see them on their 2013 visit or after. 'He knew where to find me, and he knew where to find my mum and dad, and that was it. He'd stop by for a shower and a feed really. There are a lot of gypsies out there. People living gypsy lives. Some of them keep doing it until they sustain that lifestyle; sometimes other people get greedy and they can't sustain it.'

The Stoccos had been getting greedy. And so they were when they found their way onto Burradoo that night in 2013, and then found their way into the Benders' silver Nissan Navara ute, and then drove it away. After this, Maryann reported them to the police, which she had not done before. 'I didn't give him up any earlier because I was worried about him doing stuff to me. And I'm his sister. So I know how scared those other people must have been.'

In a matter of two days, Mark and Gino had struck at least four properties, more than 1500 kilometres apart. It was quite the end to a year that had seen them bash a police officer, steal thousands of dollars' worth of property, destroy thousands of dollars more, and drive almost half the length of the country. But the noose was tightening. And a farmer from Cecil Plains was the one pulling the rope.

13

Mark and Gino Stocco, on one of their long drives north or south – this was inevitably the direction they drove, rather than east or west – may have got to discussing the predicament they were in, given their rather eventful year. The police were unlikely to take kindly to anyone who bashed one of their own, and the attacks and thefts at Redding's and in Crystal Creek were more serious than others they had committed. That was without even considering whether police in Victoria were on to them for the fires they had started at the Zipsins'.

It appears the Stoccos may have decided to spend more time in the southern states; the only crime linked to the pair in Queensland for the first eight months of 2014 was stealing a car in Stanthorpe, near the New South Wales border, in January. But if the plan was to lie low and resist any urge to lash out at those who had wronged them, this was shelved within eight months. Because, during a three-week period that August, the Stoccos reached a depravity that even those who hated and feared them did not think they were capable of. That August, they performed three of the four 'vengeful acts' that Gino would later describe as the worst they committed.

Earlier in the year, however, the Stoccos had settled in at a cattle stud in north-west New South Wales. It suited them almost as well as it suited the regal-looking Poll Herefords and Angus cattle they shared the 1300-hectare property with. The farm, near Coolatai, had an average rainfall so reliable that the cattle mostly grazed on natural feed. Ian Durkin, his wife, Shelley, and their three young children lived on the property, which was called Kargorum but operated as the Mountain Valley stud. Durkin was a fourth-generation farmer, as well practised at picking the lineage of cattle as he was at picking a trustworthy farmhand. He thought he had two of them in Mark and his uncle, John, when he hired the pair in April 2014. They soon set about proving him right. The Durkins could not fault them, and the Stoccos would stay there about as long as they had stayed anywhere in almost fifteen years.

After a solid four months of work, most of it general tidying and maintenance, including cleaning farming equipment and mending fences, with the occasionally more involved task, such as plumbing, the Stoccos let Durkin know they had to take a few weeks off. They had regularly taken a few days off here and there, saying they had been offered paid jobs building sheds or kitchens, but this was to be a longer break. Durkin had not been paying them, just offering free accommodation, so he had little hesitation letting them leave; they had worked solidly ever since they arrived, and he considered them among the best caretakers he'd had, so he wanted to keep them onside.

It was early August when he saw them on their way, telling them to come back when it suited. Durkin was not to know that the pair would be working just as hard away from the stud. But instead of fixing and cleaning, they would be slashing and burning.

The first of the most vengeful of the Stoccos' vengeful acts occurred on the night of 8 August. Gino and Mark Stocco were driving south on the Bruce Highway, not far from where the Big Melon had been, when they decided it was worth paying a visit to some old friends.

Gino and Alison Zatta lived in a two-storey house not far from the highway. A bit further to the north was the house where Gino's brother Remo lived with his wife, Joanne. Between the two houses – and in most directions you looked – was the plantation the brothers worked. The Zattas would turn their minds to Mark and Gino Stocco occasionally. They had grown up with Gino, and their children with Mark. They still knew Gino's brother Eddie, and his parents. Their mother, Elda Zatta, was in the same nursing home as Egidia Stocco. They were grateful when they got the word the pair were in the region, not because they felt they had to be particularly wary, but simply because they knew it was worth packing away anything the Stoccos could easily snatch. Certainly, the Zattas did not believe that Gino harboured any grudge against Remo and Joanne for helping Connie leave, more than a decade ago. They knew that Gino had made Connie's life hell, and that he obviously had been unable to come to terms with the separation. But all Remo and Joanne had done, to their minds, was help a friend.

Gino Stocco, however, did not see it that way. He and Mark crossed the railway tracks that ran almost parallel to the highway, and stopped a reasonable distance from Gino and Alison's place. Not only was their property closer to the main road but it was also where the family kept the machinery needed for the plantation. Inside their shed was a new tractor, a trailer and a boat. There was also a tanker full of fertiliser – enough to cause a catastrophic explosion – a diesel fuel pump and 44-gallon drums of hydraulic oil. Gino and Mark started with the fuel pump and the drums, taking a drill to both, allowing their contents to spill on the floor of the shed. Then they struck a match and fled into the night.

Gino Zatta woke to a strange glow, and troubling noises outside his bedroom window. When he went outside, he saw his shed was ablaze. He rushed out, trying to save what he could, and was burnt as he did. His efforts, which could have cost him his life, were in vain; the shed, and almost everything inside, was destroyed. But it could have been worse. The truck of fertiliser did not explode; if it had, the couple, their house and their hotchpotch collection of dogs would have been scattered across the sugar cane. When the cost of the damage was assessed, Gino and Alison Zatta found they had lost almost $1 million worth of property. And they had no idea who wished such torment upon them.

Gino Stocco felt it was all the Zattas deserved. As he headed south, again making the almost 1400-kilometre journey to the Darling Downs, he thought about all that the Zattas had done to him, how they had given Connie the means to leave, how low he had become afterwards, how hard he had fought to win her back, and how ruthlessly she had ignored him and their vows and moved on. All because of the Zattas, and the late-night lift they had given his wife in 1997. Gino believed the Zattas had intervened in the relationship. Gino said later that he and Mark did not take any pleasure from the flames. 'It was straight vengeful . . . sheer vengeance against what those people had done to me.'

*

Doug Redding had spent much of the past ten months fighting a one-man war against Mark and Gino Stocco. He did whatever he could to find other victims of theirs and make contact. This included reaching out to Sergeant Liam Duffy, a police officer who, Redding discovered, had been bashed by the Stoccos in St George while he had been employing them as caretakers. He tried to get Duffy to share as much as he could about the Stoccos and to pass on his name to any other victims he heard of around Queensland. He hoped that having the ear of a particularly sympathetic copper – given he was also a victim of them – would counterbalance the apparent indifference of the other police he had spoken to about the Stoccos.

There were some victims Redding spoke to who, even years later, did not want to be identified, even to the police, such was their concern for their safety. Redding knew the pair were relying on classified advertisements to get by, both in print and online, and so he did what he could to negate the possibility that others would employ them. This included starting a social media campaign and having people share warnings about the Stoccos on Facebook.

Redding was, in no small part, motivated in this crusade by guilt; he felt somehow responsible for bringing the Stoccos to the Darling Downs, where they had gone on to inflict carnage. He had taken as many precautions as possible since they left to improve security at his property. But it was inevitable that he had to leave sometimes; he could not simply buy enough supplies to barricade himself inside, waiting for them to return, so he could use the guns they had left behind, or that he had since acquired, to knock them off their perch.

And so, on the night of 13 August, five days after the fire at Bambaroo, Redding left his property at Cecil Plains. He realised later that Mark and Gino Stocco were probably watching him from the bush as he went.

The Stoccos walked back to Redding's shed. They opened up the fuel hatches to some of his machinery, including his tractor, and poured sugar inside, severely damaging the tanks. And they went to the gun safe, for which Redding believed they must have had a key cut. Inside they found two guns they liked so much that they stole them just for themselves, rather than to trade: an SKK semi-automatic rifle and a Remington 12-gauge pump-action shotgun. They found ammunition for both guns, took that as well, and left.

Redding returned to Cecil Plains and, for some reason, had the feeling he had just missed the Stoccos. So he took off down the road, hoping to catch up to them. He believes he got close, as he came across a ute in the night, which he started chasing at speed along an otherwise deserted road. But he realised he was out-numbered, and possibly outgunned, and went home instead to check the damage. He thought the guns were worth about $6000, and the equipment almost $20 000. The two attacks combined had cost him more than $60 000. He could have moped, or backed off, or trusted the police to arrest them, but Redding was not made like that. He doubled down on his battle to catch the Stoccos.

The way they saw it, Mark and Gino had balanced a few ledgers in the past five days, committing two of the four acts Gino later described as their most vengeful. Maybe they knew Redding had been spreading the word about them, and so were particularly keen to square up. But more than likely they were simply still upset about the pool chemical tiff. They headed south again from the Darling Downs, taking a familiar road, the Newell Highway. It is a road with its own website, and is named after an Irishman raised in the United States who became known as a pioneering roads man – Hugh Newell, who died in 1941. Head 800 kilometres from Cecil Plains, most of it on the Newell, and you arrive at a white fence and a long, straight road, which is effectively a driveway. The fence, bordering a lush farm in the heart of New South Wales, is adorned with a sign that reads 'Plenty'.

Peter Farley had found the going tough on the farm. His wife had left him. He had toiled through nearly a decade of drought and, once it appeared to have broken, invested in a modernised irrigation system, which would help him when the next one hit. But it was expensive. And, almost as soon as he bought the new system, which was powered by electricity, rather than diesel, the price of electricity went up.

He needed to pay his wife for her half of the farm. But he was already borrowed to the hilt, and the banks would scoff at any suggestion of giving him more, given he was barely making his current repayments. It was a dark time. And the only light he could see came from a troubling thought: he had to sell the farm, the property he had grown up on, that had been handed down to him by his parents. He went and spoke to them – as hard a conversation as he would ever have to have. And so, in November 2012 – a few months after he had dismissed a couple of caretakers he had employed called Mark and John – he put Plenty on the market for $3 million.

As Peter Farley pondered getting out of farming, the Tidswells were thinking about expanding. They were also third-generation farmers, and the youngest, Luke, was almost in his mid-twenties and keen to take on more responsibility. The Tidswells' first farm was given to Luke's grandfather after the Second World War – a soldier settlement of 323 hectares, about 50 kilometres south of Canowindra in Woodstock. He served as a mechanic in

Darwin and, in 1951, moved on to his new farm. Now his son, Guy, and Guy's son, Luke, were pondering an acquisition of land about as large as the soldier settlement that started it all – Plenty, the farm owned by Peter Farley.

By February 2013 – and after shelling out a shade more than $2.2 million – it was theirs. They now had more than 2000 hectares of property in the region. Luke and his wife would live on the farmhouse at Plenty, and work the sheep and grain with Luke's father. Farley moved to the Gold Coast and eventually got remarried.

Mark and Gino Stocco were not to know that, however, when they decided to stop off at Plenty, on 29 August 2014. They had planned to just fill up their ute – they were, at this stage, driving a Volkswagen Amarok – with diesel, from the pump between the cottage, where they used to stay, and the farmhouse. But once they pulled in to the driveway, they had another idea. They remembered how they had been treated by Farley, one of the first in a growing list of farmers to kick them off their properties. And the rage that had come to the surface at the Zattas', and again in Cecil Plains, spewed forth once more.

It had just ticked past midnight. Gino began to slash tyres and puncture others with a battery drill. He took to the tyres on a tip truck and a hay rake and a trailer and a quad bike. Mark was keeping watch, but slashed the tyres of a Ford Falcon while he did so. They then filled up the ute. The nozzle on the tank malfunctioned, and diesel started to pool near the sheds. The pair flicked matches into the pools of fuel.

Luke Tidswell heard his red cattle dog, Bruce, barking. He got up, walked out to the lounge and peered out the window. He could see torches near the sheds. He pulled on his boots and started out the door. By this time, he could see the sheds were on fire. He turned left out his back door to a small adjacent shed, where he kept his guns. He heard an engine starting and could not see the torchlight any more. Instead of running towards the shed, Tidswell cut across his back lawn and the front of the farmhouse, towards the gate. He knew it was the only way out.

Mark and Gino had seen the man coming from the house, and ran for the ute. They could see the fire taking hold behind them as they gunned forwards and to the right, making for the gate. They had no idea where the bloke they had seen coming was. Then he appeared in the headlights, standing near the front gate, a shotgun pointed at the ute. They had never seen him before, this young bloke with a torso so big he looked like a wheelie bin on legs. He certainly had not worked for Farley when they did.

Tidswell did not flinch as the headlights bathed him in light and the ute ploughed towards him. He had the shotgun pointed at the windscreen, and was ready to fire. But then he thought better of trying to kill a couple of blokes who had only tried to burn down his sheds. Best, he thought, to try to take out the radiator, make sure they didn't get too far down the road, and let the cops take care of them. He lowered his aim and took two shots. The driver turned sharply left through the narrow gate, the wheels vibrating over the cattle grate, before the ute straightened onto the long road leading out of Plenty and sped away. Tidswell ran back to the sheds.

Some caretakers – who had been hired by Farley after the Stoccos left – had been woken by the fire, and came from the cottage to try to douse the flames. It took almost an hour before firefighters got there. By that time, the damage had been done. They managed to save two quad bikes, but a boat, trailer and tractor were all but destroyed, and a truck, hay rake and fencing trailer were damaged. The bill was almost $180 000.

As firefighters came rushing to Plenty, the Stoccos were willing their ute to get as far as possible down the road. But it was no use; Tidswell's bid to take out their radiator had been successful, and after little more than 20 kilometres the ute packed it in. The Stoccos had made for the Nangar National Park, to the north, and they left the ute there, taking off on foot. It was found by police later that day, but the men were nowhere to be seen.

They had left something behind, though: enough DNA for a positive match to be made with Gino. They were suspects for the fire at Plenty within days.

Eventually, the Stoccos made their way back to the Durkins'. The rolling green hills of the cattle stud in Coolatai marked their return to a life far more sedate than setting sheds on fire and being shot at, as had been their lot in the past month. There were few places better to lie low than here after committing three vengeful acts.

Ian Durkin was pleased to have his farmhands back, too. 'They were really good workers – not unskilled, not lazy. They would work. Jesus, I tell ya, they worked.' Their obsession with cleanliness was something Durkin particularly valued. 'You could eat off my workshop floor,' he said. 'You could pull into the shed in the tractor, and Mark would be waiting there with the Armor All and vacuum to clean it, and he would do it every day.'

A friend, however, took a different view of the Stoccos' neatness; they told Durkin, without any doubt, that it was the behaviour of former prisoners. 'They said to me, "These two have been in jail. You're made to be that neat when you're in jail."' It may well have been that the Stoccos had become neater once they spent time inside; after all, the *Kiwarrak* was supposedly a dump when it was raided by police. What is more likely is that the Stoccos kept their surroundings nice when staying at other people's property to make it harder for them to be moved on.

Durkin certainly had no intention of getting rid of the pair any time soon. As far as he was concerned, they could stay as long as they wanted. But at the same time that the Stoccos were doing all they could to maintain their welcome at Mountain Valley, a farmer 250 kilometres north was doing all he could to make sure the pair never got work on another property again.

Doug Redding made no secret of his obsession with Mark and Gino Stocco. He went to bed each night with a loaded gun. He woke each morning thinking of them. When his eyes were open, he was with them, yet he had no idea where they were. It was as if their bearded heads were tattooed on each retina.

Redding made 'wanted' posters with their photos on them, fixing them on light poles in country towns wherever he stopped, often during driving trips to meet other victims of the pair. There were bullet holes on the photos of Mark and Gino on the posters, his message to the Stoccos that if he saw them again, he would shoot to kill. Redding took to driving long distances at night, including the almost seven-and-a-half-hour round-trip west to Roma, hoping to cross them on the road. He scanned social media, responded to emails and made phone calls. Some of those calls were to people advertising in newspapers and online for farm workers; he told them to steer clear of a bloke calling himself John who was travelling with a younger bloke, Mark. He told whoever would listen that the pair would have beards, be slight, and stink.

Redding was already predisposed to a distrust of the justice system; now his long-held fears were being realised. The Stoccos, he felt, should never have been freed, given their previous crimes. They were clearly irredeemable, and to his mind they were as certain to reoffend as he was to give them a flogging, or, better, shoot them dead, if he ever got the chance. His feelings about the inadequacies of judges, he says, go back to a murder committed by a parolee in western Queensland in the 1980s. 'This didn't just start. It has been getting worse and worse over more than thirty years. It's a situation that should have never been able to happen. They should have never been let go by those idiots we call judges.'

Redding is also dismayed by senior police, a group he calls 'the administration', who make it more difficult than it should be for boots-on-the-ground officers to do their jobs. It had been a disaster in the Stoccos' case, where the crooks were infinitely more nimble than those chasing them, he argued. 'Local detectives weren't given enough time by their supervisors to even go and visit the crime scenes.'

If Redding had headed south, rather than west, on one of his late-night drives, he may have come across someone who had seen Mark and Gino around Coolatai, and who could have pointed him in the direction of Ian Durkin. But his campaign, though undoubtedly helping dozens of people, did not reach the Durkins. By the time it did, it was too late.

The Durkins had started to notice some oddities about their farmhands. First, there was the removal of all the cupboard and internal doors in the unit they were staying in. Then they noticed that it appeared the pair were sharing a bed.

Other hosts had also noticed this about the men. They sniggered and told their spouses, but thought it simply another nomadic eccentricity. There were a few possible explanations other than that of a romantic connection between the pair. Gino, it had been noted, hated the cold; maybe he preferred sharing a bed for warmth. The pair were also paranoid; maybe they felt sharing a bed reduced the risk of being ambushed, and gave them the best possible chance to escape quickly and quietly, if they decided they needed to. Maybe it was simply about companionship. The Durkins didn't mull it over too much – they just found it weird.

Their farmhands were also weird when it came to another type of bed: the garden bed in front of their unit. It was, more accurately, a small strip of grass. Gino was fastidious about its maintenance, regularly watering and clipping it, so that it was the best-kept patch of green on the entire 1300-hectare property. There was just one problem, he told Ian Durkin: the cows and the machinery kept going across it, ruining his hard work.

That was pretty hard to avoid, Durkin told him. It was a farm, after all. But Gino wouldn't hear it, and he decided to erect an electric fence around his patch. Durkin let it go for a few days but then told him to take it down; it was awkward having to get around it, and it made no sense putting up a fence just to protect such an inconsequential plot. Gino refused. Durkin insisted. So Mark and Gino packed up their belongings, including a caravan and two Navaras, and left in the middle of the night.

In their unit the next morning, the Durkins found a note. It had been written in block letters with blue pen on a Tuesday page from a diary. 'Ian you are a fool you had two good men for the price of one but because you are argront you loose,' it read. The Durkins thought it was the last they would hear of the Stoccos. It was 30 April 2015.

Two days after the strange farmhands had left Mountain Valley stud, the Durkins returned home to find a drill had been used to puncture seventy-two tyres. Brand new fences had been cut, and bulls were found roaming around with heifers. Fuel, farm equipment including a trailer, a diesel tank and power tools, and three guns were missing. It was the guns that most concerned the Durkins: they feared the Stoccos would come back when they were home and blast them and their children away.

The family slept fitfully for five weeks, and in June the situation worsened. The Stoccos returned, this time cutting thirty-two fences and slashing the tyres on a car. The damage bill was about $80 000. It was the fourth of the Stoccos' vengeful acts, but, for Durkin, he could barely get local police to take the matter seriously. He was close to the local federal MP, Mark Coulton, who eventually shared the Durkins' experience on his Facebook page, as a warning to others. 'This is an account of a very disturbing incident that took place in the northern part of my electorate,' he posted, including an account from Shelley. The 13 June 2015 post was shared almost 4000 times. (The Stoccos had also recently worked at another farm in the electorate; a property at Terry Hie Hie. The owner knew the pair as Mark and John Karzai, and when they were told to leave the farm on 16 April, they stole keys to the house, front gate, quad bike and ride-on lawnmower, according to a report in *The Inverell Times*.)

One night, not long after Coulton had posted about the Stoccos, Durkin got a call 'out of the blue'. It was Doug Redding. He told Durkin the blokes he had employed sounded like the Stoccos. They compared notes, and it certainly seemed likely. Redding said he had made a similar mistake to Durkin's and paid almost as hefty a price. He recruited Durkin to his mission, and the pair vowed to tell as many people as possible about the Stoccos. It seemed crude, and somewhat pointless, but what else was there to do, Redding reasoned, than to have more people looking for them? He wanted to build an army of sentries on every darkened back road, so he did not have to be driving them himself. He wanted every farmer to know who they were hiring, so they could avoid having the inevitable petty argument with Gino that would unleash his fury.

Eventually, Durkin and Redding met; Durkin had found some of the other farmer's belongings, which the Stoccos had left behind, in a shed at his property. Durkin agreed with the older farmer that the police were not well-resourced or serious enough to catch Mark and Gino. 'There was nobody actively chasing them. The incidents were logged by the cops, and then they shut the book.' Durkin took to calling people who had placed classified advertisements for caretakers and farmhands to warn them. This was not as easy for him as it was for Redding, who, compared with Durkin, was bold and extroverted. 'But once you realise the coppers aren't looking for them, you do whatever you can. Some people would take it on board, but other people just hung up on me.'

He did not know what he would do if he happened to come across Mark and Gino again. He certainly wanted them caught. But he was not as hell-bent as Redding. 'When I first met [Redding], he wasn't too bad. But I think it nearly consumed him. I think it's all he thought about for a while. I'm sure he would have killed them if he found them.'

Redding did not find them. But the police did, four months after that second attack at the Durkins'. And it was owing in no small part to the big Queenslander's efforts. As bad as he thought Mark and Gino Stocco were, however, even Doug Redding was surprised when, after they were arrested, police announced the father and son were suspected of murder.

14

Graham and Peg live on the outer south-western edge of Sydney, where concrete and steel gradually melt into verdant forest. Their house is in Wedderburn, south of the Georges River, mere metres from the urban boundary of Australia's largest city. On a map, the difference between where they live and the thick warren of courts and places and drives in Rosemeadow and St Helens Park, Sydney's last suburbs, is particularly stark. Their house is a dot on a strip of road that could seemingly be engulfed by the Dharawal National Park to the south. The suburbs to their north look like the plastic maze on a skill tester, designed to be navigated with a ball bearing as they're tipped from side to side. Graham and Peg are a couple of kilometres from suburbia, and yet in the middle of nowhere.

They bought the 1970s yellow-brick veneer with three tiny bedrooms that faced the road, and that was surrounded by overgrown orchards, paddocks and a dam, as a tree change. It needed a lot of work to become their ideal retreat, but that was what they wanted; something they could spend time making perfect, rather than having to pay millions more for somebody else's idea of perfection.

First, they set about clearing land to the rear of the property, where they built a huge shed. It had space for boats and motorbikes, and living quarters: an office, and two multipurpose rooms downstairs, along with a bathroom and kitchenette, and a large bedroom, attached to a dining area with a kitchen and separate storage space upstairs. It could be lived in while the house was worked on, and then would be a place with some privacy where family could stay. Graham and Peg both had children from previous relationships, and were grandparents, so this was convenient for hosting guests.

With the shed finished, the couple turned their attention to the house. They planned to extend out the back, making the bedrooms and living area larger, and joining the property to a spacious outdoor entertaining area. The paddocks were still overgrown, but they were clearing them gradually, starting with the land immediately surrounding the house and shed. Eventually, they wanted to have space for some cows, and to rear some horses.

Graham and Peg thought, given the living quarters in the shed, they could hire workers to stay for a while, helping them with labouring on the build, and with the daunting task of taming orchards that had been neglected for years. They could pay them cash in hand, a lesser rate given they would be providing board, and get the property up to scratch more quickly than they had hoped. So in mid-2013, they placed an ad on Gumtree for labourers.

*

Mark and Gino usually trawled Gumtree using the internet at public libraries. On one such trip, they saw Graham and Peg's advertisement to work at a property just outside Sydney. Perhaps, when they saw this ad, they did a bit more research and looked at a map. It would have shown a single main road in and out, but with lots of bush behind, eventually leading to other, smaller roads that connected to a highway. Perfect for someone who did not want people in passing cars to notice them, but who also wanted an easy escape route.

They gave Graham a call. He told them they could start as soon as possible.

John and Mark looked a bit scruffy, but Graham had not expected much. After all, only a certain type of person is able to answer an advertisement so promptly to work as a live-in labourer. They introduced themselves as an uncle and nephew. Mark was quieter, taller and deferred somewhat boyishly to his uncle, given he was aged in his mid-thirties. John was probably in his fifties but had the skittish energy and need to occupy his hands of a teenager.

It did not take Graham long to realise he was getting a bargain for his $15 an hour. The pair worked hard and skilfully, and John, particularly, had a seemingly endless knowledge of how to build or fix things. They did as they were asked, and were courteous and respectful. Their work was meticulous, and they would clean as they went, an obsessiveness that extended to their living quarters in the shed, which were kept spotless.

Graham and Peg were living at their house in Ryde, and they trusted the pair to work cleaning up the property during the week, before they visited on weekends. They would pull into their driveway after the hour trip and notice more rotting fruit trees had gone, making way for paddocks that rolled away to the bush beyond.

Graham sits in his office in the shed, a simple but functional building of cinder block walls and cement floors. The room is decorated sparsely with one of those novelty signs about 'local rules' that makes reference to bringing beer and discouraging women, and framed photos of a horse he once owned, its bay nose crossing a finish line first at the Nowra races.

He is driving his tractor when I arrive, sheltered in his cab from an early autumn drenching, which has only just abated. He steps down, greets me warmly and does not bat an eyelid when I tell him why I'm there. It has been four years since he placed the advertisement, and he has been expecting a journalist to come and ask him about Mark and John for a while.

He leads me into the shed, taking his boots off before he steps inside. Soon after we sit down, finding seats among the boat and the quad bikes to carry into his office, he makes a request: he is happy to talk, but I can't use his real name. He extends his right hand, and we agree.

He is short and thick, with hard hands but a soft face, and eyes that flicker as the brain behind them tries to remember.

Peg joins Graham and me in the office after about an hour, wandering in on us after she has looked outside from the house and wondered why the tractor is still running but has nobody inside. She did not know that Graham would be speaking to me but is placated by my assurance that I will not publish their names.

She is significantly younger than Graham, and watches him carefully but kindly, as if to make sure his memory does not betray him.

The couple now know that the Mark and John they knew were Mark and Gino Stocco, a son and his father who had been answering advertisements like theirs for the past eight years and, in most instances, left the owners of those properties worse off, by either stealing or destroying their property, or both. But they do not think of the men like that, as callous and deranged waifs, floating on the breeze from one property to the next. And they do not think of them as murderers either.

Mark and Gino came and went three times from Wedderburn over a period of about two years. They stayed for the longest stretch, about four or five months, the last time Graham saw them. By this stage, he thought of the pair as his friends. Johnny, as he knew him, had a temper and was easily aggravated, but loved a chat and was a willing worker whom he respected. Mark was gentle and thoughtful, and particularly beloved by Peg. 'Johnny was sometimes a little bit moody and stuff, but the young fella was a nice man,' Graham said.

The Stoccos treated the shed as their home. In a room downstairs, behind the office where we now sit, and adjacent to the parking bay where the boat and quad bikes are stored, they set up one of three televisions they brought with them, and had a sandwich press, a fridge, an electric bar heater and a kettle. They would often have lunch there in between work, a quick break over a toasted sandwich.

At the top of the stairs, in a room they used as a kitchen and dining area, they had more cooking gear, another television on the wall, and a larger table. They usually ate breakfast and dinner here.

In the evenings, the television was almost always on. They watched the ABC and SBS – rarely commercial television – and were particularly captivated by documentaries.

On the wall furthest from the stairs was a washing machine and dryer, which Gino had installed in the corner of the room, having told Graham to buy them for him and Mark. Near the makeshift laundry area was the entry to another room, where the Stoccos kept some tools, and Graham also had odds and ends.

The bedroom was on the opposite side of the kitchen. Another television was attached on the wall between the rooms, a couch was on the opposite wall, with a heater nearby, and in the middle of the room was a steel-framed double bed. Mark and Gino slept in the bed together.

All these rooms are still exactly how the Stoccos left them, more than eighteen months earlier. The only major change is the large, dusty smears, mostly on smooth surfaces or around door handles, where police checked for fingerprints after they fled. Graham and Peg's shed has transformed into an interactive gallery exhibit, where the visitor can ponder consumerism and existentialism in the home that two men who had been without a home for fifteen years made.

What to make of the single bottle of Grolsch beer, with an old-fashioned stopper, left on the kitchen table, and the bottle of Claytons, an obscure cordial, on the fridge downstairs? The New South Wales rugby league top that a North Queenslander had regularly worn? The perfectly folded basket of washed work clothes, old jeans and polo shirts? The well-made bed with the blue and white doona? The excessive number of televisions in such a small space? The ancient blinking clock radio? The weathered Makita drill and bandsaw and angle grinder?

The cleanliness of it all? And the decision to leave all this when they fled?

Graham had worked as a concreter, and spent most of his life on worksites with other men. Some were like Gino.

'I knew how to handle him. He would think some things should be done this way, and I'd say they should be done another way. But by the next morning he was settled down. I've worked with blokes or had blokes work for me all my life, and I've realised you've got to take blokes as they are. Johnny hated anybody telling him what to do or owning any part of him. He didn't like not being right, and he didn't like not getting his own way. And he would have been like that his whole life. I don't know whether Johnny had had a hard life, or whether he had made it hard for himself.'

Depending on when they arrived and what needed doing, the pair helped on the house extension or worked in the yard. They did not wake particularly early but would often toil well into the night doing other bits and pieces, sometimes when they were asked, other times simply because they thought they needed to be done.

Gino asked Graham once about an old quad bike that was lying idle in the shed. Graham told him it hadn't run for years. Gino started tinkering with it in his spare time, and he had it fixed in a week. He became somewhat obsessed with it, riding like a demon across the property, and using it to travel even short distances between the house and the shed.

'He used to just fly across the paddocks on it,' Graham remembers. 'He would be on his little bike and off he'd go. He would get air he'd be going that fast. He'd end up this high' – Graham holds his hand about 150 centimetres high – 'off the ground.'

Graham was getting a yearling broken in once and, when the man who had done the job returned the horse, Gino seemed particularly curious. The man was a goliath, standing there with a flick whip, a smaller, gentler whip used to break horses, and talking to Graham about how the horse had gone. Gino stood there staring at him. 'He looked at the man, and then he looked at the horse. He looked at the man, and he looked at the horse. Then he looked at the man again and said, "Why do you use that?"' Gino ended up getting detailed instructions about how to care for and train the horse, which he followed meticulously, apart from one thing: he fed it too many apples from one of the few trees in the orchard that had been worth keeping.

Occasionally, Graham, who was retired, would do a job for a friend. He would enlist the Stoccos to help. It led to some entertaining road trips. 'If we saw a McDonald's, Johnny went berserk. Absolutely fucking berserk,' he says. 'He went in there, and it would probably take him fifteen minutes to order, because he wouldn't know what to get, he was that excited, mostly because I was paying.' If it was breakfast, Gino always opted for plenty of hash browns.

Graham tells me that the pair was also manic when, on the way back from a job, he stopped with them to get a cake at St Helens Park. Most Sundays, Peg would cook a meal for the pair, and Graham had decided to get dessert. 'You'd swear one of them was seven and the other was eleven. They were up and down the aisle, up and down the aisle, trying to pick a cake. And then it would be, "This one." And it would be the biggest and the one with the most chocolate.'

The pair could not resist chocolate and cakes, but otherwise ate well, if somewhat meagrely. The couple learnt their workers had regularly been eating nuts for dinner. That was partly why Peg had taken to cooking for them on Sundays; not only because she enjoyed their company, but because they rarely had extravagant meals during the week.

But they did not always eat like paupers. Once, after Graham and Peg had a cow on the property butchered, and filled a freezer in the shed with the meat, they told the Stoccos to help themselves, should they want the odd steak for dinner. 'So they ate the whole lot,' Peg says. 'I don't think they ate a lot of meat, but they certainly had a ball with that.'

Graham and Peg also found it weird that Mark and Gino shared a bed. She had noticed that, each morning, a sofa bed that she thought one of the pair was sleeping on would be packed away, and the bedding neatly folded and placed nearby. She initially put it down to their neatness, and then realised it was always packed away because they never used it. One morning, she saw that on each side of the double bed was a chair that was being used as a makeshift bedside table. On each of the chairs was a large kitchen knife.

While Graham and Peg noted that this catalogue of behaviour was decidedly strange, they largely dismissed it. 'We just thought they were from the bush,' Graham says.

The couple agree that they began to understand Mark when he was painting the house. He would spend hours alone with Peg, as she pottered about inside. They had long conversations about Mauritius, where Peg was born, and she would make him cups of tea. 'He saw me as a bit of a mother figure,' she says. 'We used to talk all the time, and he was very intelligent, and liked to read and all that, and wanted to learn about different cultures. He would ask what sort of food I would eat, whether it was all Indian influences or some European. We had little talks like that. I was very fond of him as well. He was nice to me. I really liked him.'

Mark, Graham says, struck him as someone who had yearned for maternal contact. 'It was the first time he had been next to a woman in a home for a long, long time. And they would just talk about life. Sometimes she would say something . . . and you could see his head go like this.' Graham raises his chin and cocks his ear. 'He just wanted as much knowledge as he could get. He just wanted to learn as much as possible about life. If he didn't know about something, he would ask, and was polite about it.'

Mark would retain what he was told, or what he read, with incredible accuracy. He would paint, slowly but meticulously, for hours, listening to Peg, while his father busily tended to other jobs outside. It was a clear point of difference between the pair; Mark was contented with quiet contemplation and discussion, but Gino was constantly restless. 'He was so hyperactive,' Graham recalls. 'There was always something to be done, something to be fixed.'

The relationship between the two men intrigued Graham and Peg. They did not necessarily view Gino's influence over Mark as problematic, but they were aware that the older man was dominant. It was obvious they had a close bond and knew each other intimately. '[Mark] was inquisitive, intelligent. But it was like he'd been locked away,' Graham says.

'He was open to learning new things, and very, very respectful. Both of them actually,' Peg says.

Graham thought of Mark as childlike and not only dominated by Gino, but dependent on him. 'I used to think, "You know, if something would happen to John, what would he do?"'

The couple did not know that Mark had been studying civil engineering before he became closer to Gino, and that he left university. 'He would have been good at it,' Graham says. 'He would have been good at most things he did. But his father would have certainly put a nut on that bolt.'

Mark appeared to fully understand Gino's complicated moods, and how they impacted others. Graham got the sense that Mark wished Gino was different, but knew that to try to change him was futile, as 'that was the style of bloke Johnny always would have been'.

Graham and Peg were stunned when they discovered that Gino and Mark were father and son, not uncle and nephew. 'We were flabbergasted when we found out,' Graham says.

When Mark and Gino first started working at Wedderburn, Graham asked Gino whether he had ever been married, or had children. Gino said that his wife had left at the same time as Mark's mum had left, and so they had decided to start working together. It was classic Gino: a lie wrapped around a truth.

Graham did not have to ask to find out what Gino thought of his ex-wife. He called her vulgar names in Italian that implied she was a charlatan, and so frequently and vehemently outlined his disdain for her that Graham reached a troubling conclusion: Gino hated all women.

Gino told Graham that he had spent 'twenty-five years trying to get his wife off other men', and gave him the impression she was constantly sleeping around, propositioning or eyeing off possible lovers. And, when he finally gave up his manful endeavours to change her, Gino told Graham, she took all his money. 'He said he never tried to get another woman,' Graham says. 'He just used to bag them. He didn't trust them. He was heartbroken once, and never trusted them again.'

The couple never heard Mark speak about his family.

The pair discussed other fragments of their past as they became closer to Graham and Peg. When I ask whether one of the tales they told involved a yacht, Graham's eyes widen, and he starts to smile.

'Unbelievable,' he answers, shaking his head and chuckling. 'Fucking unbelievable.' The pair had raved about the three years they had spent at sea. Gino told them that nobody taught them how to sail, so they taught themselves. To propel the yacht forward, they were reliant on using a hand-held outboard motor that was intended for the dinghy. It meant that by day they could only travel about 30 nautical miles, and they would be pushed back 35 nautical miles at night, Gino had told Graham. He also told him a fantastical tale of sailing out of Sydney Heads using the small motor, which he eventually used to sail all the way to Venice.

Graham joked with his friends, several of whom were sailors, for years afterwards, asking them whether it was even possible that a small motor could transport a yacht all the way to Italy.

Graham and Peg never had any indication that the men were outlaws. Once, they had returned to the property with a caravan and insisted it be parked behind the shed, so it could not be seen from the road. Graham did not think much of it; they had regularly left stuff behind in the shed and brought back new things in the time he had known them.

Gino explained that part of the reason he and Mark were living as they were was to avoid the taxman; a logic Graham accepted. 'That was the only naughty thing we thought they did,' he says.

Graham's son-in-law later asked the Stoccos whether, given the amount of work they did for people and how much money they would be owed, they were ever worried they wouldn't be paid, seeing as their employment was essentially illegal. After all, it was not as though they could invoice their boss, or take it up with police, should there be a dispute. 'He said something like, "You do a lot of work for cash. What do you do if someone doesn't pay you?"' Graham recalls.

'Johnny said, sort of joking, "We know where they live. We know where their fuel tanks are."'

15

In the autumn of 2015, after the Stoccos decided to flee the Durkins' cattle stud, they returned to Wedderburn for what turned out to be their final stint there. By July, the campaign by Redding, and then Durkin, started to have an impact; a detailed article about the Stoccos was published online by Yahoo7, the news website of the Seven Network.

Queensland Detective Acting Superintendent Kerry Johnson said in the article that there were dozens of victims across the three states, including some who had not formally reported crimes to police. 'These are trusting, caring people who take people into their lives. They are people who may be finding it difficult to attract employees given the current climate. These men are preying on people who have been hit by drought and are effectively small business owners doing it tough,' Johnson said. When the pair were hired by farmers, they used that property as a base before targeting other local farms, he said. And they had stayed one step ahead of police.

'You have got to remember these are also areas sparsely populated with police and residents. What they have done is not out in the open until they ripped the guts out of a place and the alarm is raised some time later – so police are playing catch up in that regard.'

At the time that Johnson was sounding the alarm about the dangerous men lurking around some of the most deserted parts of Australia, Mark and Gino were holed up only a few kilometres from the shiny housing estates of outer suburban Sydney at Graham and Peg's.

The property felt like home, and they treated it that way, quickly settling back into the shed. Gino even started tending to a small strip of grass in front of the shed as if it was the nature strip of his house; he meticulously weeded it, fertilised it and mowed it. Like the strip at the Durkins, it was the lushest patch of grass on the entire property.

Graham and Peg were happy to have them back. They trusted them completely; so much so that Peg only felt safe sleeping at Wedderburn when Graham was away if the Stoccos were in the shed. She would go and tell them he was out for the night and to stay alert, given they were usually awake later than her, for anything unusual that sounded from the blackness.

The Stoccos were put to work on the renovation. Mark again took up painting and, given his wider range of skills, Gino helped with whatever the hired tradesman needed. The extension was taking shape now, and the manpower had increased from just Mark, Gino and Graham to a rotating group of plumbers, electricians, painters, carpenters and bricklayers.

Gino did what he could, using the more than forty years' experience he had as a jack of all trades to even impart some wisdom to the qualified workers Graham had hired. But even he had some limitations, including the rather technical task of being able to complete the brickwork around window frames. For this, Graham hired a bricklayer, a Calabrian man who lived in Lurnea, an outer Western Sydney suburb about 30 kilometres north, and who had his son working with him as an apprentice.

What did a man who was suspected of murdering his wife and three children, a gangland figure who once decapitated a teenager and conspired to assassinate guests at Mick Gatto's son's wedding, and Gino Stocco have in common? They were all three included on a list of Australia's twenty most-wanted fugitives that was released on 17 August 2015.

As part of the national Operation Roam, Crime Stoppers, in conjunction with all Australian police forces, generates and publicises a list of the most-wanted fugitives. The operation runs for about two weeks and is acclaimed for getting results by increasing public awareness of a small group of crooks who have repeatedly avoided capture. Since 2011, when the first operation was held, an average of about eight arrests have been made each year. A different state police force collates the list each year, and in 2015 it was Queensland's turn.

Gino was in serious company. Stuart Pearce, also on the list, was suspected of setting his family home in Adelaide alight, with wife Meredith and three of their four children inside. They had all been killed before the flames took hold. Pearce had been on the run for twenty-four years, and was the subject of an Interpol warrant, with police believing he had started a new life overseas.

Another high-profile fugitive on the list was Graham Gene Potter, recognised as the most-wanted man in Australia. He was twenty-three years old and on his bucks night in Wollongong in 1981 when he horrifically killed and mutilated teenager Kim Barry. He was jailed for life, but he was released fifteen years later, and in 2008 he was suspected of conspiring to murder two significant mafia figures at the wedding of Mick Gatto's son, and of being involved in the world's largest ecstasy bust, a shipment of 15 million tablets with an estimated street value of $440 million, which police found in tomato tins in Melbourne. The seizure led to some of Australia's most senior Calabrian Mafia figures being jailed. Potter had fled Queensland Police in 2010 and been on the run ever since, with sightings reported across the country. He was considered a master of disguise who had adopted a variety of aliases.

Also on the list was Brady Hamilton, an enforcer for the Comanchero outlaw bikie gang who was suspected of beating a man to death in 1999 because of a dispute about the exchange of a Harley with a Triumph. So was a bloke who had escaped on day release from a Western Australian prison and still had eleven years on his sentence, and various rapists and drug traffickers.

Gino was listed as wanted for property offences committed in Queensland in 2012 and 2013. While the majority of other fugitives included in the operation had police or prison mugshots of them released, Gino's image was a photo of him taken in a light red shirt, seemingly by a swimming pool, with someone's arm around him. Crime Stoppers Queensland chief executive Trevor O'Hara told the *Townsville Bulletin* that Gino was suspected of burglary, arson and fraud. His most serious suspected offence was the arson at Bambaroo, but he was also suspected of offences in St George, Chinchilla, Theodore, Euramo, Yuleba and Stanthorpe. There had been sightings of him in Ingham, Dalby, Chinchilla, Townsville and New South Wales, with more recent sightings of him north and south of Brisbane. Mark was not mentioned in relation to the recent offending, but it was noted that he and Gino had been jailed in Victoria in 2007. 'He is not deemed a violent offender,' O'Hara said. 'But it is important we do get people looking out for him.'

Gino Stocco's crimes could not be compared to those committed by others on the list. But his inclusion among such a gallery of rogues showed just how badly police wanted him caught. It was a significant shift; he was no longer simply a thorn in the side of local coppers like Barron, nor merely hated by people he had wronged such as Redding and Durkin. Gino Stocco was a national fugitive.

On 17 August, Mark and Gino spent the day as they spent many of their days in Wedderburn – with the younger man painting and his father 'cowboying', as Graham liked to call it, around the paddocks. That night, a Monday, they retreated to the shed to watch television and tinker.

Graham and Peg, as they usually did on weeknights, watched the 6 pm news on either Nine or Seven in the house. During a segment on the most-wanted men in Australia, Gino's image and name were plastered on the screen: the man in their shed was staring back at them.

It hit Graham right between the eyes. But he did not think long about what to do. He went out to the shed and told Mark and Gino they had to leave. He would give them until morning, and then tell the police.

'Both of them broke down and cried,' Graham says. 'Especially Mark.'

They thanked him, and told him they would be sad to leave but did not want to get him and Peg into trouble. Graham left them alone to pack up, and never saw them again.

Peg remembers the final night with Mark and Gino somewhat differently. She says she and Graham did not see the pair on television on 17 August, but that early the next day her daughter called her because she had seen Gino on a morning television show. Peg then saw a link to a story about Australia's most-wanted fugitives on Facebook, and Gino was on the list. She says that she and Graham checked the shed, but the pair were already gone. So they called the police.

A detective who was one of those first called to the property says it is possible that neither, or both, accounts are correct. The detective thinks it is likely the Stoccos were tipped off; whether it was just by Graham, or that Peg also knew, is unclear. Peg's version checked out, as she and her daughter gave convincing accounts of how it occurred, but Graham may have seen the program the night before and warned the pair without telling his wife.

Gino himself would later tell a psychiatrist that Graham had warned them. For various reasons – including the fact that the Stoccos rarely used the internet or watched commercial television – it is unlikely they found out themselves that Gino was on the list. And, if Graham had not warned them, it would be a strange brag for him to concoct, given he is essentially admitting to a crime.

When Graham and Peg did call the police, the authorities responded swiftly, with officers from Campbelltown arriving within an hour. One detective who responded said they did not realise until much later how perilous the situation could have been. They did not even know that Gino was on the list of Australia's most wanted, or that there was a strong possibility the pair were armed. Instead, police cannoned down the only road to Graham and Peg's house, planning to take a statement about the two blokes who had just left their garage. The detective shuddered weeks later when they realised how dangerous Mark and Gino were. The police could have been driving straight into an ambush.

After the Stoccos fled Wedderburn, leaving behind tools, clothes and their three televisions, among other items, they moved in with a man whom they had met only a few weeks earlier: the Calabrian bricklayer from Lurnea.

The Stoccos set themselves up in the garage of the bricklayer's modest house. Life was not as good for the pair as it had been at Wedderburn – they had just been turfed from one of the places in which they had felt most at home in the past fifteen years. But at least the Stoccos had become friends with the bricklayer, and they socialised with people who came and visited him. He also found them work with a friend just down the road in Casula Mall. They were not living as isolated a life as they had in Wedderburn, but they hoped to hide in plain sight in the Western Sydney sprawl, partially by fitting in with other Australian–Italian tradies like the bricklayer.

Someone who visited the bricklayer was a short and stocky bloke who spoke broken English and had known the Stoccos' host for about forty years. His name was Rosario Cimone, a retired butcher who was isolated from his family but still living in an area where he had raised three children and owned a business for decades. Rosario had been asked by another man who was a mutual friend of his and the bricklayer's whether he was free to do some work. The man already knew the answer. Not only was Rosario available, but he had decades of experience doing the job he wanted him for – and it wasn't butchering. He wanted Rosario to work as a marijuana crop sitter.

There was little time spent deliberating. Rosario agreed to the job in early September 2015, about a fortnight after the Stoccos left Wedderburn.

16

You can almost imagine a gavel-clutching auctioneer wrapping his shiny teeth around the words to the real estate advertisement for Pinevale, his eyes prowling for bidders as he shouts that it's 'the property for you', the 'perfect rural property for that perfect weekend escape or for a change of lifestyle' with 'something for everyone'.

The 385-hectare block with two houses near Elong Elong, about forty minutes from Dubbo, was listed for sale at $490 000 in early 2014. 'This property has the rural feel you need to escape to when you have had enough of city life,' the advertisement read. 'There is plenty to do on this property as there are a number of motor bike tracks and horse riding tracks to explore. Great to get your mates together for a hunting weekend or just for some peace and quiet away from the rat race. So whether you are looking for a tree change close to Dubbo, Mudgee, Newcastle and Sydney or a weekender with mates this property is for you.'

As it happened, the buyer was not looking for a tree change or a weekender, but the advertisement worked regardless. He bought the property on 6 May 2014, and it was settled in July – less than five months after it had gone on the market.

The vendors, who had owned Pinevale for more than a decade, had recently finished building a three-bedroom house there. It was simple but comfortable – a white, steel-framed, homestead-style house with front and back balconies, a small kitchen and two bathrooms. It was not far from the original house on the property, a three-bedroom cottage with air conditioning and a large family room. An adjoining shed had a cool room. Each house had a storage area, a workshop and a carport. Surrounding them were five dams, stockyards, rainwater tanks and newly fenced paddocks.

The main attraction of Pinevale – its isolation – was hard to spell out in an ad. The only road in ended at the front gate, so there was no passing traffic. And the property was bounded by the Goonoo State Forest, which in turn joined the Goonoo National Park, a home to the critically endangered regent honeyeater and several other rare bird species. While the advertisement claimed that the 120 hectares surrounding the houses were suitable for 'hobbyist' cropping or livestock, locals considered it a difficult area to farm. But the man who bought Pinevale was a bit more bullish about its potential for agriculture. He planned to use it for growing cannabis.

The man who bought Pinevale had links to the Calabrian Mafia. The organised crime group, known as 'Ndrangheta, had long been associated with cannabis cultivation in Australia. The heartland of this pursuit had originally been Griffith, about 460 kilometres south-west of Pinevale in the Riverina, with its warm climate, fertile soil and irrigation channels. Now, the 'Ndrangheta grew cannabis anywhere there was water, electricity, space and privacy – and, of course, trusted workers to harvest it and pass it up the chain for distribution.

While the man who bought the property either owned it himself or had bought it on behalf of somebody else, he was not responsible for organising the cannabis operation. That fell to another man and Rosario. They set to work relatively quickly. Within a year, or possibly even earlier, Pinevale was being used to grow hundreds of cannabis plants. One of the sheds was converted into a hydroponic operation, and plants were also growing in pots at the back of one of the houses.

A crop could be harvested about three months after planting. Each plant was worth as much as $3000, which meant, for example, that even if only 100 plants were harvested at a time, they could make $100 000 a month, before expenses.

For such a lucrative operation, the syndicate needed a steady pair of hands. Some crops could be largely left to their own devices, but, perhaps to allow better, greater harvests on the considerable property, or because it was more than four hours from Sydney, they decided to install someone there permanently as a caretaker. They asked Rosario. Within days, the 68-year-old grandfather left his home in Green Valley, in outer Western Sydney, for Pinevale.

As it happened, the bricklayer knew of two others who would be well suited to working at Pinevale. Not only could Mark and Gino Stocco help their enterprise, but also the pair could do with some privacy, since Gino had appeared on the most-wanted list. It was win–win, so the Stoccos made their way to Pinevale too, arriving around 2 September.

*

That September was the driest month in the region for almost two and a half years, with less than four millimetres of rain falling. It was the driest September for eight years. But it was not oppressively hot, with an average temperature of only 21 degrees, and no day warmer than 28.

This was ideal weather for work, which is exactly what the Stoccos were at Pinevale to do. Neither was thrilled with his predicament; they had felt as if they had little choice but to accept the offer, given Gino's new status as a high-profile fugitive, and did not enjoy being involved in growing cannabis. Both men had claimed to have never taken illicit drugs – Gino said he had never even had a cigarette, let alone a joint. Mark later said the pair had known they would be growing cannabis when they went to Pinevale, but Gino seemed to indicate that they were talked into it once they got there, and planned to only stay a short time, using it as a hideout. Gino had also claimed they had 'traded their way' on to the property with stolen guns. Either way – and, given Gino's relationship with the truth, I'm more inclined to believe Mark's account – the pair did as they always did: worked to earn their keep.

Mark and Gino stayed with Rosario in one of the houses on the property, and the owner, during his spasmodic visits, stayed in the other. The Stoccos and Rosario, or 'Ross', ate together most nights. Perhaps, at some point, Gino and Rosario, who were ten years apart, discussed all they had in common: both were Italian and spoke the language, or at least a dialect, both had grandchildren they wished to see more, both had been divorced, and both had long been on the wrong side of the law and watched their only sons similarly stray.

Their days were filled with odd jobs, some more clearly linked to the crop than others. The Stoccos helped set up an irrigation system, performed electrical work and built a pergola, along with doing general cleaning and maintenance. Gino, Mark said, fixed a television and some sliding doors, and installed a bypass wire that would allow them to use diesel on the property. Work on the crop included stirring a mixture of chicken manure and dirt into pots, and cutting and bagging the dried cannabis.

In mid-September, Mark would later tell police, a man whom he described as being in charge came to the property with the property owner to harvest a crop. Given the timing, it must have been planted in July, at the latest. About seven kilograms of marijuana – probably worth almost $70 000 – was taken to Sydney soon after this point.

Also around this time, the Stoccos went away for about four days. It was probably the last week of September; Mark told police later he thought he had been there about three weeks when they decided to take off for a few days. He did not elaborate on the reasons, but it is possible they drove to an area where they kept belongings, which they may not have been able to access while in Sydney.

Mark said there had been no disputes with Rosario, or any of the three other men, and that he and Gino had been kept busy. Everything was going fine at the property. This was somewhat miraculous, given the volatility of the situation – a stubborn fugitive who domineered his son helping grow a commercial marijuana crop on a farm in the middle of nowhere, which was owned and operated by four ageing Calabrian Mafia figures. It was a delicate equilibrium that could not last.

The Stoccos returned to Pinevale in late September and within days started to find Rosario and the others grating. They lacked the work ethic, regimentation and initiative the pair valued. A new crop was not starting, and the other men seemed more interested in drinking than in rectifying the situation.

'We found them, yeah, sort of irritating,' Mark told police. 'They just wanted to just party all day, all night. We couldn't see a crop or anything develop, not that we were that interested in the crop anyway but we just . . . we just want order and discipline with everything we do. And we could just see that they were just like, yeah, they weren't doing anything, they were just lazy.'

It seems the main source of their frustration was the man who was pulling the strings, but who rarely spent time at Pinevale. When he did, it would be to drink. Police found that the owner and another man visited the property more regularly, 'consistent with them keeping an eye on their investment and employees'.

The Stoccos thought about leaving again and not coming back. 'That's why we sort of felt like we didn't want to stay,' Mark said. '. . . the main sort of guy. We used to complain about him and say, "What's he, what's he do?" Like he comes in, he just burns everyone . . .'

Less than a week after their return, the Stoccos left again. It was far less certain this time that they would come back to Pinevale. 'At that point we were virtually sick of them. We were thinking [of] entirely not coming back at all,' Mark told the police. 'They weren't running things properly or doing things. We didn't feel like we were being treated well.'

But Rosario convinced them to return, Mark said. 'Ross sort of wanted us to come back. He said, oh, he, he really liked us, he wanted us to come back, so then we came back and then, yeah, that was it.'

17

The first weekend in October 2015 marked the climax of the AFL and NRL seasons. Hawthorn would claim its third premiership in a row and a place among the greatest teams in history when it knocked off West Coast in the AFL grand final on Saturday. The next day, the Brisbane Broncos and North Queensland Cowboys slugged out an incredible finale. In extra time, when any score would win the game, the Cowboys' Johnathan Thurston, standing just beyond the 20-metre line, called for the ball. He watched it fall into his hands, took three short sharp steps before planting his left foot so as to transfer all his momentum into his right, which was thrust into a perfect but terrible arc, like the swing of an executioner's axe. He cut through the ball, which cut through the posts, and his helmeted head was swamped in the girth of other men, bigger men, as most all of them were, right near the VB logo on Sydney's Olympic Stadium.

Mark and Gino returned to Pinevale. The pair spent the latter part of the week with the 'main guy', who had become their least favourite of the four men linked to the property. Together, they installed pipes and a pump, which would be used to run water from a dam to the shed where the crop would be. He left before the weekend, but his mate and the owner arrived by Friday with some family and friends. It was the Labour Day long weekend in New South Wales, and the group planned to spend it drinking and shooting kangaroos at Pinevale. They were blessed by the weather; for the first time since April, the temperature hit 30 degrees. There were also a couple of big football games to watch. But Rosario did not appear to embrace the festive mood. The owner later said he was agitated.

The brickie's mate and the owner left on Monday 5 October. And the Stoccos and Rosario got back to work. It hit 34 degrees that afternoon – the afternoon in which Gino and Rosario started arguing.

Gino thought that Rosario was ruining the tractor, and told him so. The men had a dispute about how best to water the crop, including how to fit pipes properly and operate the pump, and they bickered about Gino wanting to water other parts of the property during the heatwave.

The arguments were just between Rosario and Gino, focused solely on the operation of the property, and did not escalate to threats or violence, according to Mark. But the pair were arguing 'really hard about a lot of issues', Mark said later. He related that Rosario 'pulled rank' but Gino would not hesitate to tell him he was out of his depth. Essentially the conflict boiled down, as it often did with Gino, to his distaste for being told what to do, and his conviction that he knew best. But Rosario was a veteran at growing marijuana, and had been appointed by his mates to oversee Pinevale. He was also a barrel-chested former butcher, not the type to take a backward step when confronted by a moody little fugitive who, among his odd traits, shared a bed with his adult son.

The stand-off, as Mark called it, continued into Tuesday. The Stoccos stopped sharing meals with Rosario. They only spoke to each other when necessary. Meanwhile, the heat kept building; Tuesday would be even warmer than the previous day.

Rosario spent the day taking cannabis cuttings, Mark said. It is unclear what the Stoccos were doing, but there is little doubt how they were feeling while they did it: they feared that their time at Pinevale was coming to an end, and were frustrated and annoyed that they were again about to be turfed from a farm they had toiled long and hard to improve. How could these ingrates continually fail to see the merit of their work, and the brilliant ingenuity of Gino? 'A similar pattern developed,' Mark later said. 'We felt we were being used and abused.'

By 7 October, the fifth day in a row of temperatures reaching more than 31 at Pinevale, it appeared that spring would be only a month long. Summer had pushed it aside, and planned to stay until late April.

Mark was out of bed by about 8 am. His father and Rosario were already awake. When Mark went to join them in the yard, they were having another scrap. Rosario wanted Gino to move cattle from the area immediately surrounding the owner's house to another yard. The pair walked back to the house where they were living, and the argument continued. By this time, the argument – as often happens – was about something completely different, having morphed to encompass the festering disdain Gino had for Rosario's incompetence.

'Dad was always telling him off about the tractor and how he couldn't drive the tractor, he busted the tractor and stuff like that,'

Mark said. 'Yeah, it was like voices raised, he's saying, "Ross, you're useless, you can't, you shouldn't even be driving that tractor," just stuff like that.'

Rosario was at breaking point. He was constantly being told he was useless by a bloke he and his mates had done a favour for. Every day was spent in dust and heat and choking isolation. The other three men involved in the plot were coming and going from Sydney as they pleased, yet here he was, stuck babysitting a fledgling dope crop with two people he increasingly despised.

He decided to go to Sydney to talk to the bricklayer and sort it out. Pinevale couldn't keep being run the way it was. Rosario and the Stoccos both felt as if they had been backed into a corner. 'It sort of came to a bit of a boiling point,' Mark told the police.

Rosario packed his white Mitsubishi Magna and left, saying little to the Stoccos other than that he was going to Sydney. The five-hour drive started with the dirt track leading from Pinevale. But he only made it to the front gate. It was padlocked, and he didn't have the key. He tore back up the dirt track to Pinevale, and soon was arguing with Gino in front of the house, demanding the key to the lock. They blued about who had changed the lock, and where the key was. Rosario rummaged around the house before ordering Gino to find it and storming back out to wait by his car. During this rant, Rosario told the Stoccos he would be calling the bricklayer to 'sort this out', and that his mate wanted 'to get rid of youse'.

The Stoccos had started packing when Rosario left, knowing he would not get very far and expecting their time at Pinevale was ending. Now that he had returned, and another spat had erupted, they knew it was over.

As Rosario stood by his car waiting, Gino and Mark went inside. Rosario thought they were looking for the key, but they had no intention of helping him leave. Within minutes of his returning to Pinevale, the Stoccos said later, they had decided to kill him.

The Stoccos' anger was like a bucket under a dripping tap. And Rosario Cimone was the drip that made it spill over. When it finally did, it is curious that Mark, not his father, was the aggressor and took charge. He told Gino to kill Rosario; he was going to talk to the others and have the Stoccos kicked off Pinevale. It was the latest injustice in a litany of woes, and Rosario had to pay.

Later, the pair would say they feared that Rosario and the other men were going to harm them, and that because of their mafia links they believed they were capable of anything. This may have been contrived to make it look as though Gino had acted in self-defence, or perhaps they were trying to convince themselves. But it is clear that when Mark recounted the actions of 7 October to police three weeks later, he was motivated by fury, not fear. 'Dad didn't even want to do it. He just said, "Tie him up or fucken let's leave," and I said, I just, I just snapped,' Mark told police. 'I just said, "Kill him." And then he – probably because I said that, Dad got the courage to do it.' Gino described it later as caving in.

Under their bed was a 12-gauge Remington 870 pump-action shotgun. The pair had stolen it from Doug Redding in Cecil Plains. It was such a reliable and stylish weapon that Remington claimed they had sold 11 million of them, making it the best-selling shotgun in history. It was loaded with five or six rounds of two different types of cartridges, which had also been stolen from Redding. The cartridges contained tiny metal pellets: one type had eighty-eight pellets; the other had 150 pellets, which were slightly smaller – not even the size of half a pea. Pumping the shotgun loads a cartridge. Pull the trigger and the pellets are set forth, dispersing wider and wider with each millisecond, until they find something to careen into.

Mark reached under the bed, grabbed the black Remington shotgun and handed it to Gino. He thought it was best that his father shot Rosario since he was more adept at handling and loading the gun. 'I'd used it once or twice but it had a safety on and I wasn't sure, you know, when you're about to shoot someone, you want to be sure you're going to fire the shot off, I suppose,' Mark said. 'So, yeah, I actually handed him the gun and said, "Yeah, you shoot. You know how to use the gun better than me."'

Gino walked out of the house with the shotgun, with Mark following. Rosario looked at them bemusedly from where he stood near the car; it was as if he thought it was a joke, or that the pair were only threatening him, Mark felt. Gino removed the safety and pumped the shotgun. He walked towards Rosario. When he was two metres away, he fired.

Rosario flinched just before Gino pulled the trigger. Now he was doubled over, his body burning as dozens of perfectly round metal spheres ripped through it. He had an entry wound about the size of a 50-cent piece in his large gut, just to the left of his belly-button. As he bent over, struggling for air, trying to make sense of what had happened, Gino pumped the shotgun again. Rosario would not have seen it, but he would have heard it; the spent cartridge being expelled and another being loaded into the chamber. Gino shot Rosario again. This wound was smaller and higher and to the right, just below Cimone's ribs. Dozens more pellets buried themselves in his flesh, and he fell to the ground. A small amount of intestine protruded from his abdomen. He started to froth at the mouth. Then he took his last breath.

One of the Stoccos' projects at Pinevale had been building a carport. They dug holes for the posts and erected string between them. It would be close to the new house, allowing a car to be parked permanently in the shade rather than in the baking sun. But they never finished it. They had a more pressing task to attend to, as splayed just near the string lines was the body of Rosario Cimone.

The pair tried to lift his body into the tray of a ute, but it was too heavy. So they dragged him to a raised concrete platform, propped him up, and then backed the ute up to the platform and transferred the body to the tray. They drove about 50 metres along a path and then turned into the scrub, where they drove for another 80 metres, just past a makeshift rubbish tip. They dragged the body off the tray to the ground, then took hold of Rosario's hands and legs and dragged him into thicker and lower scrub. Mark removed Rosario's clothes, so he would blend better into the bush, and then covered his naked body with leaves and branches.

The Stoccos then drove back to the house. Once they got there, they placed the clothes in a 44-gallon drum, poured methylated spirits and diesel on them, and set them alight. They took Rosario's belongings from the house and burnt them too, but kept $50 they found in one pocket. They also kept the work boots Cimone had been wearing when he was shot; they were, the pair said later, 'good boots'. The spent shotgun cartridges were also thrown in the fire.

Mark set about cleaning the ute. It was not as difficult a task as it could have been, because Cimone had barely bled. 'The way he shot him there was bugger all blood. It was like – it was amazing, actually, how little blood there was. There was just a tiny splotch of blood, like not even a hand size on the back of the ute, so I just washed it out. But even if I wouldn't have washed it out, you virtually wouldn't have noticed because there was bugger all blood.'

Mark hosed out the tray, and then jumped in the driver's cab. He reversed the ute down a slight hill and parked, allowing the water to drain from the tray, until it was nothing more than a drip.

The Stoccos conceived the murder of Rosario Cimone when faced with the dilemma of a seemingly impending eviction from Pinevale. But killing him didn't solve this problem. It bought them time, and meant they could leave on their own terms, but they had damned themselves to the very thing they had hoped to avoid: returning to a life on the run. And they would do so not only as fugitive arsonists and thieves but as murderers.

Both men seemed somewhat perplexed by the logic of murdering Rosario when asked later why they did not just leave Pinevale. 'It's a hard feeling to describe why we didn't just leave,' Mark told the psychiatrist. Gino said it was a 'total misjudgement' – it was a 'really bad call to do what we did'. Their answers illuminate a distinct possibility about the morning of 7 October: that both men descended into a fog of rage so thick that they could no longer see reason and, when looking to the other to provide some, instead found only more motivation to act.

This would be an unavoidable conclusion – that the men were so angered by Rosario, and by their history of being 'used and abused', as Mark put it, that they lashed out – were it not for one small detail: the locked front gate. Mark was vague when interviewed by police about why the gate was locked. He said

Gino knew about it, but that, in essence, the bricklayer and Gino had agreed to change the lock, and then Rosario hadn't been happy with the replacement. A detective I spoke to had another theory: that the Stoccos had locked the gate after fighting with Rosario on Monday to prevent the other men from arriving, or Rosario from leaving.

Whether they also planned to kill Rosario is less clear, but, if they had deliberately planned to contain him, it is logical they would have considered what might happen if he had tried to leave.

The Stoccos left Pinevale under cover of darkness, within hours of the murder. And they did so seemingly un-haunted by Rosario. Gino says it lingered on him for a while, but he blacked it out. He was soon occupied with little more than day-to-day survival, being, as he described it, 'on the road again'.

18

The Stoccos laid low for nine days after leaving Pinevale. It had been about seven weeks since Gino had been named one of Australia's most-wanted fugitives. Stories had been prominent for the first few days after the list was released, but it was no longer being widely circulated. Some of the men on the list were caught, but often the related media stories did not name those who were still on the run. Gino had outlasted at least three of the men named as part of Operation Roam: an alleged sex offender, a parole breaker, and an alleged burglar, who was wanted in Queensland. After the burglar was caught, he revealed he had actually spent a month in prison since the offence but was released again.

Gino said later that the pair camped on the roadside in New South Wales immediately after the shooting. That is not unlikely; police in New South Wales were on the lookout for them, given they had only narrowly avoided capture in Wedderburn, but they would not have known much about the car they were travelling in, or whether they were even still in the state. The Stoccos may have feared that Rosario Cimone would be found dead, sparking a more aggressive manhunt, but it was probably not a major concern: they had made it look like he had left the property; they knew he had few close connections who would report him missing; and even if those at the property stumbled upon the body, they would be unlikely to report it, given marijuana was growing there.

Mark and Gino had, over the past fifteen years, spent periods of several weeks camping. Most of the time, this was probably out of necessity, rather than choice, because the Stoccos were on long drives in between jobs, were trying to flee a region where they had committed an offence, or were merely out of work and needed to be frugal. When they were not camping, they appeared to be preparing for it; Gino told one family he worked for, when they enquired about his habit of seemingly rationing dinner, that he was 'in training'.

There is no evidence the pair had bush survival skills. They were merely canny and competent thieves, able to easily make or pilfer anything they needed when money was low. The Stoccos had also hoarded items they had stolen over the years. One such stash was in Glen Innes, in the New South Wales northern tablelands, but police and victims believe, given how much territory the Stoccos covered, and how much property they stole, that there were probably more. The Stoccos may have intended to visit one of these stashes after they left Pinevale. They may have even done so during one of their two short trips away from the property.

But had the Stoccos driven five hours north, either via the Newell or New England highways, to Glen Innes, they would have been disappointed: police had raided their stash there in August.

After eight years on the run, the net had tightened. New South Wales detectives had visited a property within hours of the Stoccos leaving Wedderburn and had uncovered goods in Glen Innes that the pair had undoubtedly hoped to rely upon when they were unable to find work and somewhere to stay. Inside the industrial shed, which had probably been filled during the Stoccos' time at the Durkins', police found a car loaded with firearms, camping gear and other equipment. Around the car was an eclectic range of stolen items that, when catalogued, ran over several pages. The Stoccos had stashed a number of pumps, boxes of tools, generators, a lawnmower, a whipper snipper, camping goods, jerry cans, gas cylinders, an air conditioner, televisions, a battery charger, a box trailer, radios and street directories.

Police returned some of the property to its owners but could not trace a large amount of it; some of it had probably not even been reported missing, given how worthless it was. But it was obviously valuable enough to the Stoccos that they tucked it away for when it was needed. Unfortunately, now that that time had come, the property was being audited by New South Wales Police, rather than being loaded into the Stoccos' ute and driven to their next hideaway.

The Stoccos were travelling in the silver Nissan Navara they had stolen from Gino's sister, Maryann, during a late-night trip to her cotton farm in Chinchilla, west of Brisbane. They were armed with the shotgun they had used to kill Cimone. And, sometime after leaving Pinevale – given both men stated that the only guns on the property were shotguns – the pair armed themselves with a semi-automatic SKK rifle that they had stolen from Doug Redding at the same time as the shotgun, along with 1500 rounds of ammunition. It was loaded with 7.62 × .38 millimetre calibre rounds that could travel a kilometre and pierce police-issued ballistic vests. It was a Chinese-made version of an SKS, a Soviet rifle first developed in 1943, which was similar to, but superseded by, the well-known AK-47. The rifle had been hidden somewhere while the Stoccos were at Pinevale, but it was now in the ute with them as they tried to lie low. The shotgun had already shown its value at close range; the rifle would be useful when the Stoccos were confronted by an enemy who was further away.

Constable Benjamin Kerslake was driving his highway patrol car through Henty, a small farming town about halfway between Albury and Wagga Wagga. He was based about 45 kilometres south-east at Holbrook, but he would often go on circuitous routes around his region; it was better than being parked at the side of a road, waiting for a hoon. Besides, a big part of the job as a highway patrol officer was visibility and deterrence; seeing a cop car could make people change their driving for the rest of their trip, and stop them wrapping themselves around a tree further down the road. It was 2 pm on Friday 16 October 2015. But there was no early knock-off to start the weekend for those working around Henty; it was only weeks from grain harvesting season.

Kerslake drove his police car south along Railway Parade. The road becomes the Olympic Highway, which continues south until it joins the Hume just north of Albury. It was so named because the Olympic torch was carried along that route on its way to Melbourne in 1956. To Kerslake's left was a strip of houses, small businesses and industrial sheds, and beyond them a few blocks of houses. A railway line ran alongside the road to his right, and on the other side of the railway was the rest of the town. Further still to the west was Doodle Cooma Swamp.

As Kerslake passed Fourth Street, a silver Nissan Navara ute turned right out of Yankee Crossing Road on to Railway Parade and started driving towards him. Kerslake's car – like all New South Wales highway patrol cars – was fitted with automatic numberplate recognition software. It detected the numberplate on every car he passed and fed the details through a database. It could tell him if the numberplate matched records of those that had been stolen, if it was unregistered, and if the suspected driver had outstanding warrants, among other things. Only a few years ago, Kerslake would have had to take down the plate details, radio them in and then wait while they were checked. But the software can scan six numberplates a second, without him even needing to push a button.

Kerslake's car and the ute were less than 300 metres apart, and closing on each other. His numberplate system sounded a warning: it had detected that the plates on the ute, CVS95L, were stolen. They had been taken from a grey Suzuki Swift parked in Orange, more than 360 kilometres north, about seven months earlier.

Kerslake did a U-turn, turned on his lights and siren, and started pursuing the ute. The video recording device in his car automatically activated.

Gino was driving west along Yankee Crossing Road, his son in the passenger seat of the Nissan Navara they had stolen almost two years ago. The flat grain paddocks of southern New South Wales stretched behind him, and the town of Henty in front. When Gino hit the intersection with Railway Parade, he decided to head right, which would take him north towards Wagga Wagga: straight and he would have crossed the railway line and headed along the southern edge of the town; left and he would have headed towards Albury.

Gino looked both ways down the expanse of Railway Parade, and turned right. Before long, he realised he had made an error – he was driving directly towards a New South Wales highway patrol car. Had he been five seconds later to the intersection, the cop would have driven along Railway Parade directly in front of them, and not given the ute a second thought. Gino would have given way to the officer, shared a wry smile or even a chuckle with Mark, and been on his way. Or, if Gino had gone straight, instead of right, the police car would have passed behind him. But now he was watching the police car in his rear-vision mirror, hoping it continued towards Albury. Hoping it would not slow. Hoping it would not explode in red and blue, turn back across Railway Parade and start chasing them.

But Gino saw the brake lights come on. And then the lights. And then heard the sirens. For the first time in two months, since he had become a fugitive of national importance, Gino Stocco was being chased; not by a detective in North Queensland, nor by a farmer he had slighted, and not by the shady friends of the man he murdered, but by someone who existed in a world other than his thoughts; someone he could touch and see, and someone who could touch and see him.

Kerslake noticed that the driver of the Nissan Navara with the stolen plates slowed for a moment after he began his pursuit, but then quickly sped up. They were travelling back along the same section of road he had just driven down, past houses and businesses, but the driver of the ute accelerated to 90 kilometres per hour – almost double the speed limit. Near the edge of town, he turned right down Sladen Street and headed east, along the Henty–Cookardinia Road. Within minutes, they were outside Henty, careening along roads bounded by paddocks.

The driver of the ute was reckless; at one point, when he crossed over to the wrong side of the road, he forced a farmer, who was slowly towing equipment in a ute in the opposite direction, onto the dirt shoulder to avoid a collision. But he was not driving at breakneck speed – only about 117 kilometres per hour now on a road with a 100-kilometre-per-hour limit.

The pursuit continued along the Henty–Cookardinia Road, past the southern edge of the site that hosts the renowned Henty Field Days, until the driver turned left down the dirt Kreutzbergers Road.

Gino slowed for a moment after seeing the police car in his rear-vision mirror, but then he accelerated, speeding along the streets of Henty next to the railway line, before turning right and heading east. He was now driving parallel to Yankee Crossing Road: the road that would have kept him safe, had he not turned and come across Constable Benjamin Kerslake's highway patrol car and his automatic numberplate recognition software.

As the road angled north and Henty disappeared behind him, Gino asked Mark to take the wheel. The pair swapped seats as the ute careened along the Henty–Cookardinia Road. Mark jammed his right foot on the accelerator, and Gino picked up the rifle, which he had taken to keeping close at hand. If it was not already loaded, it soon would be.

Mark swerved off the bitumen and down a dirt road. The Stoccos said later that they were used to officers stopping when they went down dirt roads. But this police officer didn't – he continued to follow them.

Mark dropped the speed to between 80 and 85 kilometres per hour, but this was still fast enough to be somewhat perilous on a dirt road. They were sure the cop would give up soon – he had been chasing them for just under twenty-five minutes, and more than half of that had been on the dirt road – but he just kept going.

They were on a straight and wide stretch of the dirt road when Gino asked Mark to come to a stop. As soon as the Navara was stationary, Gino leant out the passenger side with the rifle and took aim at the police car.

Footage from the video camera inside Kerslake's car shows a dark mass in a cloud of dust on a road almost three cars wide, with eucalypts lining the road, paddocks beyond them and a steely sky above it all. The dust makes the Stoccos' ute hard to see, but you can make it out, 50 to 100 metres in front of Kerslake, heading north. The sound of road underneath the police car can be heard, the crackle of the radio, his screaming sirens.

At 2.21 pm, the dust settles, and you can see the ute in the road, almost completely stopped about 60 metres in front. 'Stand by radio, he's almost come to a stop,' Kerslake says. The ute starts to move again, dust building as it begins to fade from view, but it's still there. Still close. Less than two minutes later, it stops again in the middle of the road. An odd sound, like someone slapping a pool of water, cuts through the sirens and the radio and the tyres on the road. There is no mistaking the next sound: Kerslake shouting into the police radio, the voice of a man who thinks someone is trying to kill him.

'Urgent, urgent, urgent, urgent, he's firing, shots fired, shots fired. Shots are fired, shots are fired. He's armed and dangerous, he's got a rifle.' Kerslake's car is hit again. He adds to the cloud of dust as he reverses the car, swearing. The ute disappears from view as Kerslake does a three-point turn and speeds back towards Henty.

Gino steadied the rifle and took off the safety. Stopping the car gave him a better shot. The police car slowed, but was still moving towards them. He wanted to scare the copper off. He squeezed the trigger. And again. And again. In total, the SKK let off five shots, maybe six. Gino was fairly sure he hit the car at least twice. Regardless, shooting at the cop had the desired effect; he had backed away, and then driven back the way he had come. Back towards Henty.

At 2 pm on 16 October, around the time that Kerslake started following the ute with stolen numberplates, Senior Constable Matt Shaw was visiting his son at primary school in Wagga Wagga. Shaw worked for the Highway Patrol in the town, and had been rostered on since 6 am that day. Things had been steady, but he found time to check in on his boy, who had been sick the day before. Shaw's wife, Nicole, was also a police officer; she was the general duties station supervisor rostered on at Wagga that day. The plan was for Shaw to pick up the kids from school, and Nicole would be home in time for dinner, all being well.

Shaw stayed at the school for about fifteen minutes. As he left, he heard a job on the police radio. Nicole would have heard it too. There was a pursuit, and the ute that the police were chasing was heading north, towards Wagga Wagga. Shaw radioed that he was on the way; he planned to head the ute off, by putting spikes on the road to stop it. He drove towards Mangoplah, a one pub and one shop town, about 30 kilometres from where the pursuit had started.

That one shop is run by a bloke called Paris. He is the newsagent and the postman, and he smiles at you with a cracked right front tooth, shakes your hand with cracked hands and makes you laugh with his cracked humour. His hair is trying to escape from under an ECM Livestock bucket hat, and he's wearing a grey sloppy joe and brown slacks. He remembers the day that police cars came speeding past his shop from Wagga Wagga: a convoy so loud and bright it was as if someone had shot fireworks down the main street. The first car he would have seen or heard was Shaw's.

On the drive from Wagga Wagga to Paris's shop, two emus pop their heads up from feeding in a paddock next to the road. They are jarring, like a weird art installation. Paris is sort of the same thing: too outrageous to be in such a setting. He is behind the counter when I go in, but it looks like his favourite perch is the plastic furniture out the front. There is a coffee cup on the table, stained with the remnants of a thick black brew, one Winfield Original left in his pack of 25s and yesterday's *Sydney Morning Herald* spread out.

As he's contemplating where exactly the Stoccos shot at police, saying he could draw me a 'mud map', a man in his late teens or early twenties comes in. He grabs a 1.25 litre bottle of Coke and a can of Coke, and wants a pack of twenty cigarettes. 'Now, you look like a young go-getter,' Paris says to him. 'So I'm going to let you know that you can get that bottle' – he puts his hand on the Coke – 'for $5.50, or you can get that big two-litre bottle' – he points at the drinks fridge behind the customer – 'for the same price.'

The go-getter takes this in. Without saying anything, he takes the bottle from the counter with a smile, replaces it in the fridge, grabs the bigger bottle and comes back, all while Paris explains that he got a better price on the two litres and doesn't want to rip people off. 'Don't drink it all at once,' he says, as the go-getter wanders out.

Shaw had not even reached Paris's shop at Mangoplah when he heard Kerslake say the ute was slowing. The next dispatch was more panicked: 'Urgent, urgent, urgent, urgent, he's firing, shots fired, shots fired.'

He feared for Kerslake's safety. 'All I could think of was that I had to get to the officer as quickly as I could to give him support,' Shaw said later. 'My greatest concern was that he had been shot and was alone on the side of the road without any help.'

Kerslake had not been shot, but he was alone on the side of the road, with his car disabled. Gino Stocco had shot the car twice. A bullet had struck the bumper bar, just above the fog light, and another hit the wheel arch wall on the front passenger's side. This bullet severed the brake hose behind the front wheel, and, after driving a few kilometres, Kerslake's car came to a halt. He radioed that he was unharmed but his car had stopped.

When Shaw heard this, he was relieved, and the fear he felt for Kerslake quickly turned to anger. Shaw drove past Paris's shop and was south of Mangoplah when he saw the ute, which was also travelling south, back along Henty Road. So Shaw did what Kerslake had about thirty minutes earlier: he gave chase.

*

Gino Stocco was back behind the wheel of the Navara. He decided to turn around and drive back towards Henty. He and his son were closer to Wagga Wagga than to Albury, and perhaps that figured in their reasoning: that they were better to try to keep away from either of the two larger towns and avoid the cavalry of police who would surely respond to one of their own being shot at.

But barely five minutes after they had shaken one police car, another appeared. And then another. Gino turned left down Paper Forest Road. It was bitumen, and he could have driven faster than he had when being pursued by Kerslake. But, within minutes, he started to slow the ute again. He crossed to the wrong side of the road, and then turned, so the passenger window was facing the way he had come, towards the police. He told Mark the rifle was still loaded, and to take aim.

Senior Constable Stephen Woolatt was based at Holbrook with Kerslake. He was driving a police four-wheel drive when he saw the silver ute on Mangoplah Road. At the same time, Shaw came up behind him and overtook him to pursue the ute. When Shaw noticed that the Navara had slowed, he kept his distance. He had heard what had happened to Kerslake.

He was about 200 metres from the ute, which was parked across the road, with the passenger-side window facing him, when he saw movement at the window. Then there were two loud cracks. A puff of dust shot up from the roadside just in front of his police car. He did exactly as Kerslake had done: reversed as quickly as possible. But this time the driver of the ute did not continue along the road, away from police. He came towards Shaw, and Mark let off two more shots. Shaw heard them but did not see them. He was looking over his left shoulder out the back window as he reversed away, hoping it would not be the last sight he ever saw.

Shaw and Woollatt both reversed until they were back on Mangoplah Road. At some point, the ute had stopped coming towards them and had started to again head east.

Nicole Shaw had heard everything unfold on the police radio; she was the officer in charge of dispatching most of Wagga Wagga's police that day, and yet she was utterly powerless as her husband was fired upon. And then she heard him say he was going back after them.

Woollatt followed as Shaw continued the pursuit. But they stayed even further from the ute this time. The Navara continued east along Paper Forest Road. The only break in the landscape of flat paddocks was Burkes Creek, its meandering progress to the north of the road marked by the trees lining it. Beyond that was the Livingstone National Park, renowned for its wildflowers.

The driver turned left onto Pulletop Road, the bitumen again replaced by dirt. They crossed Burkes Creek, following the road that tracked along the south-eastern edge of Livingstone. And Shaw soon lost the silver ute in a cloud of dust.

It had been about an hour since Kerslake had started chasing the ute in Henty. Just when it appeared they might have lost them for good, they spotted the ute again, stopped at the intersection of Pulletop and Cheviot Hills roads. Shaw radioed to say he was again on the ute's tail.

The driver of the ute went slowly past the intersection, and Shaw and Woollatt followed. But then the ute reversed quickly and turned into Cheviot Hills Road, passing a sign that read 'No Through Road'.

Shaw waited for more police. It was one thing to pursue men who were willing to shoot at officers on an open road. It was quite another to follow them into what could be an ambush.

Cheviot Hills Road winds for another 13 kilometres before stopping at the front gate of North Wandoo, a sheep farm owned by the Robinson brothers. Roy, eighty, and Ivan, seventy-nine, were known as local eccentrics – 'a pair of funny old buggers', as one neighbouring farmer put it to me.

The Robinsons' story about how they found the front gate of their farm padlocked and chained shut one Friday afternoon probably would have been met with some cynicism. That is, until police later confirmed it. The Stoccos had come to the end of the road, driven onto the Robinsons' property and locked the gate behind them. Gino and Mark had worked on a property to the rear of North Wandoo before. They knew that it backed on to the Hume Highway, a possible escape route given there was no way police could close the major road.

As the Stoccos snapped the lock behind them and continued driving towards the Robinsons' farm, Shaw and Woollatt were still waiting for support back at the intersection. Specialist tactical police from Sydney had been requested, as had air support, but both requests were declined for 'logistical reasons'; they would not make it that far south in time. More police were still expected to arrive. But the lack of specialist officers meant that, regardless of how many police officers turned up, the Stoccos would still have the most powerful weapon, and a vehicle that was equal to any that police could access.

At 3.40 pm – about forty minutes after the Stoccos had careened down the no through road – police discovered the locked gate at the Robinsons'. A search of the farm started about an hour later. Fresh tyre marks and recently cut fences were seen. Almost another hour later, police spotted the Stoccos. Mark and Gino were in a gully with the Navara nearby. There was a decision to be made: move in and try to arrest them, or wait to see if the cavalry arrived. They decided to wait.

Detective Inspector Darren Cloake from Wagga Wagga didn't know it yet, but he was about to work for three weeks straight. Within hours of the Stoccos shooting at Kerslake, Shaw and Woollatt, Cloake was thrust into coordinating the New South Wales hunt for the pair. It was not his decision for police to hang back once they had spotted Mark and Gino in a gully at the Robinsons', but it was the right decision, he said, because the gun had scopes that could spot a target 450 metres away, and was so powerful it would knock over a cow at that distance. 'How Mark and Gino would have reacted if confronted by police, who had a limited capacity to return fire, was something not worth risking,' he said.

Ideally, specialist support from Sydney should have been made available. But it was not forthcoming, so the officers had to wait for back-up from Victorian and ACT police. 'We could have done better there,' Cloake said. 'Any job like that is not going to go to plan, so you just adapt and overcome.' But by the time reinforcements had arrived, the Stoccos had slipped away. It may have seemed a miraculous escape, but in reality 16 October 2015 was the day that Mark and Gino tightened the noose around their own necks.

19

Walk south through the rolling green of the Robinsons' farm, North Wandoo, and you will come across the northern boundary of Wandoo, another sizeable sheep property. Mark and Gino knew this; they had spent a couple of months working on the property. But Bill Wearne, who owns the farm with his wife, Joy, can't exactly remember when this was. His only point of reference is that, when the Stoccos arrived to work, they told him they planned to be in Tasmania for Christmas and, later that year, he saw a news report about them being rescued in Bass Strait. He is adamant it was them, but nobody else I speak to has heard this sensational story of the Stoccos being plucked from the icy waters between Victoria and Tasmania. Other than this odd revelation, Bill Wearne's experience of employing the Stoccos is like that of many other farmers: their work was great, their behaviour was weird, they left after a minor disagreement and they stole from him when they did.

Bill needed some carpentry done in his woolsheds, so he put an ad in *The Land*. He got a call from a bloke called John. He and his son stayed in a cottage on the property while they completed the work. The pair were clearly unusual, Bill said, but not to the point of worrying him. The Stoccos were trusted to use his account at a supermarket to buy groceries. They ate healthily and did not drink. They kept the cottage tidy; it helped that they were only sleeping in one of the beds of the cottage, which had at least four bedrooms. They worked hard, they worked skilfully and they worked closely together. Bill called them Zig and Zag, because they went everywhere together. 'If one of them needed to get a hammer from the tool box, they would both go.' It was not just being close physically, while working and sleeping, that characterised the relationship between the two men. Gino was frank with Bill about his marriage breaking up, and Mark was staunchly behind him. 'Mark felt his dad had a hard time, and that he would stand by him and look after him. I thought that was a good thing.'

I can hear the hum of a ride-on mower, being driven by Joy, as Bill speaks. He is barefoot, in jeans and a long-sleeved RM Williams Stockyard chequered shirt, the sleeves rolled up, his face a dark pink and his eyes a sharp blue, shining under heavy lids. His voice is disarmingly soft. Bill is watching over his young daughter, her eyes watching him back from under a shock of hair, as he occasionally pushes her pram back and forth. Halfway through the conversation, his staffy, all smiles and low-slung muscle, with a bright red bandanna tied around its neck, trots up with blood streaming from the top of its nose. 'Jeez, it's knocked itself about there,' I say, noticing that the whole snout is coated in claret. After a strangely long delay, as if he'd been pondering and then systematically calculating the probability of every scenario, Bill says, 'Probably went after a rabbit or something.'

Gino told Bill, as he told many people, about the impending collapse of the world. But this version had a few more shades of the Rapture. Gino would talk at length about the Bible and quote passages from it, giving Bill the impression that he and Mark read it nightly. Bill also soon quickly learnt that the pair had no trust of authority and were paranoid about being watched all the time. They were convinced there was a conspiracy whereby a small number of families in the world were in charge of all institutions, particularly political parties and banks. They both seemed to truly believe this, and it didn't seem Gino had influenced Mark to do so. 'I'm a reasonably strong person, so I asked a few questions, but you can see with certain people that there's no point because they're not going to change their mind about anything.'

One afternoon, Bill left them at Wandoo and told them he'd be back the next morning. The following day, he was busier than he had expected, and he didn't make it to Wandoo until the afternoon. Gino seemed irrationally upset. The next morning, the pair had gone, taking an esky and cheap, old tools, such as a shifter and screwdrivers. 'The value of what they took wasn't even worth calling police,' Bill says. 'And it probably wasn't even worth what I owed them for the work they had done anyway.' He felt bad enough about them leaving that he 'called them, because I was just going to say sorry it didn't work out, all the best, and I wouldn't have brought up the missing stuff. But I never spoke to them.' A mechanic who worked for Bill wasn't so conciliatory; he said during a media interview that if he saw the Stoccos again he'd break their jaws, so angry was he about Gino borrowing a tool of his.

Bill had some concern when he learnt that the Stoccos were on the property the afternoon they shot at police. But he was not too worried; his family live in a house on another property on the other side of the Hume. But as police searched for the Stoccos around Wandoo, the men lay in a creek bed not far from Bill's house, waiting for nightfall. The perfect time to steal a ute.

For farmer Paul Rogers, Sundays are rubbish days. And 18 October 2015 was no different. Rogers drove his white Toyota LandCruiser ute up and down Four Mile Lane, picking up wheelie bins from across his 280-hectare property Yarranalla, loading them in the tray and then taking them to the tip. His cattle stud is in Little Billabong, on the other side of the Hume, about 18 kilometres from the Robinsons' property, across rolling paddocks and four lanes of bitumen.

Rogers's property is the Centennial Herefords stud, where he breeds coffee-brown cattle with white heads and underbellies. His bulls look like they would hit as hard as his ute, and they cost almost as much: $40 000 for the best of his sires, Nova Saffron G09. They soon pay for themselves, however: a 0.5 millilitre straw of their semen is worth as much as $50. Most cows are artificially inseminated; it's quicker and safer than waiting for brutes like Nova Saffron to sidle up to a suitor. But it is a fickle business, genetics. Read the lineage of a sire wrong, or get unlucky, and you've got a very expensive steak on your hands. And then there is the weather, and its blessings and curses.

Rogers didn't know it as he pulled bin after bin into his ute that Sunday, but the spring weather was about to end; by the end of the month, days would start regularly hitting 30 degrees. Still, the weather in the Riverina was more forgiving than at the property Rogers had previously farmed, about 560 kilometres further north, not far from Pinevale.

Just as Rogers could not have known about the weather, he could not have known that, as he drove along the dirt lane, wheelie bins echoing in his tray, he was being watched.

It was not the closest Mark and Gino had come to capture in the past eight years; after all, Mark had only been saved from arrest in St George because of his father bashing Sergeant Liam Duffy. But the predicament the pair found themselves in – behind a locked gate on the Robinsons' in a stolen ute, bouncing across the paddocks, knowing that the police would be coming for them – was certainly acute. And there was the small matter of Rosario Cimone's murder. Did police know about that? Was that why they had chased them in the first place?

The pair parked the Navara in a gully on the Robinsons' property. From here, they may have been able to see police watching them in the distance. Certainly, after a while, they would hear helicopters. They decided to wait until nightfall, leave the ute and set out on foot to the south. Towards Wandoo, the farm they had worked on. They took the SKK rifle with them, and some food and water. But they left behind the Remington shotgun, which they had used to kill Cimone nine days earlier. And they started to walk.

North Wandoo, and the properties surrounding it, is prime farming land. That dictates that all that stands on these fertile paddocks is felled: trees first, and then, in turn, the cattle that take their place. But there was some cover for the Stoccos, mostly along small creeks, their dry beds shaded by remnant bushland.

And there was thicker bush to the south-west, licking the foothills of the Great Dividing Range, which rise to Mount Kosciuszko, about 110 kilometres away. It is not inhospitable country, and the temperature was mild. It would dip only as low as 17 on their first night as prey in the wild.

It is unclear how far the pair made it that night. It must have seemed weeks since Kerslake first started chasing them along the main street of Henty, but it had been less than four hours between then and when they had finally shaken police. Two hours later, darkness would fall, and they could move stealthily across the paddocks, cutting fences when they reached them, and getting closer to the Hume. It would make sense to move then, even if they were weary from their day of evasion. They would look for another vehicle and, if they couldn't find one, lie low as dawn broke, and then wait out the sunshine.

Later on Saturday 17 October, they were on the move again. They probably crossed the highway this night and, before dawn, settled down in Four Mile Creek with hessian across their bodies to make them harder to see from the air. They were about seven kilometres from where they had last been seen by police.

Sometime the next day, when they heard the crunch of tyres along the gravel lane to their south, they peered out. And they noticed a white Toyota LandCruiser ute with wheelie bins in the tray.

Paul Rogers unloaded his bins at the tip, filled up the 145-litre diesel tank on his ute and made for home. He turned left from the Hume into Four Mile Lane, the Four Mile Creek running parallel to the lane on the passenger side. Rogers went back to drop off the bins and then turned into his long drive, went up a slight rise and parked the ute, a 2012 model with a distinctive white bull-bar, in a shed behind and to the left of his house. He shut the driver's side door, leaving his wallet inside and his keys in the ignition. He then walked about 40 metres to his back door and stepped inside. It was nearly 7 pm.

Down in the creek, the Stoccos watched as the ute was driven away from them and up a driveway, and then tucked behind the house. They knew farmers. There was a good chance that whoever was driving that LandCruiser would not lock it. And they would probably leave the keys inside. All they had to do was wait a couple of hours until nightfall and see whether they were right.

They slunk up the driveway, past hundreds of thousands of dollars' worth of cattle, and Rogers and his wife sleeping in their bedroom, and tried the door of the ute. It was open. And the keys were inside. So was a wallet. Perhaps their luck was turning. They put the white ute into neutral and pushed it out of the shed. It was straightened up, then rolled down the decline of the driveway, onto the road. When they started the engine, out of earshot, the Stoccos were pleased to see that the ute had a full tank of fuel. They eased it into gear and into the blackness.

Paul Rogers was out of bed by 6 am the next day. He had to give a bloke who was working for him keys to the gates on his properties. The bloke was waiting for Rogers outside, near the shed. Rogers walked out the back door to his ute to fetch the keys. But when he got to the shed, it was empty. He looked at the shed, then looked at the bloke, and said, 'Where's my ute?'

20

Gino Stocco was raised by parents who were considered 'other', foreigners toiling on the land to make a living. It was an upbringing that contributed to his belief that society was gravely unjust. He felt victimised by the establishment when he railed against these injustices. He was a petty thief who became a murderer and shot at police who tried to arrest him.

Gino shared all these traits – not to mention his beard – with a man who had died 135 years earlier: bushranger Ned Kelly. It was not these factors, however, that would lead to the comparisons between the pair. When Mark and Gino slipped down Paul Rogers's driveway and then turned onto Four Mile Lane, they headed south. Into the region of north-east Victoria mythologised as Kelly Country.

It was not long after the Stoccos escaped police at Wandoo that senior New South Wales and Victorian police worked on a strategy to capture them. There was no shortage of intelligence available for the force to trawl through about the history of the pair, but little of it was concrete or offered guidance about where they could have fled to. All the intelligence did was outline the extent of the challenge facing police: the fugitives were cunning and resourceful, loyal only to each other, with no strong ties to any property or town; they travelled long distances, often at night, and were known to have visited five states; and they lived completely off the grid, with no known phone, bank, car, licence or address details. Not to mention that they were armed with at least one high-powered firearm, which they had already proven willing to use.

Police would do what they could to monitor known haunts, including properties they had previously worked on, and speak to relatives and the few acquaintances they could find, but they came to the conclusion that the public would be their greatest weapon in the hunt for the Stoccos. Their crime spree may have lasted eight years across three states, but there was little widespread awareness of them, even despite Gino's inclusion in the list of Australia's most wanted. That would change within hours of the pair shooting at police.

By that evening, they had made headlines and nightly news bulletins in Australia's two main media markets, Melbourne and Sydney. The update to the story two days later would be irresistible: the bearded outlaws who had shot at police to avoid capture were spotted filling Rogers's stolen LandCruiser with petrol in Euroa, a town dripping in bushranger folklore since the Kelly gang robbed the local bank. Police embraced the poeticism, and referred to the Stoccos as 'modern-day bushrangers'.

The only thing Euroa reveres as much as its bushranger history is its history of war heroes: three Victoria Cross winners hail from the town, and there's a statue of each of them in its memorial park. There is also a Wool Fest, which is on when I visit.

Binney Street, the main drag, is closed to traffic and has a stage set up on the back of a truck at one end. A maypole is erected in the middle, and local girls dance around it to Taylor Swift. Further up the street, near the sheep display and the fire trucks, is a man selling raffle tickets. I ask him which service station in town the Stoccos were seen in, and he points with his right hand, down the other end of the street to the Shell. Before I head there, I duck into the visitor information centre to buy a map. A volunteer, Kevin, lays one out that's $11.95, which he later tries to give me for free.

He wants to show me where the Stoccos could have gone. There is a clutch of small roads that branch off soon after leaving the Shell, most of which lead away from the Hume and towards wilder country. 'Follow this all the way,' he says, running his finger along a mountainous track, 'and it takes you back to the Tanner show.' He's referring to Denis Tanner, a former detective caught up in the deaths of two women: Adele Bailey, a sex worker, whose body was found in a mineshaft near his property to the south at Bonnie Doon, and Jennifer Tanner, his sister-in-law, who died from gunshots to the head in an apparent suicide. He was never charged with either, despite being linked to one or the other, or both, for about half of his sixty-one years.

A further hour and a half up the Hume lives Paul Dale. Dale is probably the only former Victorian copper from the past two decades as notorious as Tanner. The former detective was raised in Yackandandah and moved to Wangaratta after he was booted from the force, also under a cloud for his links to two murders. The Dale story is murkier, with more links to the gangland war, high-ranking police and suppressed evidence. But the Tanner story got more people talking. Particularly the death of Ms Tanner. She had been found to have shot herself twice in the head with a bolt-action rifle, which she must have had to fire using her toes, with the gun held in her feet, before reloading and doing it again. She also had gunshot wounds to her hands.

Kevin points at the narrowing rings of topography and the darkening green, which stretch away from Euroa to the west and north. This is where the Stoccos went, when they left a Maccas and a Shell on one of Australia's busiest stretches of freeway. Footage of the pair at the service station shows Gino filling Rogers's white LandCruiser. Mark can be seen walking out of a blue-walled corridor leading to the toilets. His arms are positioned somewhat oddly by his sides, the collar of his white shirt up, sleeves three-quarters down, the front of the shirt tucked into jeans. His left eye is obscured by the peak of a dark hat, which his sunglasses perch on, and he has light stubble. If he'd kept walking straight and to the right – rather than through the service station to the ute – he would have ended up at a tourist information booth for Euroa. Plastered above the brochures is a slogan: 'Lose yourself a stone's throw from Melbourne.'

The service station staff were none the wiser while the Stoccos made their understated getaway. 'The team member who served them didn't watch a lot of TV,' Sheryle, who is behind the servo counter the day I visit, says. Just before I speak to them, Sheryle and her colleague Lorraine are goading the man at pump 11 about his thirty-fifth wedding anniversary. Sheryle sings an impromptu happy anniversary song down the microphone. He pays at the pump to avoid coming in.

The women know the story of the Stoccos, but they weren't working that shift, and the woman who served them doesn't work there any more. The Stoccos paid for everything, including some ice. The only hint of something unusual was when Mark returned the keys to the ice box. 'He got spooked by something and dropped the keys down there by the coffee machine and took off,' Sheryle says, gesturing.

After leaving the service station, the Stoccos drove east, away from the Hume, took a left and passed the Euroa Lawn Cemetery. The cemetery lay between them and the shaking city-bound lanes of the freeway. The Stoccos idled past Kevin's house on Faithfuls Creek Road, so slowly that his wife heard the engine and decided to take a look out the window. She noticed the white LandCruiser from the news, and was still watching their headlights as they turned left at Mckernans Road. Along this road, you cross over Faithfuls Creek, bitumen becomes dirt, and then you hit Sheans Creek Road. From here, the Stoccos probably went east, away from the Hume. If you keep tracking in that direction, and then to the south, for about 100 kilometres, negotiating the Strathbogie Ranges along the way, you may happen upon Stringybark Creek: the place where Ned Kelly, his brother Dan and other members of their gang gunned down three policemen in October 1878.

Within hours of the footage of the Stoccos in the white LandCruiser being released, Paul Rogers's phone started to ring, and it didn't stop for days: he was the owner of the most infamous ute in Australia, the getaway car of two violent fugitives. 'For two weeks after it happened, I was getting so many calls . . . I couldn't keep my phone battery charged for a full day,' he said. 'I dunno how many times I can say to people, "They took my ute."'

So it is not surprising that he is wary when I pull into his driveway, just behind where his new ute is parked, about a year later. Rogers's skin is coloured by years of dirt and sun. Once I've introduced myself and he invites me in, I drag a chair next to where he has been sitting, outside the back of his house, looking on to his fruit trees and flowers, the back of his shed, and the paddocks stretching to our left, some recently cut for hay, others still green. It has been wetter this spring than last, the year the Stoccos were here; Rogers's tractor cut up the wet ground a few days ago while carting hay.

The Stoccos would be on the run for ten more days after stealing the ute, and, after they were shown with it in Euroa, it became a symbol of their skills of evasion; the trusty steed that was faster and craftier than any beast used by police – as though they were riding the colt from old Regret. 'It was just a rising two-year-old V8 LandCruiser four-wheel drive ute. Half the farmers in the country have got them,' Rogers said. 'But, I suppose, for driving the back of scrub and stuff, it's one of the best vehicles for that.'

It was the wallet, rather than the ute, that Rogers was worried about losing. 'I was thinking, if they don't catch these blokes, eventually they'll try and claim my identity.' But the wallet was found before the Stoccos were, with only the cash missing, although it took Victoria Police ten months to return it.

When Rogers heard that the Stoccos had been spotted in his ute in Euroa, filling up with diesel less than twenty-four hours after they had stolen it, he thought, 'How have they burnt 135 litres of fuel in a day and only ended up less than a couple of hundred kilometres down the road?'

It would not be the last time his car would feature on the news. The Stoccos headed as far north as Dubbo and as south-east as

Bairnsdale, the car a constant, but the numberplates rotating through a collection stolen from Victorian, New South Wales and South Australian drivers. It rammed police cars out of the way, ghosted through other seemingly tight police cordons and took its occupants to hideouts beyond the reaches of the exceedingly well-resourced officers who hunted them. 'Everyone wanted to make sure I got the ute back because it was famous. Someone said we could use it at B & S balls as some sort of draw card.'

Other farmers in the area didn't take the theft so lightly. 'Most people here were purposely leaving their keys in the car because they didn't want [the Stoccos] to come inside looking for them. I told the coppers during the interview that was happening and they took a dim view of that.'

It is impossible to untangle the mystique of bushrangers from the national identity. Their larrikinism, indifference to authority and sense of a deeper fairness not associated with the law are seen as inherently Australian characteristics. Rogers does not think of the Stoccos as bushrangers. To him, they are simply crooks. But people were interested in them for the same reason they were interested in bushrangers; because, Rogers thinks, most people like to see police fail. It is often overlooked that Kelly and his gang murdered the police at Stringybark Creek, an ignorance that continues to grate on the descendants of those killed. But it is rarely overlooked that the Kelly gang spent years on the run, giving police the slip – just like Mark and Gino.

'They made a mockery of the police forces. They made the New South Wales and Victoria police force look like idiots. They kept having sightings of them and then they let them through their fingers,' Rogers says. 'Generally people don't like the police force, so if someone is making a mockery of them, they enjoy it.

And these blokes got made up as folk heroes because they kept evading police.'

Rogers had his ute replaced by insurers within days, as they knew how important it was to his farm. The stolen ute is probably already being driven around by somebody else, who bought it at a police auction oblivious to its bizarre history.

Occasionally Rogers looks out from under the peak of his Centennial Herefords hat towards his paddocks, which are glowing now in the afternoon sun. The pastures may be tame and neat and sown with grass native to a land tens of thousands of kilometres away, but they are a green as rich as the rainforests of Far North Queensland. And this is why he sold that dusty farm near Pinevale.

But there is something missing from his paddocks. All around the region, from late winter to mid-summer, many of them shine with a purple flower: Paterson's curse. 'Don't have that here,' Rogers says. 'I might see half a dozen plants on my travels. And I pull them out.' If only it was so rudimentary weeding out the Stoccos.

As it happened, the police were right to concentrate their search on regions where Mark and Gino had previously worked. Not only had the pair left the stolen Navara ute on a property neighbouring one they had worked at, which they then trekked across before stealing the LandCruiser from Rogers, but, after leaving Euroa, they gradually headed back towards another familiar enclave. It was as if they were having a farewell tour.

In reality, it just showed the breadth of their travel across the eastern seaboard – there were few regions they had not worked in during the past fifteen years. Internally, police circulated a document about the Stoccos the day after they were seen in Euroa. It was issued by the fugitive task force, and marked as sensitive and not for public release. It detailed that a round recovered from the Mangoplah shootings showed the pair were armed with a high-powered rifle and, as such, that police should exercise extreme caution. The police circular read:

> *These rounds WILL penetrate vehicles and police issued ballistic vests. They are utilized in centre fire military caliber rifles and can travel for over one kilometre. Members are requested to be vigilant in relation to their own safety and to also report any sightings, stolen vehicles, stolen plates, farm house burglaries and thefts; along with any reports of persons fitting their description – in and around camping areas. Also note that Mark and Gino Stocco have been known to travel through various parts of Victoria in the past and can be unpredictable in their movements.*

The images that the police released of Rogers's LandCruiser, taken from the CCTV footage, showed that the tray of the ute contained camping chairs and a lime green esky. They also showed the Stoccos as clean shaven, or close to it, compared with previous images where the pair had long, unkempt beards.

Almost fifteen hours since they left the service station, after a detour to Tumbarumba, on the western edge of the Snowy Mountains, where they stole numberplates from three cars, the Stoccos reappeared, little more than an hour from Euroa, to the south.

21

Punch north and east through the sprawl of suburban Melbourne, past the vineyards of the Yarra Valley, preened and prepped for weddings as much as for wine, over the Yarra Ranges to where the land flattens, and you reach the farming settlement of Glenburn. Mark and Gino first worked in the region in 2009, and possibly earlier. And they had returned in October 2012 and January 2013 to light fires at the Zipsins' cattle farm. From Euroa, there are multiple ways to get to Glenburn, but it is impossible to get there without, at some point, driving on or very close to the Melba Highway, a major road.

The pair well knew the warren of fire access tracks that cut across the mountains and through the deep pockets of bush between the towns, and may have spent several hours in there, after news of the Euroa sighting broke. They had several methods to avoid detection while they stopped. One was to place hessian bags on the roof and tray of the ute so it was less visible from the air.

Another was to do as much as possible to avoid their registration plates being seen, including standing or setting up camping chairs in front of them, as this looked less suspicious than removing the plates entirely. Once they hit the road again, a favoured tactic was to turn off as soon as they noticed a car behind them. It meant the driver behind would not get close enough to take down their plates. But there were limits to what they could do to avoid detection. And, at about 9 am on 21 October 2015, the pair were spotted on the Melba Highway just outside Glenburn, heading south.

The Euroa sighting triggered a blitzkrieg in Victoria. A strategy to deal with major incidents – established in response to the failures exposed during the Black Saturday bushfires – was put into effect. Police swarmed into Yea, where an incident control centre was established, and got to work. The Stoccos were in the huge chunk of Victoria from Cobram in the north to Phillip Island in the south, and all the way east to Mallacoota, that was – and still is – under the watch of Assistant Commissioner Rick Nugent. His major concern was that, after shooting at police in New South Wales, the Stoccos would not hesitate to kill one of his officers on a deserted back road somewhere in the bush. He knew there was some risk to the public, but police who came across them were likely to be the main target. There were other judgements, based on intelligence and the Stoccos' background, that Nugent and his men made. It was highly likely that if the Stoccos were cornered, a siege would start. They also considered it likely that they had supplies – including weapons – hidden somewhere in the Victorian bush, or might know people who would help them. Other scenarios – such as the possibility that the Stoccos could start a fire to hamper police – were considered, but discounted.

As police pored through what they knew about the Stoccos, and used it to forecast the risks, Superintendent Paul O'Halloran, who, alongside Nugent, had a key role in the search, had a staggering realisation: he had never dealt with crooks who drove like the Stoccos. Maps based on intelligence were drawn up showing where the Stoccos had been sighted and how far they could travel. The area was enormous. 'You're talking about the size of England,' he told me in an interview. 'And it's in the bush.'

While O'Halloran and Nugent got up to speed with the Stoccos, Detective Inspector Ian Campbell from the fugitive task force told media about the 'credible' sighting on the Melba Highway in Glenburn. He said the Stoccos 'had quite a good knowledge of the area'. 'Potentially that is a reason why they have headed in this direction,' he said. 'We're certainly appealing to them to hand themselves in. It's only a matter of ringing the nearest police station or ringing triple-0, and we're appealing to Mark and Gino to hand themselves in.' Campbell stressed that, while it was believed the pair were armed and dangerous, the public should not fear harm, despite the shooting at Mangoplah. 'There's no suggestion that any member of the public is in any danger. However, what we are doing is appealing to every member of the public to be vigilant to keep an eye out for the vehicle.'

As the day went on, police became increasingly confident they had Mark and Gino cornered. Nugent, who has worked as a homicide detective and been involved in several major operations, including hunting for prison escapees and, earlier that year, the search for an autistic boy lost in the bush, could not tell me later what technology or methods police used to reach this conclusion. 'Operationally there were a whole lot of tactics and different equipment we use, which I can't talk to you about,' he said. 'We believed . . . they were absolutely within this spot in the bush.'

A huge dragnet spanning more than 170 square kilometres was set, from the command post north at Yea, east to Marysville, south to Yarra Glen and west to Kinglake. Police checked to make sure they had as many roads covered as possible, and the heavily armed Special Operations Group (SOG) were ready to respond. And, whatever secretive methods Nugent and his team were using, they were right: the Stoccos were surrounded. The pair were hunkered down in the LandCruiser, probably on a secluded bush track in the Yarra Ranges, not knowing where to go next.

Night fell. It had been five days now since the Stoccos had shot at police near Mangoplah, and two weeks since they had killed Rosario and buried him in a shallow grave. About this time, the Stoccos started to bicker. Gino wanted to give up, police believe, but Mark kept talking him round. Back and forth, back and forth: why run from something that was so much faster and larger and could come from all directions? Why give up now, letting the system win?

Outside the cab of their stolen ute, hundreds of police waited for them in the black. Some of them, too, had doubts and fears, about the two blokes armed with the serious guns and, even more dangerously, armed with the hate to use them. What was to say they weren't watching them right now?

At a police cordon on the Melba Highway near Castella, about 15 kilometres from where the Stoccos were last seen, two officers waited in a patrol car. Blue and red lights danced across the road and the trees before drowning in the dark. About 1 am, the Stoccos came across the police car. Rogers's ute was flying beneath them, any thoughts of surrender long gone. They gunned straight by, heading north. The two officers gave chase, but the white ute was not for catching – it quickly reached more than 140 kilometres per hour. If they had tried to keep pace, there was an even greater risk of a car crash. The Stoccos – if it was them being chased – could easily pull up around the next bend and pick them off as they drove towards them. The police were told that the SOG had been deployed just up the road. If Mark and Gino wanted a shootout with them, the officers thought, good luck. The pursuit ended.

Nugent and other senior police were comfortable that the cordon would hold, and that the Stoccos would soon encounter the SOG. They waited and waited. But Mark and Gino did not come. The net had a hole. 'Sometimes people luck out,' Nugent said. 'I don't think it was planning on their part. They just ended up finding this little track that came out, and we missed them. But you get that.' Gino and Mark had slipped away down an unmarked logging or fire trail, and were bumping along, eyes on the rear-vision mirror, the fuel gauge and the bush that held them to her bosom.

It did not take long for speculation to grow that the Stoccos were the latest beneficiary of Victoria's messy police pursuits policy. After forty-three people died in police pursuits in twelve years, Coroner John Olle made sweeping recommendations about how to stop the carnage. One of the cases reviewed by Olle was that of Sarah Louise Booth, a pregnant seventeen-year-old who died when a car she was in, driven by a 24-year-old man who was high on ice and speed, crashed into a tree at 140 kilometres per hour while being chased by police. The recommendations were adopted by police in July 2015. But within weeks, police started noticing something: they were being goaded into chasing drivers, or openly taunted, as word spread about the relative impotency of the new policy. Only five months later – and two months after the Stoccos chase was called off near Castella – senior police conceded in *The Age* that the force had suffered a 'reputational hit'. A review of the new policy was announced. But Nugent and Campbell dismissed suggestions that this policy helped the Stoccos, though some police, particularly New South Wales officers, remain sceptical.

Nugent's officers kept a firm gaze on the bush, optimistic that Mark and Gino were still trapped inside. There appeared no way the pair could beat the cordon again, given where they had last been seen, and police had intelligence that suggested they could have found another lair, though Nugent will not detail the nature of this information. It is still not entirely clear how, but as a small army of police waited and watched the verdant green of the Yarra Ranges, the fugitives were driving towards the patchwork of paddocks in north-east Victoria. They were just up the road from the Big Ned Kelly, a six-metre, one-and-a-half-tonne fibreglass statue in Glenrowan, when they next came across police. About 2 pm on 22 October, two Cobram highway patrol officers pulled over a white LandCruiser for a routine check on a road near Lake Rowan, north of Benalla. The officers were pretty sure it wasn't the Stoccos: the car looked to be an earlier model, and the numberplate was different. They were also almost 200 kilometres away from where the pair had last been seen, about thirteen hours earlier, and police down that way were pretty sure they still had them cornered. But, as the officers were getting ready to get out of their black patrol car and speak to the driver, he abruptly reversed, smashing the LandCruiser into their car, and sped off.

The officers saw that there was a passenger inside the ute, too. Both men were wearing high-vis vests, and a light had been placed on the dash, as if to warn about a wide load travelling behind. It all happened so quickly, though, that the officers did not notice much else. The LandCruiser, with its towbar, had disabled the patrol car on impact, so they could not give chase even if the new pursuit policy had allowed it.

Police quickly hosed down speculation that the incident at Lake Rowan was linked to the manhunt. 'Police don't believe the Stoccos were driving the vehicle involved in the ramming of the police car near Lake Rowan,' a spokeswoman said. 'As confirmed earlier, we will continue to focus our search for the wanted father and son in the Yea area. We will also increase patrols in the Lake Rowan area searching for the vehicle involved in ramming the police car.' Media described the ramming as a red herring.

But it had been Mark and Gino, and, the next day, the police conceded they had got it wrong. 'We can now confirm that it is our view both Stocco and Stocco, the father and son, were in the LandCruiser that reversed into the police car,' Nugent told media on the morning of 23 October.

As Tony Wright wrote in an article in *The Age* headlined 'Gino and Mark Stocco – will o' the wisps in Kelly Gang country', 'A red herring had, you might imagine, turned into red faces.' The information that proved the Stoccos had backed into police came after a sighting was reported in Bairnsdale, in East Gippsland, hundreds of kilometres from where police had been focusing the search. The pair had been seen leaving a supermarket, and were driving the same LandCruiser, but not with Rogers's plates. They were using Victorian plates stolen from near Wagga Wagga – the same plates seen on the ute involved in the ramming. Inside the supermarket, a person had heard the pair arguing, they would later tell police.

An air of vaudeville surrounded efforts to catch the Stoccos. Twice, they had been so close that police could almost touch them. And yet they had slipped away both times – once after literally running into police. The Stoccos had managed to drive from the New South Wales border to the north, to Bairnsdale in the east, almost 400 kilometres away, at least once while supposedly surrounded by a police cordon. The increasingly familiar images of the pair at Euroa, two blokes who looked like farmers driving a farmer's ute, were juxtaposed with images of heavily armed police, some in camouflage gear, as if on safari or in a war zone, wandering around regional Victoria, seemingly waiting for one of the Stoccos to leap from a paddock, so they could take a ping.

One online news story featured a photo of a single police car in a country town, an image as telling as any other about the futility of the search: the Stoccos could be anywhere, so the police may as well be too. On social media, people were transfixed, and Stocco memes were quickly created and shared. 'Where's Wally?' was modified to 'Where's Stoccos?', the pair were declared 2015 Hide and Seek champions, and Mark and Gino's heads appeared on top of the leaping silhouettes borrowed from Toyota's 'Oh What a Feeling' campaign. Most of the material was at least indirectly critical of police. One popular meme featured Chief Wiggum, the bumbling police officer from *The Simpsons*, saying the fugitives were pinned down in an area bordered by Mallacoota, Perth, Broome and Thursday Island.

The mockery of the force was, as Paul Rogers alluded to, something many Australians took particular glee in. But there did appear some grounds for concern about how the search for Mark and Gino was progressing. In the days since the Stoccos had shot at police in Mangoplah, and they had become the most sought after fugitives in the country, hundreds of police had been tasked with finding them. But there were holes appearing in the force's knowledge of the pair, and in the plans to capture them.

What chance did the public have of spotting the pair if two policemen who had their car backed into were not even able to recognise them or their vehicle? How many stolen numberplates did they have access to? Had the Stoccos been underestimated from the start?

'They are organised, they're cunning, and they're working very, very hard to ensure that they are not apprehended by the police,' Nugent said at the time. They were again compared to bushrangers, and Nugent lauded their survival skills. The police command post was to be moved north from Yea to Wangaratta, as it would give police a better overview of the north-east. It had been five days since Rogers's ute had been taken. The Stoccos had been able to travel thousands of kilometres, and police had no idea where they were. By Sunday – a week after the ute was taken – journalists were asking Nugent if it was possible the Stoccos were in South Australia.

The search was certainly being watched closely in other states. Darren Cloake, the detective inspector from Wagga Wagga, was monitoring the hunt in New South Wales. He spent his time keeping abreast of how Victoria Police were tracking, while speaking to as many people as possible who knew the Stoccos and could give information about where they might show up next. It quickly became clear to him, as it had to his Victorian counterparts, that these were no ordinary fugitives. They had no safe place, no family to lean on and no particular region where they felt more at home than anywhere else. There was nothing electronic that could be traced or checked to see if it presented patterns, about where they shopped, who they interacted with on social media, who they regularly spoke to via mobile or which phone towers they regularly pinged.

How to catch two recluses, who trust only each other, have no need for electronics or comfort, and have a knowledge of country roads akin to that of the most dedicated local copper? It became clear that old methods of policing were just as ineffective as new ones. There was no place to visit to try getting family to pressure their loved ones into turning themselves in. And there were no phones to trace, bank records to be seized, or metadata to plunder, which could help find them. 'They're a clear example of those living off the grid and the methodology we have to use,' Cloake said. 'We would usually be looking at close relatives, places of significance, habitual stuff. They were completely unique . . . because they didn't maintain any normal trends.'

Cloake had been working on building the brief against the Stoccos in New South Wales, while touching base with police in Victoria. He closely analysed reports of stolen numberplates, hoping one could point him in another direction. He discovered that a shell casing found in Mangoplah matched the ammunition that had been stolen from Doug Redding; an important piece of evidence tying them to the shooting.

Fifteen warrants against both men were active in New South Wales, and that was before the shooting at police offences were even considered. In theory, Cloake's job was as simple as making sure he kept in contact with Victoria Police about the hunt for the Stoccos. In reality, it was far more difficult. A strike force, codenamed Kalkadoon, had been established after the Mangoplah shootings. Cloake was in charge, but he was also required to do the heavy lifting. 'I basically worked every day for three weeks straight.'

Despite the hard work, Cloake knew that catching the pair would ultimately come down to one thing: ensuring the public knew who the Stoccos were and reported any sightings. He did not buy into their characterisation as bushrangers, and thought that most people in the community would help to catch two crims, despite their lauding of Kelly and his ilk and their delight in the failures of the police. The ability of police to reach more people than ever before with this message was one thing in their favour – the modern equivalent of a 'wanted' poster could be seen by tens of thousands of people in an instant, not to mention accessed at any opportunity, including immediately after a possible sighting. 'We wanted people on the street who were aware of these two and engaged in social media and watched the news – that was the ideal,' he said. 'The community were getting involved and understanding there was no romanticism about these two. They were criminals who, at that stage, had committed serious offences. There was no looking at them [with the] inference they were modern-day bushrangers. They were basic criminals. Certainly our ability to share information these days is tenfold on what it was in days gone by.'

Redding, in Queensland, and Ian Durkin, in northern New South Wales, were also two keen interstate watchers of the Victorian search. Redding had been overcome with anger once news of the Mangoplah shooting reached him, and now he was scarcely able to contain himself. Every day, another report reached him of police seemingly wallowing in ineptitude. And Mark and Gino were nowhere to be found.

It was another manifestation of the coppers on the ground fighting with one hand tied behind their backs because of the failures of those higher up the chain, Redding reasoned. It was the same ailment that prevented the Stoccos being caught sooner; local coppers wanted to properly investigate crimes the pair were suspected of committing on their patch, but were weighed down and discouraged by the 'administration', as Redding calls senior police, and so eventually let them slide. The failures in leadership made it impossible for the community to respect the police pursuing the Stoccos, Redding said, hence the scorn heaped on the hunt for the fugitives. 'We have a disdain for authority that does not perform,' he says. 'There's a difference between a Dad's Army and an SAS regiment. We're not run by a professional mob who know what they're doing.'

Redding was one of the few victims of the Stoccos who had been identified, and so was being regularly contacted by journalists. In one particularly memorable interview, he said the Stoccos stank like polecats, and outlined their South Sydney Rabbitohs refereeing conspiracy. He described them as mongrel dogs and gutless. But behind the bluster was real fear. Fear he shared with Durkin. The Stoccos could kill someone. And they could, as they had before, travel thousands of kilometres in a night and find their way back to either of their properties. And this time, they would have even less to lose, and had shown they were even madder than anyone had thought, given the shooting at Mangoplah.

Durkin took to secreting weapons and ammunition in hiding places around his property, and taking a loaded gun with him each night while he checked the gates. He had reason to be fearful. He did not know it yet, but the Stoccos *had* killed someone. And they were driving north again.

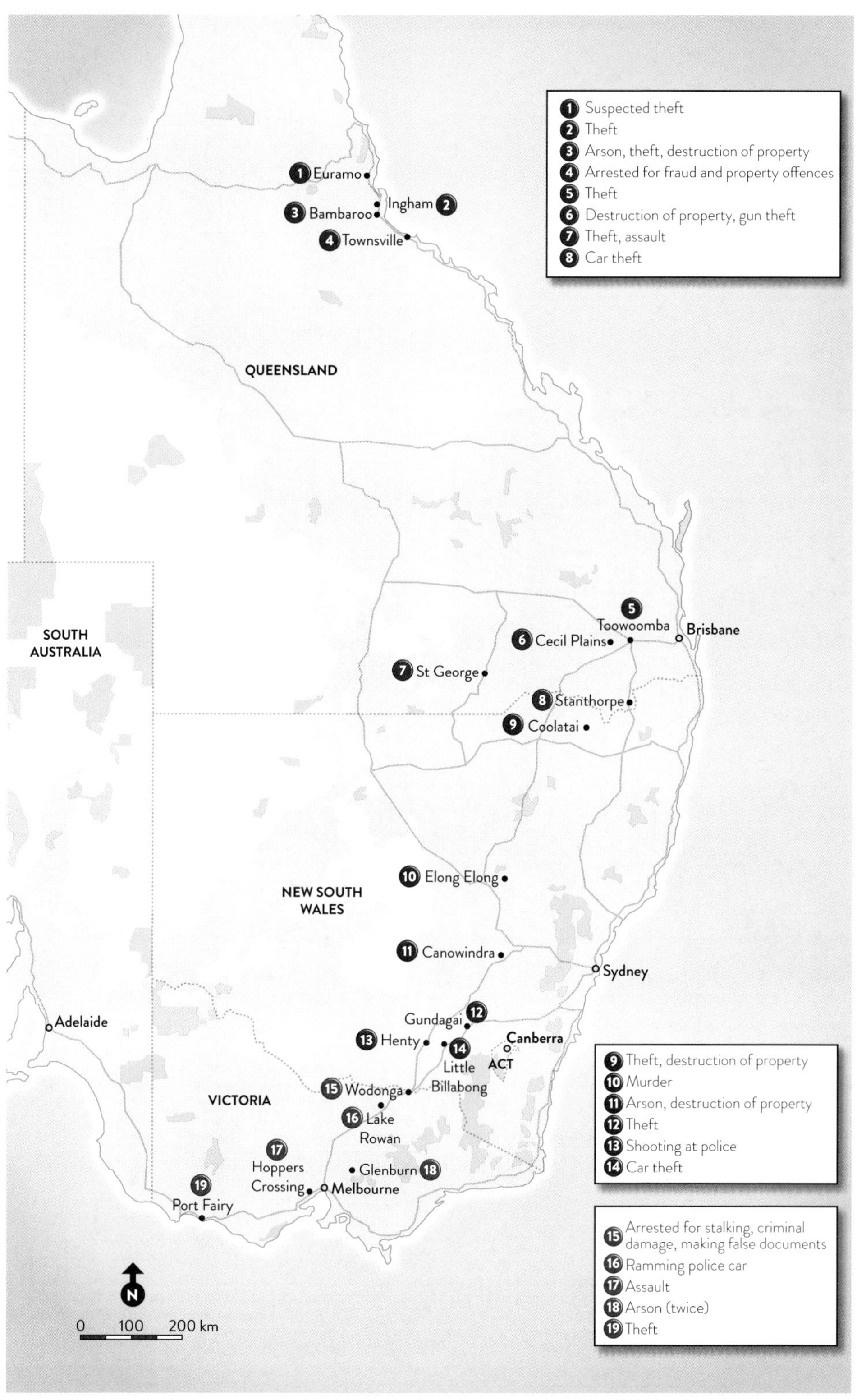

Mark and Gino travelled up and down east-coast Australia committing a variety of offences.

Gino and Mark Stocco. The photo of Gino accompanied his inclusion in the list of the most wanted fugitives in Australia in 2015. (New South Wales Police)

Peter Stocco's home in Toobanna, Queensland. Mark and Gino Stocco were thought by police to rely on the place as a safe haven while on the run. (Photo supplied by author)

The Moyne River in Port Fairy, Victoria. The Stoccos moored their yacht, the *Kiwarrak*, on the town side of the river, to the right of the picture. The yacht club they later robbed was on the opposite bank. (Photo supplied by author)

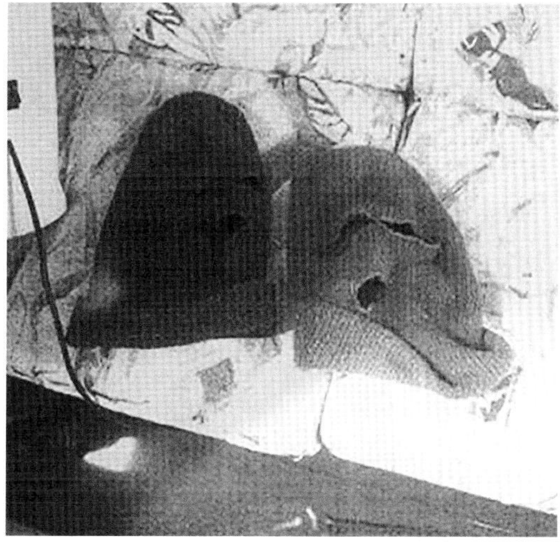

Balaclavas, numberplates and tea towels seized by Victoria Police from the Stoccos' yacht after it was raided in Apollo Bay. The pair pleaded guilty to robbing Port Fairy Yacht Club, but they maintained their innocence for years afterwards. (Victoria Police)

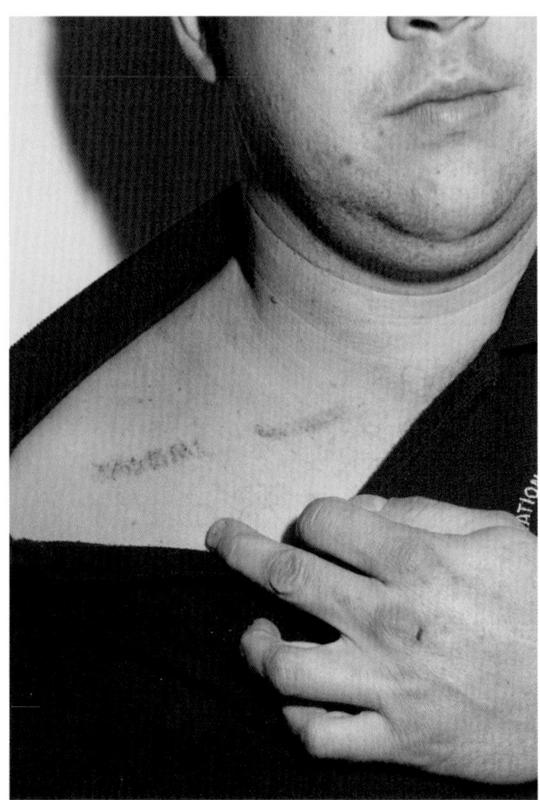

St George police sergeant Liam Duffy escaped serious injury when he was bashed by Gino Stocco while trying to arrest Mark in south-west Queensland in 2013. (Queensland Police)

A shed at the Zipsin's property is destroyed by a fire lit by Mark and Gino Stocco. The property in Glenburn had survived the deadly Black Saturday bushfires. (Glenburn CFA)

The dirt road to Pinevale and other properties in Elong Elong, NSW. The Stoccos worked on the remote property cultivating marijuana, and Rosario Cimone's body was later found there. (Photo supplied by author)

Detective Inspector Darren Cloake speaking at a press conference outside Wagga Police Station, 25 October 2015. Cloake was one of the NSW police tasked with tracking the Stoccos. (Kieren Tilly/Fairfax Media)

A police roadblock at Big Springs, after the Stoccos shot at officers who were pursuing them, in 2015. (Les Smith/Fairfax Media)

The Stoccos evaded police after fleeing through the property of elderly farmers Roy and Ivan Robinson and padlocking the gate behind them. (Peter Lorimer/Newspix)

Captured at last: Mark and Gino Stocco arrested at Pinevale, 28 October 2015.

Police swarm Pinevale in the hours after the arrest of Mark and Gino Stocco. (AAP Image/David Moir)

THURSDAY, OCTOBER 29, 2015 $1.40 (inc GST) HERALDSUN.COM.AU WE'RE FOR VICTORIA

Herald Sun

STOCCO BANDITS NABBED

GINO STOCCO

MARK STOCCO

IT'S BLOODY OVER

An eight-year reign of terror by father and son fugitives Gino and Mark Stocco ended in an armed police swoop, a short bloody struggle and the shock discovery of a body, shot three times, in a shallow grave on a farm in western New South Wales.

REPORTS & PICTURES, PAGES 4-7

FREE SAMSUNG GALAXY TABLET DETAILS PAGE 25

NEW DVD COLLECT THE SET DETAILS PAGE 2

LATEST NEWS - SPORT

FULL DERBY FIELD

MOVIES & MUSIC GIRL HIT POWER

The capture of the Stoccos made headlines across Australia. This is the front page of Melbourne's *Herald Sun*. (News Ltd/News Pix)

22

Any fugitive can be caught – even a fugitive who is friends only with darkness, and shuns hunger and paranoia and fear and fatigue. Who ignores the whispers that salvation is only a surrender away, and has no longing for family or friends or lovers. Even one who believes wholeheartedly that all he does is just and all those against him are not, and is motivated by this undeniable truth yet untarnished by hubris. Even this fugitive can come unstuck. It can be a mere oversight, a minute failing that renders a lifetime of precision utterly worthless. Or being pitted against an uneven foe, so mighty they crush the firmest resistance and straighten even the most crooked bend. Or there can be a compounding of happenstances that brings about their end; like the sun shining on an empty stubby in the bone-dry bush and starting a raging inferno. Such was the end of Mark and Gino Stocco.

The pair were travelling at night, finding places to stop at dawn, on the move again at dusk, and taking turns to sleep where they could. They had been able to make do, for the most part, with the food they had bought in Bairnsdale and the fuel from Euroa. It was too fraught now to do the 'shopping' they had been used to doing before the shooting at Mangoplah. People were already looking for them. But eventually they would have to take a risk. Money was low. They had not been prepared to flee when Mangoplah happened, and they had been unable to settle ever since. If they had other hiding places, similar to the storage shed at Glen Innes, it was unlikely they were stocked with fuel and food, given neither of those were found in the shed that the police had already discovered.

They also no longer had the option they had regularly relied on: dropping back in to a property where they had previously worked, or answering an advertisement for workers, and using that as a base. They had, of course, also used these opportunities to restock on things they did not have – usually by stealing them – and to offload things they did not need but wanted to keep safe. Police and farmers have theorised that this also gave them an excuse to drop back in to places, even those from which they had departed acrimoniously, as they had a seemingly legitimate reason to call in and reclaim what had been left behind. This door was also closed to them. They had begun to feel the fingers of desperation around their throats when they decided to kill Rosario Cimone; now, those fingers were starting to squeeze.

Someone watching the hunt for the Stoccos would not have got the impression they were starting to feel desperate. Even Cloake, watching from Wagga Wagga, feared the pair could get away from them. 'I thought they could go a lot longer,' he said. 'Look at Malcolm Naden.' Naden was the first Australian to have a bounty on his capture since Ned Kelly and had been on the run for almost seven years, eventually caught by New South Wales police hiding in dense bush near Gloucester in the Upper Hunter in 2012. He was jailed for murdering two women and shooting a police officer. Naden, however, was in far thicker bush than the Stoccos, and was even wilder and more desperate: a scavenger who broke into and lived in the Western Plains Zoo while he was on the run. Like Mark and Gino, Naden was an opportunist, rather than a survivalist. The difference was that he was willing to go to even greater lengths than the Stoccos to take those opportunities.

Police in Victoria were essentially in a holding pattern, waiting for the Stoccos to show up, so they could reengage. They had a detailed plan for their capture, and closely monitored incoming intelligence, but were almost entirely reliant on them slipping up. Little did they know, a police officer in New South Wales had the first strand of information they needed to catch the Stoccos. The problem was, the police officer didn't know it yet either.

The bricklayer began to suspect something had happened to his old friend, Rosario Cimone. He had been back to Pinevale with another man involved in the dope crop on 9 October. The property was empty. Mark, Gino and Rosario had vanished. The house was cleared of their belongings, and instead of three men toiling over a lucrative marijuana crop, he found a hauntingly deserted farm in the middle of nowhere.

This was problematic on several fronts. He and three others knew that one of Australia's most-wanted men and his son were working on a property growing dope. They knew that when the job was offered to the pair, they had little choice but to accept it. At the time, the risk of involving the Stoccos was counterbalanced by the security of knowing you had workers who could never go to the police and tell them about the grow house. But that roll of the dice had fallen the wrong way.

The bricklayer knew there was tension between the Stoccos and Rosario; on his last visit to Pinevale, it had hung in the air as pungently as a freshly harvested dope crop. He had known Rosario for forty years, and two things were clear: he did not back down from a stoush, and he did not abandon his mates. Putting those two truths together led him to a troubling conclusion: the Stoccos had done something to Rosario.

The bricklayer and another man cleared up any remaining evidence that there had been a marijuana crop at Pinevale, and left the following day. Only a few hundred metres from the now empty shed, insects and small animals were devouring the naked body of Rosario Cimone, feasting on his internal organs as he started to mummify in the heat of a dying spring.

On 17 October the bricklayer decided to tell the police about the Stoccos and Rosario. The previous day, Mark and Gino had shot at police near Mangoplah. He knew that the police wanted any information they could get about the Stoccos, but it was still difficult working out what exactly he should tell them; how could he let them know he knew of a property where they had been and that his friend was missing without letting on too much about the circumstances? But he decided it was worth the trouble; police were appealing for any scrap of information about the Stoccos, and this could help him find out what had happened to Rosario.

He went to his local police station in Green Valley and said he knew the Stoccos had been working on a farm near Dunedoo, and that a friend of his who had been there with them was missing. But the probationary constable struggled to put together what the bricklayer was saying. Part of the problem was the bricklayer's broken English and thick Italian accent. Also, police were not so interested in places the Stoccos had been as where they were now; and what exactly did this have to do with Green Valley? The bricklayer could not even find Pinevale on a map. The officer further found it odd that the person reporting Rosario missing was a friend, not a relative. He had last seen the man a month ago but, by his own admission, only regularly saw him once a month. The bricklayer also held back some information about Pinevale and Rosario. This combined with his accent meant the young constable found it impossible to understand that the man was linking the Stoccos, a remote property near Dunedoo and his missing friend. Certainly, the bricklayer gave no impression that he thought Rosario had been harmed.

The officer, after speaking with his sergeant, lodged a report: that a man named Rosario Cimone had gone missing; he was last seen at a remote property in western New South Wales; the Stoccos had also been there before; and a friend had reported him missing. That same day, the bricklayer decided he should tell Rosario's family he was worried about him.

As Cloake sifted through hundreds of pieces of information filtered to him from the real-time intelligence centre in Sydney – which, as the name suggests, uploads intelligence gathered by police as it is received and triages it based on possible relevance and merit – he came across the report lodged by the probationary constable from Green Valley. He immediately thought there was something in it.

*

Only hours earlier, the bricklayer was telling Rosario's family what he had told police: he was worried about his friend. The family contacted the police themselves, and were able to lodge a missing persons report, complete with a photo. They later said they believed it was their missing persons report that had sent police to Pinevale; in reality, it was the information provided by the bricklayer. Police were already aware of Pinevale and the Stoccos' connection with it when the family reported Rosario missing.

Detectives had also received other information that the Stoccos had been working on a marijuana property. Combined with what the police already knew about Rosario and his criminal history, the pieces were starting to come together. Had the Stoccos been involved in the disappearance of a retired butcher, grandfather and middling Calabrian Mafia figure from Western Sydney, who had last been seen cultivating a remote cannabis crop? And was the answer to that question down a dusty track and behind a locked gate at a property called Pinevale?

Mark and Gino Stocco had managed to lie low for two days following the Lake Rowan ramming. That incident had taken another day for police to confirm it was linked to them, and no new information had been released since. It was now 24 October.

Some police, privately, at the very least, started to wonder how long such a significant number of resources could be allocated to the search, and whether command had even the slightest inkling where the pair were. It was one of the largest searches ever undertaken in Victoria; hundreds of police deployed over an area of 46 000 square kilometres, taken from uniform branches, crime command, the elite Special Operations Group, and the Critical

Incident Response Team and Operations Response Unit. The next year, Victoria Police were so chuffed with their effort that they published an overview about the search in the annual report, under the heading 'Working with Our Stakeholders'.

But, as of that day in October, it had been for nothing. The Stoccos were still on the loose, and the trail had seemingly gone cold. What only senior officers in Victoria and New South Wales were privy to was that there was a possible lead involving a secluded property near Dunedoo. That morning, the Stoccos were spotted at Sale, west of Bairnsdale, in Gippsland. Then, at 9 pm, Victoria Police realised the pair had left the state: they did a drive off from a petrol station in South Gundagai, about seven hours away from where they had been seen that morning. The Stoccos were still driving the ute, but it was now fitted with stolen South Australian numberplates. They were about an hour up the Hume from where they had stolen Rogers's ute almost a week earlier, and about 400 kilometres from Pinevale.

As they again travelled along the Hume, a road they had driven perhaps more than any other in Australia during their odyssey, Mark and Gino were exhausted. They did not know how much longer they could cope with the constant fear of capture. Gino was on edge and felt he was being noticed everywhere. They had limited food and water, and had spent significant periods walking in the bush in the previous six days. It is unclear whether parking the ute and walking into the bush had been a strategy to avoid capture, or whether Gino exaggerated the extent of the hardship the pair faced. Regardless, both men knew they needed rest. They made a decision: to return to Pinevale. There was food in the freezer and diesel in a tank. It was remote and secluded, so they could sleep easy in the comfortable bed they had left not three weeks earlier.

And nobody would know where they were; they were sure Rosario's mates would not have mentioned to police that their friend was missing.

As it happened, the morning after the Stoccos were spotted in South Gundagai, two other men linked to the property returned to Pinevale. Perhaps the Stoccos were watching from the bush as the men made another quick check of the premises, before leaving.

The next day, 26 October, the Stoccos were camping in the bush in the Goonoo Forest, possibly making sure Pinevale was clear before returning. It was about lunchtime, and the two men were moving around their ute and a makeshift camp, when park rangers came upon them. One of them flipped the tailgate down to cover the numberplate, and there were hessian bags on the roof so the ute could not be seen from the air, but it was no use: the rangers were sure they had just spotted the Stoccos. It was a perilous situation; the rangers were alone and unarmed, had no mobile phone or radio reception, and had just stared two ruthless fugitives in the face. They reversed and made their way out of the park, frantically watching in the rear-view mirror to make sure they were not being followed.

Once the rangers called the police, they organised a rendezvous and sting: the police would use the rangers' car to drive back into Goonoo and past the campsite to check whether the two men were the Stoccos. They drove back down a narrow dirt track deeper into the forest and found the campsite empty, the makeshift tent still there. Car tracks seemed to lead out of the forest towards a bordering property: Pinevale.

There were now three clear signs pointing the way to Pinevale: the report of the bricklayer; the evidence provided to other detectives, which would remain secret; and the sighting at the camp and the car tracks in Goonoo. That was enough for police to plan a major raid targeting the property. The next night, 27 October, Rural Tactical Operations Police crept towards Pinevale. They did not use lights and barely spoke as they inched their way through the black. Eventually, they came to a point several hundred metres away: close enough to have a good view of the house, but far enough away that the Stoccos could not see them. It was around midnight, and Pinevale had sunk into the unnerving blackness of the desolate landscape around it, a lighthouse barely visible through a stormy sea. They lay still in the bush, and waited.

Each Tuesday night, Darren Cloake plays water polo. It's a fairly niche sport wherever it is played, but particularly so in the country. On the Tuesday of 27 October 2015, just before Cloake was about to jump in the pool, he received a phone call. 'It was a copper, and he's told me, "We're at this property, we're pretty confident the Stoccos are here, but we have to do more surveillance before an arrest."'

In some ways, the property was perfect for a covert arrest operation, since there was nothing else around; this meant there was almost no possibility of members of the public being caught in the middle. The property was surrounded by bush, with only limited tracks leading in or out, so it would be easy for police to cordon off. And there was no need to rush: as long as the property was monitored, there was little prospect that the pair could escape, if, as police suspected, they were inside.

But in other ways, Pinevale represented a horror scenario. They were trying to capture the Stoccos on their own turf. The forest around the houses could be booby-trapped, as could the houses and sheds on the property. The whole thing could be an ambush, with the Stoccos just sitting back and waiting for police to walk right into it, while they picked off officers with their rifle from a perfect crow's nest. They could even be hundreds of kilometres away, hoping that Pinevale had created a diversion and given them clear air for a few hours.

As surveillance officers kept watch over Pinevale, dozens of other police were making their way towards the property from Sydney. These officers included the Tactical Operations Unit – as close as a police officer can get to being in the military. It is a long road to get there, involving advanced weapons, tactical and equipment training, and gruelling mental and physical tests, as well as psychometric testing of psychological and behavioural limits. Ten months earlier, some of the officers had been responsible for storming the Lindt Cafe in Sydney's Martin Place after Man Haron Monis took eighteen people hostage.

It is hard to imagine two more different settings than Pinevale and Martin Place. But they had something in common, the day the Tactical Operations Unit were called: they were both occupied by crazed gunmen who did not think twice before shooting at police.

The Tactical Operations Unit were joined by robbery and serious crime squad detectives and uniform police at a muster point about ten kilometres south of Pinevale. Among the police were Detective Chief Inspector Mick Banfield and Detective Inspector Virginia Gorman – the two officers who would be charging the Stoccos, should they be at the property. It was the morning of 28 October, and Pinevale had been watched for at least eight hours. Still, it was no clearer whether the Stoccos were inside. Banfield, Gorman and tactical police kept waiting for a signal.

The Stoccos liked a sleep-in. And so it appeared that morning. The police who had lain in wait around the property overnight finally radioed through at 9.20 am. A man had been seen. Fifteen minutes later came the description: he was in his fifties and wearing a grey shirt. It looked like Gino Stocco. Over the next forty minutes, the officers watching Pinevale decided to change position. Then came the next dispatch: a white ute could be seen on the property, tucked in behind a Navara. The signs were promising, but not firm enough to trigger a move. At 10.45 am, another man was seen. He looked like Mark, but the officers had not been as sure as they were with Gino. They were asked to firm up the sighting, and did so. By 11.05 am, a decision had been made to move in.

Tactical police made their way to 300 metres south of Pinevale. They found the gate padlocked and decided to cut through the fence. At 11.30 am, their progress was halted again: they had lost phone coverage, so they had to pause while waiting for their radios to come back online. Ten minutes later, they moved in.

Mark and Gino had been inside the farmhouse at Pinevale, but something made them go outside. At 11.43 am, the Stoccos walked from the house and were swarmed by police, semi-automatic rifles pointed at their heads, shouts of 'on the ground' echoing in their ears. But Mark and Gino did not give in; they spent their last seconds of freedom trying to steal more time, not face-down in the dirt waiting for cable ties to tighten around their limp wrists. Their final resistance, however, was quickly subdued with blows to their heads.

It had not been straightforward for police: at least eleven hours of waiting in the bush, weighing up the risks of raiding an isolated house with two armed men inside who they suspected would be willing to kill them, before storming the property and having to violently restrain them. But it had not been the Lindt Cafe or Stringybark Creek either. 'They did not surrender to police or hand themselves in,' acting Assistant Commissioner Clint Pheeney said. 'There was some resistance to the arrest.' For the first time since 2007, the Stoccos were in custody. 'They knew the bush very well, they knew all the ways and times to avoid police,' Pheeney said. 'But it was . . . only gonna be a matter of time before we tracked them down.'

The pair may have fought until the end and been left bloody-faced for their trouble, but Banfield and Gorman felt that, once the reckoning came, they were grateful. 'You could just see it was . . . a relief off their shoulders,' Banfield told me. 'The pressure had been on [and] they were just like broken men. They knew it was over.' Gorman said they seemed thankful. Mark later said he accepted that it was the 'end of the line', and he did not want to hurt the police who came to arrest him. Gino wanted the dream to last forever, but also had no plan to harm the police who were destroying it. 'We knew it was going to end, but we didn't want it to end,' he said.

Banfield and Gorman became the first police officers to have meaningful conversations with two of Australia's most-wanted men in eight years. It did not take long for Banfield, a bear of a man known to his colleagues as Bandy, to experience some of Gino's wiles. Shortly after making his way from the muster point to Pinevale, he asked Gino, 'Where's Rosario?'

'I think he's in Sydney,' was the response. Banfield repeated the question. 'I'm pretty sure he's in Sydney,' Gino replied.

Banfield tried again. 'Gino, where is he?'

He finally relented. 'Oh, he's over there,' Gino said.

Mark and Gino led police away from Pinevale towards the body of Rosario Cimone. Flies were starting to cake themselves to Gino's bloodied face, and Banfield took his hat off to wave them away, but Gino cowered, fearing he was going to be hit. 'I've never seen flies like it,' Banfield said later. 'There were billions of them.'

Police were also swarming around the property. They found a 44-gallon drum, with shotgun cartridges and items belonging to Rosario mixed among the soot and ash. There were the remnants of another fire, where shreds of clothing could still be seen, and a shed, empty save for dozens of small, black, plastic pots. It took Mark and Gino a bit longer than police expected to direct them to the body. But up an access track running away from the houses was Rosario Cimone, lying on his back, arms overhead, his empty eye sockets pointed at the sky.

News of the Stoccos' arrest broke within hours. Their capture after eight years on the run, and twelve days after shooting at police, would have been an enormous story in itself. But the discovery of a body, and the expectation they would be charged with murder, was stunning. The mirth at the Stoccos' exploits and at the seeming ineptitude of the police had taken a dark turn.

By that evening, the nation saw footage of Mark and Gino, their wrists cable-tied behind them, lying on the ground outside the farmhouse. When photos of their faces were shown, Gino looked as though he had been struck on the right side of his face, his eye black and jaw swollen. Mark had got a blood nose, leaving dried red stains on his face and hooded jumper. Soon, the dead man was revealed to be a caretaker at the property, Rosario Cimone. Later that night, more information about Rosario was given, including his history as a crop sitter with links to the 'Ndrangheta.

Peter Stocco was at his home in Toobanna when he heard the news. Soon after, an ABC television crew arrived. The 87-year-old stood there, on the grey tiles of his patio, speaking in Italian about the ills that had befallen his son and grandson. 'He was last here three years ago and I haven't seen him since,' Peter said of Gino. 'He doesn't want to call because he says if he calls, they can find him.'

Peter spoke again about the separation – 'The son remained with the father and the daughter with the mother' – and about accepting jobs on farms, which had led to conflict, and then to the life on the lam. 'They would give them something to eat and a place to sleep. The landlord would tell them, "Go build the fence, watch the animals," and later, they had some arguments.' Whether his feelings were understated in translation, or an accurate reflection, is impossible to say, but Peter did appear genuinely troubled by the pair using a gun. 'Listen, they did wrong by having a weapon. They did really wrong there.' And he also wished to emphasise, as he had in other interviews, that he had done what he could to right Gino's path. 'And I know he did something wrong because I always told him, "Change your way. Change your way and do something."'

23

Mark Stocco made a full confession to murdering Rosario Cimone within hours of his capture at Pinevale, and had helped police find the body. But it was not so straightforward when it came to his father. Gino, as always, had a story to tell.

He said that the pair had feared Rosario would kill them in their sleep with his shotgun. On the morning of the murder, Rosario had produced a gun after an argument and given them an ultimatum to put up with his instructions on the farm or leave. The pair feared for their lives and killed him. 'And, um, or when he produced, ah, a gun, we didn't know what to do, it was just like, um, an ultimatum,' Gino told the police the day after their arrest. When the police told Gino that Mark had given what appeared to be a more truthful account, he dropped this tale and agreed that his son's version of events was accurate. The pair were both interviewed twice on the day they were arrested, firstly at Pinevale, with the interview recorded on a police officer's mobile phone, and then later that afternoon at Dubbo Police Station. They were charged the next day with murder and other offences.

Mark said that he and his father decided to kill Rosario because they feared they were going to be told to leave. They resented Rosario for doing what many others had done: failing to properly acknowledge their contributions to their properties, and then wanting to discard them, like topsoil blown over the paddock by a stiff summer's wind. The Stoccos felt particularly cornered by their situation at Pinevale. They had to agree to grow dope at the property because they were among Australia's most-wanted fugitives and had nowhere else to go.

'It's probably just a build-up of years and years of just always being booted out of places. We just got sick of it and we said, "Oh that's it, kill him, fuck it,"' Mark told police. 'The basic reason was, like I said, just after years and years of just like working on properties, feeling sort of like we had built up, like a place to stay, maybe. It's probably a bit hard to explain but, like, we'd come and gone from properties and um, yeah, just always having to scream with the farmers and it was, like, this was like the final straw for us.

'We'd cleaned up the whole place – the place looks a lot cleaner than what it was when we first got here, just stuff like that. Um, we felt like, yeah, we'd built a place to stay and then, and then we've always got to leave, like just at the moment you feel like you've gotten . . . organised a place to stay, you've got to leave. And then it was just like, yeah, just, for me that's how it felt for me, anyway.'

The Stoccos' angst about being asked to leave the place they called home oddly reminded me of a theory that Thomas Friedman, the *New York Times* columnist and Pulitzer Prize winner, had about the rise of Donald Trump. 'The most neuralgic feeling a person can have is no longer feeling at home,' Friedman said. 'The sense of home is the most powerful feeling we have.' Had losing their sense of home driven the Stoccos?

Something had been building in them. And in their eyes, Cimone, first by trying to leave for Sydney, and then by saying he would sort out Gino's insolence by calling the others, made it spill over. 'Oh, we just, we just took that to mean it was curtains for us, we're going to have to leave the property,' Mark told police about the phone call. 'If you want to look at, like, a motive of sorts, it was just like after all the farmers we dealt with and all the places we've been it was, like, as if . . . it was like the straw that sort of broke the camel's back. Um, yeah, like it's just another property, we've got to leave another property after all these people we've dealt with and all these good things we've done, so we, well, in our minds, the goods we thought we had done.

'Dad had fixed a million things for them and sort of got the property up and running, got everything functioning again and they want to get rid of us, like. And to us that had been like a recurring theme. Well, a lot of the properties we, we just gotten everything up and rolling and then it was time for us to go, like, and, and it was sort of like as if Ross took the brunt of all the anger. For me, that's how he felt for me, anyway, that Ross took the brunt of all the anger of all the places we've been, like.'

Mark and Gino did not appear to regret the rush of blood that led to Cimone's shooting, neither in the sense that they had taken a life nor that they had been caught, even though both thought there was a reasonable chance they would get away with the murder. This theory was based on either one of three beliefs, or a combination of them: that police would never be told Cimone was missing; that the others involved at the property would cover it up because they were growing marijuana; or that the death would not warrant investigation because of the marijuana.

Mark said he would not have shot someone like Ian – most probably referring to farmer Ian Durkin – because he was a better person than Cimone. 'But with Ross I felt like, oh, yeah, he deserves it and he's [. . .] a person you can even partly maybe get away with it 'cause he's linked with drugs or, I don't know. We'd been on the run for so long and we were so wanted it seemed like killing him was just, like, felt like nothing because it felt like we were wanted anyway.

'And then I thought too that, like, if, if we had to kill him – not that it was a premeditated thing as such, like I thought in my head 'cause I was sick of him the way he was treating us – but I thought, oh well, they're going to keep it hidden anyway because they're, they're involved in drugs, so.'

Gino was even more blunt. 'He's nothing but an old druggo who threatened us and I said, "Oh, no one's even going to miss him" – apparently someone did. He's harassed us so hard and intimidated so hard that I felt it was justified what we'd done in the end.'

After the Stoccos were interviewed at Dubbo Police Station, they were given something to eat, Detective Inspector Cloake remembers. They were then told they would be charged with murder. Both men just stared blankly. Soon after, the pair, who had been interviewed separately and had not seen each other since being arrested earlier that morning, were led into the same police cell. They embraced warmly, holding each other for a long time.

During their police interviews on the day of their arrest, the Stoccos also admitted to shooting at police near Wagga Wagga, and explained where they had dumped the weapons they used. In December, they were questioned about the arson at Plenty, the

Tidswells' property in Canowindra, and they admitted to that, too. Around this time, the Department of Public Prosecutions was told by the Stoccos' lawyers that the case was unlikely to proceed to trial; the Stoccos planned to plead guilty.

Detective Inspector Gorman is a Scandinavian crime-noir tragic. She reckons the murder of Rosario may have seemed as confounding as one of those mysteries – the body of a man with a long and interesting past, found on an isolated property, weeks after he was last seen – were it not for the Stoccos being captured at Pinevale, and their confessions. (Banfield could have even played the grizzled nearing-retirement-age detective, she joked.) But the Stoccos had helped them avoid all that, even if it did mean some questions remain about Rosario and his background, and about what the Stoccos did between shooting him and shooting at police: a nine-day gap in an otherwise fairly clear chronology. If the Stoccos had not confessed, all these details would have had to be painstakingly confirmed, despite the fact that the investigation had already proved that – like Scandi noir – the explanation was fairly straightforward, Gorman said.

Gorman and Banfield were still able to clear up a few things. Between the killing and the Mangoplah shootings, the Stoccos had camped, mostly in caravan parks in small towns around southern New South Wales, including Bega. And they looked into Rosario's past, but not in great depth – a point that would aid his family's growing conspiracy theories about the murder. The bricklayer was spoken to again, but it was clear to Gorman and Banfield that he and the other men who knew about Pinevale were not involved in killing Rosario. 'Everyone who gets murdered . . . there's potential other lines of enquiry . . . and Rosario had a few I guess,' Gorman said. Even without the confession, however, she was confident she could have built a case against the Stoccos. It just may have taken longer.

She found the bricklayer to be genuine in his dealings with them. '[He] and Rosario had been friends for a very, very long time,' Gorman said. 'They were old Italian mates who had drunk together and done whatever else together for years and years and years.' His main feeling about the Stoccos, and the fate that had befallen his friend, was, according to Gorman, 'guilt that he introduced them'.

As police in New South Wales worked on investigating the murder, Nugent and his team in Victoria were assessing how the operation there had worked. Despite how it may have looked publicly, police felt they had done everything they could. And they took some ownership in the Stoccos' capture – it may have occurred hundreds of kilometres from Victoria, but the pressure of police there had forced the Stoccos' hand, Nugent felt. 'It's really important when people are on the run like this to maintain a certain amount of pressure,' he tells me. 'You want them getting tired. Constantly looking over their shoulder, constantly. We can change shifts. We have people come on, go home, sleep, shower, so part of our tactics is we need to maintain pressure. If we don't maintain the pressure, then it just fizzles.

'While I would have liked them to be caught sooner . . . they were caught nine days after we set up . . . it was a nine long days, but in nine days we actually got them. It was just a matter of time.'

Nugent has one main regret: referring to the Stoccos as modern-day bushrangers in a press conference. He had been asked by a television reporter whether the men could be described as bushrangers – a well-worn technique to hopefully get the interviewee to repeat that exact word on camera. Nugent fell for it.

'I made a blue . . . as soon as I said it, I walked off and thought, "What did I say that for?" I just fell into that at the end of the interview. But it wasn't helpful.'

It may have fed into the community sentiment that the Stoccos were leading police on a merry dance, but, in a perverse way, that was helpful: with every meme being shared on social media, the number of people who knew who Mark and Gino were grew.

Police had workshopped several scenarios to trap them without a shootout; Nugent will not go into detail, but it is understood this meant a rapid response when the pair were seen at a service station or public toilet, for example.

And Nugent found the snippets of the men that emerged fascinating: at one point, it was confirmed that Mark had used the public library in Shepparton to read news reports about their escapades, while Gino waited in the car. New South Wales Police also passed on some reports that the Stoccos may have planned to ambush highway patrol officers during toilet stops at roadside rest areas.

But ultimately, fate meant the Stoccos would be caught in New South Wales. And, aside from the bushranger comment, Nugent did not think much would be done differently. The Stoccos were not too good for them. Just lucky. 'But you make your own luck, don't you,' Nugent says, with a knowing smile.

At the end of a eucalypt-lined road, about 60 kilometres south of Pinevale, is a large brown-brick building: the Wellington Correctional Centre. Three small hills dotted with the same eucalypts stand sentry over the prison. Look long enough, through the high perimeter fence, and you might see an inmate loping between buildings, a forest-green leaf rolling gently in the wind across a dusty ground. Aside from paddocks and hills and Goolma Road, the only other notable surrounds to the prison are the makings of another: a $150 million, 400-bed, dormitory-style prison, which the New South Wales government funded to be built rapidly in a bid to ease overcrowding.

Somewhere down that eucalypt-lined road on the other side of the reinforced steel perimeter fences and through those brown-brick walls are Mark and Gino Stocco. They could not have known when they left Pinevale on 7 October 2015 that their years-long odyssey, covering almost half of Australia, would end here, only a short drive from where they committed the crime that made them infamous.

24

It is logical that a prison cell would swiftly break the spirits of two nomads, who for the past fifteen years had a highway or an ocean stretched in front of them, and no decision to make other than which point of the compass to follow. When this prison cell also separates you from the only person you have had any meaningful contact or relationship with for that same fifteen years, the shock must be even more violent. But this was not the case with Mark and Gino Stocco.

Perhaps it was a sign that living with nowhere to call home, nowhere to feel safe, becomes a cage. In prison, Mark and Gino had nothing left to run from.

Case notes on both men prepared by the New South Wales Department of Corrective Services attest to how quickly they settled in. The notes date from their first night behind bars, on 29 October 2015, to January 2017 – only months before their sentencing.

It appears that Gino found the first few days in prison harder than his son. The pair both had to spend their first two weeks in segregation; common practice for new inmates charged with serious offences. On the second night in his cell, Gino asked a guard to turn his television off, as he could not sleep. 'When the outer cell door was opened the inmate ran to the back of the cell and hide [*sic*] under his own arms as if he was scared?' the guard wrote in Gino's case notes. 'I turned his TV off and told him to relax. No further issues.'

The same day, when more was being explained to him about the process of segregation, Gino stated 'on numerous occasions' that he needed 'to be housed with his son'. The guard added, 'Inmate was advised that as co accused this was not going to happen. Inmate continued to request he be housed with his son.'

It was policy that co-accused on remand in the New South Wales prison system were not to be housed together. Gino would ask again that day and was again told that he would not be able to share a cell with Mark, but stated 'that this was okay and that he will do absolutely anything we ask in order to progress to mainstream population'. A New South Wales detective would later tell me they believed part of the reason why the Stoccos pleaded guilty at such an early stage was to hasten the process of being able to share a cell, such was their devotion to each other.

Gino was given access to the prison yard for the first time the following day, and again on 1 November. By this stage, his notes are already flecked with terms describing his fairly seamless introduction to prison; words such as compliant, courteous, respectful and polite are used, indications that not only had he settled but he was also considerably more at ease than he had been when he was free. By mid-November, both men had been signed off on their segregation orders and were 'settling well' in their pods within the general prison population. They were no longer alone, but they still did not have each other.

As the Stoccos settled in at Wellington, police across the east coast of Australia kept looking for answers. Detectives worked on establishing how many crimes the pair had committed, who their victims were and where, exactly, for more than eight years since being released from prison in Victoria, the pair had been. The majority of the work was being done by Queensland and New South Wales detectives. Victoria Police were also working on a warrant relating to the crimes the pair had originally committed in that state, including ramming the car at St James, and the arson at the Zipsins' in Glenburn.

South Australia Police did not suspect the Stoccos of committing any offences there, and it was believed that the situation was similar in Tasmania, although a spokeswoman for Tasmania Police refused to confirm this.

It meant that police from as far north as Cairns and all the way down to the Victorian–South Australian border were investigating the Stoccos. Journalists were also trying to find out more about the pair. And so, about the time when the Stoccos usually considered heading south for the summer, a steady stream of people headed in the other direction. Towards Ingham.

In a small town just north of Townsville, at the end of a cul-de-sac, live Christina Stocco and her husband, whom we'll call Stuart. There's a rugby pitch on the way into town, and termite mounds line otherwise empty paddocks. Like Christina, many of the people who live here commute to Townsville for work, but were drawn to the town by the larger blocks and tighter community.

Nobody is home when I knock on the couple's door. But as I turn to leave the house, I see Stuart walking from a shed to the side of the property. He is fairly nonplussed by my visit, and barely pauses before motioning to the front of the house, the direction in which he is walking.

Stuart is rendering a small section of his front fence, and he talks to me in the yard while patching it up, occasionally pausing to think, or to make a point more firmly, or to listen. He is thoughtful and cautious, only agreeing to speak to me if I do not reveal more detail about the family; only their closest friends know they are related to Mark and Gino, and their young children are also unaware of their infamous relatives. He fears them being bullied. Only the eldest child has any real recollection of his uncle and grandfather; once, during their spree, Christina's husband asked the child whether he recognised the man on television. It was Grandpa Gino. 'We've lost friends because of it,' he says, 'not friends that were that close, but people who know we're related.'

Christina and the children are out. Stuart is wearing a high-vis shirt, a broad-brimmed hat, shorts. It is almost midday and in the high 30s, and there is no shade. The render dries quickly on the fence, and he has to continually stir the small container he holds in his left hand to keep it from setting. Stuart ruefully recalls how, after eight years of Mark and Gino committing crimes, including against himself and Christina, nobody – let alone the police – seemed to care. Then they shot at police. The next day, everybody knew of the Stoccos. Journalists started arriving at their home.

He reckons he has seen Mark and Gino about three times in the past decade. They had long worn out their welcome, and the couple considered their relationship with them to be irreconcilable, even before they were charged with murder. 'We were a long way past that,' he says. Gino had such an indifferent relationship with the truth that he didn't 'even know when he lies', Stuart says: 'it's that normal now'.

Gino had been keen to break up Stuart and Christina. He vandalised Stuart's brother's house and, in what was clearly a favoured tactic, wrote insulting letters about them to their friends. Stuart thinks Gino was motivated to break them up because he had always stood up to him. Once, when Gino knew the couple would not be home, he stole from their shed. There was an argument, and Stuart demanded Gino return what he had taken. On the night the Stoccos stole Maryann Bender's four-wheel drive in Chinchilla, they also punctured eight tyres at Stuart's parents' property. Gino had behaved this way for most of the time Stuart had known Christina. But it was vindictive, petty and dishonest crime, not the offences of a madman. And Mark was not like his father. How they became murderers, Stuart says, is a 'monumental story'. 'Gino wasn't a murderer in my eyes, when I first met Christina. But obviously . . . it's gone too far. It's just tragic.'

It is clear that Stuart has given most thought throughout the saga to what has befallen Mark, and that he is genuinely sad about his fate. '[Gino] had sociopathic tendencies which have got worse over time, and it's just a shame Mark was a sheep, I suppose.'

He wonders why Mark did not flee. How a man about the same age as him could become so entangled in the fate of his father. 'I wonder why, when they were splitting up and driving different cars, Mark didn't think, "I could just go my own way."'

Christina and Stuart are victims of Mark and Gino. Not merely because of the items that were stolen, but also because of their loss in a broader sense: a loss of privacy, of family, of being able to identify as Stoccos. And, in Stuart's eyes, the police did not do all they could to minimise this. Other victims had it far worse than them, he acknowledges. But, in a common refrain from those touched by the Stoccos, he has had his eyes opened to the failures of the police force. He speaks about them in the same way as other victims I've spoken to, with an air of 'never there when you want 'em, always there when you don't'. 'It's not like TV when there's an obsessed bloke who works thirty-six hours straight until he catches them,' Stuart says. 'They just do what they can on their shift and go home.'

Their contact with Mark and Gino since their capture has been minimal. Mark wrote once, but his letter contained no great revelations. Stuart gives the impression that Christina would have been happy to have never spoken to them again. But she had to speak to them twice in their first year in custody. She had to tell them Egidia and Peter had died in Ingham.

Linda, who is the wife of Peter and Egidia's eldest child, Mario, would later tell me that the saga contributed to her in-laws' deaths. But Stuart does not say he thinks Mark and Gino's exploits in any way hastened their passing; Egidia had been in a nursing home for years as dementia took hold, and, shortly after she died – as is common with couples married for more than sixty years – Peter died of a heart problem. He had outlived her by just seven months.

Mark and Gino's reactions to the deaths of Peter and Egidia are outlined in their prisoner case notes. Their entries on 27 February 2016 regarding Egidia are identical. 'Inmate was upset but stated that she was very old and it was expected,' the case notes read. When Peter died in September, Gino and Mark were working together in the prison's printing shop. Gino 'appeared shocked by the news but said that he was okay'. A ten-minute phone call was authorised so he could speak to Christina. There was no entry about Peter's death made in Mark's case notes.

Peter Stocco had spoken to several journalists about his son and grandson. Eventually Christina drove north to take the family photos away because her grandfather kept allowing them to be published by journalists who came to the house. In one interview, Peter, who spoke only rudimentary English, tried to describe the torment that enveloped Gino after his break-up with Connie, which Peter said started Gino's descent into serious crime. Peter used the phrase 'he married the wrong woman', which then became the headline on an article about the case, and rightfully attracted outrage when it appeared that Connie was being blamed for the rampage committed by her former husband.

During the same interview with Fairfax Media, Peter said he was grateful the pair had been captured alive. He said he had tried to get Gino to see a psychiatrist when he was young, but he refused. He visited Gino during other prison sentences and he had been constructive, once building a garden. He planned to make contact with Mark and Gino in prison this time, too, but it appears this did not happen: on both sets of prison case notes, the only contact Mark and Gino have with anyone is when Peter and Egidia die and they speak to Christina, and when they are interviewed by police or meet their lawyers. It is noted that they have had no visits, letters or phone calls.

I had hoped to speak to Peter myself about what had happened. He had been a lone voice from the family in the media about the case, even angering some relatives with his inability to say no to an interview. He did not appear frail on television, giving no impression that I had to rush to Ingham to see him. He was the best hope of asking what Gino was like as a boy, and how he was different to his siblings. I had wanted to hear firsthand the story of Gino pissing in the inkwell. Peter could describe what Ingham was like when he arrived; whether he ever had the sense he was not welcome, or missed Italy. I wanted to know why he had ended up there. And how life in North Queensland had contributed to Mark and Gino Stocco being the men they were.

Two of the numerous mostly dry creeks along the Bruce Highway between Townsville and Ingham are called Easter and Christmas. They are both decorated accordingly: the Christmas Creek sign with fresh tinsel and a cut-out of a tree; the Easter Creek sign just with 'Happy' written on cardboard and placed above it.

Peter had lived in a house in Toobanna, on the east of the highway, just south of Ingham. It is 20 kilometres further north from Bambaroo, where he had once owned property, and where the Big Melon was squashed. Closer to Townsville, there is still big fruit on the highway: a three-metre mango, advertising a cafe known as the Frosty Mango. Bambaroo has little indicating its existence other than a slight thickening of the houses by the highway, and a school, tucked down a service road. The school was founded in 1924, according to a sign outside, which also features its crest: a white bird, possibly a white-bellied sea eagle, atop four heads of crops.

Peter's house is on a service road. There are palm trees between the house and road, in his front yard and along the nature strip. It is brick, painted white, with a double garage and an under-cover front porch. A large frangipani is flowering, dropping pink stars onto yellowed grass. Everything is neat; white plastic chairs tucked precisely under a plastic table adorned with a vase of garish fake flowers.

Attached to the fence is a large yellow sign. 'House 4 Sale. Genuine Enquiries Only' has been written on it in black permanent marker, the first line and 'only' emphasised. The mobile number on the sign is Eddie Stocco's. He lives with his wife along one of the wide streets of Ingham, in a second-floor unit. When I go there to speak to him, he answers the door warily. His face reminds me of his brother, and his eyes are like his, too; it is as if they do more than watch, but are also listening, and would talk too, if they could. They are so clearly the most animated part of his face that the rest appears superfluous. He initially seems keen to speak with me, and then, when he shouts back inside the unit to his wife about who I am and what I want, he decides against it. When I speak to Stuart months later, he says that Eddie told him I wanted to write about Mark and Gino as 'heroes'; a strange and entirely inaccurate retelling of our conversation.

North of Ingham, the tropics begin to close in. There is little but forest and sugarcane and banana plantations, green on green on green, only the hue and brushstroke changing. The land has barely an undulation but then is shocked with a mountain, coated in the deepest tone of all. Later in the afternoon, the cloud thickens and rounds and settles behind these single peaks, creating the illusion that an entire range stretches far beyond the horizon.

Occasionally, at the roadside, shapes appear, sunglasses and hats and fluoro colours coated in sweat and mud, standing in gravel at the base of machinery, working to stop bitumen from disintegrating, or widening it against the scrub.

Houses appear otherworldly. Even those that are low-slung and surrounded by undergrowth look like flotsam in the ocean. The Queenslanders, with their long legs, appear especially out of place. They look as though someone has grabbed the pitch of the roof and pulled skywards, trying to pick them up and plonk them back down somewhere where they would better fit in.

North Queensland still feels as if it is being colonised, as if another Ingham could come here seeking to make his fortune. The jungle appears ready to swallow everything up, retaking 160-odd years of European settlement in a few days of decent rain and unmolested growth; all the roads and houses and people, covered in a thick green sea.

Perhaps, when the tropics take a human mind, it is not the heat or the rains that don't stop for weeks that cause it. It is not turning to drink to cope with it all. It is not the maddening, impenetrable darkness of the jungle whispering that it could take you and begging you to step inside. It is the unarguable truth that this land was not to be settled. And the mere thought of doing so in the first place was madness. For some, this causes their mind to close in on itself, like the jungle that surrounds it, until all is black.

During this drive north to Cairns, surrounded by the jungle and sugar cane, I thought of something else I wished I could ask Peter: why did his son decide to leave North Queensland? Did Peter think Gino had started to feel the wild closing in?

25

On 15 June 2016, Mark and Gino Stocco pleaded guilty to murdering Rosario Cimone and to three other charges relating to shooting at police and the arson at the Tidswells' place in Canowindra. Charges of attempting to murder police had been dropped – a decision that frustrated some officers but that seemed a logical move given the Stoccos insisted they had merely been attempting to disable their cars and had made full admissions to the other offences.

Mark and Gino Stocco were due to appear for the first time in a Sydney court a few weeks later, on 5 August. They had appeared in Dubbo's local court since their arrest, but the arraignment hearing in Sydney would see the matter pass for the first time into the jurisdiction of the Supreme Court, and formalise their earlier pleas.

There is a rainbow in Sydney on this morning; an almost perfectly straight strip of colour cutting through the heavy grey that hangs low to the west. I wonder whether cities make the Stoccos skittish. Whether this had been an unspoken truth between them, or something they mulled over and kicked about. Perhaps they were just indifferent to cities; if you have dedicated a life to working on the land, a city doesn't offer much. Only buildings taking the sky, cars and trains taking the silence, relentless masses taking the freedom to move.

There are almost seventy chairs in Court 13A, and they are full by 10 am. People keep arriving, bow at the door, and just stand there, waiting for a seat. The first case heard before Justice Peter Johnson SC this morning is about a woman who died in a car accident on 29 July, but who was supposed to face trial in Dubbo later this month. The next is a man accused of murdering a woman in a bedroom, where he had been alone with her for some time. The issue will be about what caused her death, his lawyer says. The man looks on from a television screen to my right – the justice's left – perched above the dock.

Justice Johnson is matter-of-fact, bordering on brusque. His face is a shade of red barely lighter than his robe and his beard the same colour as his wig. He speaks from his chest, not boomingly deep but with a light huskiness at the end of most words. Above his head is the New South Wales crest, with the Latin inscription '*Orta recens quam pura nites*', which translates to 'Newly risen, how brightly you shine'.

Cases for arraignment keep ticking over, barely five minutes spent on each: a woman, appearing under a pseudonym, is being charged in relation to the death of her child, who had a medical condition. She is one of those standing by the door, without a seat, her umbrella in hand, her other hand raised briefly when Johnson asks her lawyer if she is present. The next case involves a man, who appears on the television screen with an A4 piece of paper Blu-tacked on the wall behind him reading 'Long Bay jail video room three'. He is comically framed by the camera in a way that makes him appear tiny, even in a room seemingly no bigger than two phone booths.

At 10.24 am, the Stoccos are called. Despite court staff insisting to me that they would appear in person, they too appear on the television screen – where everybody has already seen them before. Mark sits to Gino's right, wearing a green bomber jacket. Gino wears a dark crew-neck jumper. I don't see them enter or exit the room on the screen, and can't read the paper behind them that states where they are. Both men are still bearded, but they look less ominous; instead they seem almost impish. Mark is slightly taller than Gino, it appears, while sitting. Gino sits with his arms crossed, scratches his nose with his left hand, raises his chin and stares towards the top-left corner of the room, beyond the camera. Mark stares straight at the camera, as if waiting for a passport photo to be taken. They could be anywhere: the movies, a football match, a church pew.

Unlike the others who have appeared on the screen today, they don't look like criminals: their faces are softer, less worn. They also seem curious, whereas the others appeared almost too familiar with it all; another court hearing, another prison. But the Stoccos are bright-eyed. Perhaps they see the packed court and think it's all for them. Perhaps they can't see the court gallery at all.

In five minutes, maybe less, it is over. The Stoccos have not spoken, and the next court date has been set. The screen goes dark, and I am left thinking about how they looked: Mark with hair parted to the right, with some poking out from behind his right ear. Gino looking neither older nor younger than in previous images, but perhaps more rested, less robust. Less weathered, but softer featured, as if age has mellowed him.

And what of them after the black screen? Back to their cells; maybe a quiet word to each other first. An all-too-brief moment alone together.

This hearing, the arraignment, is the first time Rosario Cimone's family have attended court for the Stoccos' case. And, standing in the lobby outside the court shortly after the hearing, they are told again why police believe the Stoccos killed their father. A police officer tells Cimone's daughters, Maria and Vincenza, and their partners, that the Stoccos killed Rosario because he was going to kick them off the farm. She tells them that while there was no marijuana found there, there was evidence to suggest that's what the property was being used for. And she says that the Stoccos killed Rosario because they thought they would get away with it.

The Cimones don't buy it. They demand answers. On the lift down from the thirteenth floor, and while pausing in the lobby downstairs, they curse the futile hearing as a waste of time and taxpayers' money. They rubbish the links between Rosario and the Calabrian Mafia. 'There's no such thing as the Calabrian Mafia,' Maria says.

I tell them about the book and that I would like to speak to them more at some stage, before giving them directions out of the building. Several months later, I am told a somewhat bizarre theory that helps explain why the Cimones don't believe the police: they are convinced that the Stoccos had another motive to kill Rosario, or, maybe, that they did not even pull the trigger.

*

Maria and Vincenza, along with Filippo Cimone, come face to face with Mark and Gino Stocco for the first time during the sentencing hearing.

The hearing, designed for both sides to outline to Justice David Davies what punishment befits the crime, begins on 30 January 2017. For the Stoccos' lawyers – Ian Nash for Mark, and Mark Ierace SC for Gino – it's essential that their arguments focus on the early admissions of guilt, the contents of psychiatric reports about their clients, and the prison case notes, which demonstrate the Stoccos' exemplary behaviour since capture.

Crown Prosecutor Wayne Creasey SC will counter by outlining the lack of remorse shown by the Stoccos in their police interviews, and the victim impact statements of the Cimones and Senior Constable Matt Shaw. The Cimones will then read their statement to the court, with Mark and Gino watching on from the dock. Creasey will also refer to sentences in similar cases to provide examples of where the Stoccos' offending fits within a spectrum of case law.

Nash and Ierace could not be much happier with the material in the prison case notes, which provide regular updates of how the Stoccos have fared in custody, their engagement with training, and their dealings with staff and other inmates. It is hoped that Justice Davies will view them as evidence that he should not deliver crushing sentences, which would offer no prospect of release. Nash and Ierace contend that the notes show the Stoccos are already beginning to rehabilitate and that they have been 'model prisoners'. It is hard to argue with this: both inmates are regularly commended in the extensive New South Wales Corrections case files. But there are some entries regarding Gino – other than the strange behaviour with the television and the repeated insistence that he be able to share a cell with Mark – that provide a more complex picture.

In February 2016, Gino asked to change cells because he and his cellmate were 'not seeing eye to eye'. He was told the move would happen discreetly, and, when it did, it was noted there were no issues with the former cellmate. It was also noted that Gino was making repeated requests for dental care, and expressing concerns that this was not being provided. After Gino had been raising this issue for several months, Mark's case notes show that he also made a similar request.

When Peter Stocco died in September 2016, Gino was reprimanded for trying to convince the chaplain to make a phone call for him to Christina – a call that, because it originated from the chapel, would not have been recorded. The chaplain sought permission from prison management, which was refused because of Gino's classification as an Extreme High Security inmate. 'Inmate spoken to in the presence of chaplain and warned that . . . should he attempt this again he could be denied access to the chapel,' a case note reads.

But the prison notes are overwhelmingly positive. There are repeated references to the Stoccos' behaviour, demeanour and work ethic, and it is noted on both their files that the men hope to remain at Wellington after they are sentenced.

By this January, the Stoccos have begun working in the print department. Mark is particularly enamoured with the job, and his case notes read, 'Inmate is keen to undertake a traineeship in printing once he is sentenced. Inmate states he is happy to be housed in Wellington to complete traineeship.'

The pair perform odd jobs around the prison without being asked, including picking up rubbish from lawn areas and around their pods, where they are housed, and cleaning the urinals. 'Neither Stocco are asked to attend to cleaning, they both do it off their own back,' one case note reads. On weekends, the Stoccos have painted cells, the prison reception area and the rooms where inmates like them appear on video link for court hearings.

'Their work ethic is outstanding,' another note gushes.

'They work methodically without any complaint, both Stoccos seem to enjoy working and take pride [in] their results,' yet another says.

'The Stoccos rarely complain and quietly go about their business without getting involved in gaol politics – both could easily take advantage of their notoriety amongst the other inmates however neither want to draw any attention to their situation.'

This notoriety is referred to again in relation to a television program on the Seven Network's *Sunday Night* about their time on the run. Gino was asked whether he was concerned that the show could cause the pair problems in prison. 'Inmate stated "no" saying the inmates are more or less congratulating them on the show being aired,' a case note reads.

26

Detective Sergeant Dave Barron can scarcely believe that the two local scumbags he was warned about when he started in Ingham eight years ago have become national news. He was initially irritated by them, like a splinter in his thumb, before the arson at the Zattas' in Bambaroo; after that, it was as if the thumb had become infected, and he wanted to lop the whole thing off. Then came the shooting at police. 'I remember sitting at home watching the news, thinking, "Wow, now they've really put the heat on themselves, hey?"'

And now, years after he first heard their names, and months after they were caught, he got to sit across from them in a windowless room in Wellington prison. Barron and other Queensland detectives had warrants out against the Stoccos for about thirty offences, and they hoped to get them squared away. It had been painstaking work, traversing the countryside getting people to make statements, often about crimes that had happened more than five years ago. In some cases, Barron was perplexed by the reaction of those he called up – people he'd heard could be victims of Mark and Gino. 'They would say, "Those boys were really good people, don't you call me up about them,"' he said. 'One old chook, she gave me a massive bake, saying how happy she was with a massive deck they had built her.'

But far more people were grateful that Barron was finally taking their concerns seriously. It was unlikely that Mark and Gino would be walking out the prison gates any time soon, but if they did, Barron wanted to make sure they were whacked straight back in cuffs and hauled up to Queensland. He separated the Stoccos and set to work.

Mark admitted everything that the police put to him; he was so helpful that, at some points, Barron would simply put a date to him, and Mark would tell him what the pair had done that day, such was his recall for numbers. There was something deeply unusual and not a little disturbing about his accounts, however. 'There was no remorse, but he was owning up to everything. That pissed us off, really,' Barron said. 'He was talking about it like it was algebra: "This plus this equals we burnt their house down."' But at the end of it, Barron was left not only frustrated by Mark; he pitied him. 'You just walk away thinking, "You poor bastard."'

He did not feel the same about Gino. 'You just feel like reaching over the table and choking him,' he said. Gino also did not show any remorse; he simply made Barron think that he believed every crime they had ever committed against any Queenslander could be justified by what they had done to them first.

There was one question that Barron had always wanted to ask the pair, should he ever be lucky enough to get the chance, so he took the opportunity then: 'Did you share a bed because you were in a relationship?'

Mark flatly denied it. Gino 'arced up', as Barron put it, and then almost started crying, before saying, 'Everyone is really jealous of my special relationship with my son.'

The only person who has visited Mark and Gino Stocco in prison, other than detectives and their lawyers, is forensic psychiatrist Dr Jonathon Adams.

Adams submitted three reports about the Stoccos. The first is a report on Gino, the second a report on Mark, and the third is a supplementary report, requested later by the defence, that outlines their mental state at the time of the murder, the development of the Stoccos' 'belief system' and their prospects of rehabilitation, given their 'positive post-arrest behaviour'. The Stoccos' lawyers submitted the reports to give insights into their offending and their mental states, and, as neither Stocco gave evidence during their court appearances, they are critical pieces of evidence.

Adams did not assess the Stoccos together. He based his assessments on his prison visits and interviews conducted by video link, criminal records, video and transcripts of police interviews, among other things. Ultimately, Adams's reports state that neither Stocco has a mental condition; a finding that staggered police and victims.

'I've been pretty sane my whole life,' Mark told Adams. It is a strange declaration, even in the context of a psychiatric report. And it shows the limitations of what the assessment will achieve; Adams is almost completely reliant on the responses of Mark and

Gino for his report. These responses are far from truthful; both men claim the shooting of Cimone was their first real violent act, for instance, despite the bashing of Sergeant Liam Duffy and the vicious mugging of Connie. Their explanations for destroying the farms of those who slighted them for such trifles as being asked to move a fence are framed as little more than rational and almost logical responses.

Adams appears to accept that these acts were not impulsive. Mark told Adams that he normally has a 'pretty good, pretty balanced' mood, which did not frequently change. He denied persistent periods of low mood, or of mania.

'He told me he was good at controlling his emotional state,' Adams wrote. Mark defined his self-esteem and self-confidence as 'pretty reasonable' but also described himself as generally a 'shy person'. 'He said he tended to avoid large social situations, but confirmed that he was able to do so if required. He denied any significant concerns forming stable relationships,' Adams wrote. 'He referred to himself as a "well-considered" person, and did not believe he engaged in impulsive acts, commenting, "I don't do anything without thinking."'

He denied any significant concerns trusting others, stating, 'You've got to give people a chance to see what they're like.'

Mark said he had never used illicit drugs, was a social drinker with no history of abusing alcohol, and his only significant medical problem was having to have an inguinal hernia surgically repaired in his early twenties. Adams reported that Mark believed his mood had been 'pretty good' in custody, and that he was glad he had been housed in the same prison as Gino, as 'it would be hard without it'. Mark had been trying to function to the best of his ability.

Mark had used his time in custody to come to terms with his behaviour, Adams believed. While initially claiming he had acted in self-defence when deciding to murder Cimone, Mark now accepted that pride, anger and fear also played a role. Adams said that Mark clearly articulated how becoming closer to Gino in 2001 had caused his descent into crime, but that he insisted there had never been any pressure for him to adopt his father's anti-establishment views. Adams wrote that Mark accepted he needed to change his views, and to 'stop turning away from problems all the time'. He intended to live a 'normal life' that was not 'always in survival mode' when he was released. He hoped to 'do the right thing by the system, not the wrong thing'.

'[Mark] Stocco highlighted how his situation altered significantly during his parents' relationship difficulties and eventual separation in 2001,' Adams wrote. He continued:

> *He gave a clear description of how this precipitated his closer relationship with his father, whom he said he had a close attachment to. From this point on Mr Stocco revealed the heightening importance of his anti-authority viewpoint, which he shared with his father. Mr Stocco said at no point did he feel threatened to share this belief system. I explored the form and content of Mr Stocco's anti-authority belief system in detail, and I did not elicit any evidence to suggest that his beliefs were indicative of symptoms of mental illness, such as delusions.*
>
> *Mr Stocco accepted the need to alter his anti-authority belief system going forward, and appeared to accept that he would need to continue to do so in order to lead a more stable existence in the community.*

Adams reported that Mark understood how this anti-authoritarianism had impacted his behaviour, leading to the murder, shooting at police, and arson offences, and added:

> *In terms of his level of insight, in my view Mr Mark Stocco had a reasonable understanding of his trajectory over recent years. It is evident that the offending behaviour leading up to the murder charge in October 2015 was set in the context of [his] increasing time with his father, relative separation from society, and escalating anti-authority standpoint.*
>
> *He explained the property damage offences in terms of their response to . . . being asked to leave a property without being paid satisfactorily for the work they completed. Mr Stocco accepted that this behaviour could be viewed as wrong and illegal, but he justified it in terms of their overriding anti-establishment views.*
>
> *[The murder] could be considered inconsistent with his past behaviour in terms of violence towards others. Mr Stocco explained this in terms of their overwhelming fear for their safety, and need to remain undetected by police.*
>
> *It is clear that Mr Stocco's endeavours to avoid arrest escalated over a significant period, and were perpetuated by his underlying belief system.*

Adams outlines the limitations of his assessment, including that he did not have access to sources of collateral information such as school reports and general practitioner medical records, and he did not speak with corroborative sources. He said he would review his opinion if contradictory information was provided, but that he was of the view that Mark Stocco was not experiencing a major mental illness at the time of his offending. Nevertheless, he said that Mark could benefit from long-term psychological therapy to understand his role in offending and how his trajectory altered, to challenge his anti-authoritarianism, and to understand how he became so violent.

In essence, the report's value to the defence is summarised in one sentence, which underlined that Mark was remorseful: 'Mr Stocco appeared to have a good understanding as to the wrongfulness of all of the offending behaviour, his role in it, and the impact upon the victims.'

Adams's assessment of Gino was based on similar material, and essentially has the same outcome. But it is easier to see instances of Gino fibbing in his assessment. He made regular claims that the pair had not been violent before killing Cimone, saying he had never even been in a fist fight before – despite the St George incident and police confirming to me that he was also suspected of punching a woman while camping in Victoria's Otway Ranges with Mark years earlier. He lied about the extent of his criminal history. He probably understated his drinking history, given he had clearly offended at least once while drunk. He said some farmers kicked them off their properties for no reason at all, after they had performed exemplary work – a claim for which there is no evidence. And he said he only killed Cimone because he felt threatened, as Cimone and the other men at Pinevale were armed, and they were 'under siege' – a claim the prosecution later proved is false.

When Adams asked Mark and Gino whether they can be impulsive, they both responded exactly the same way: 'I try to be a thoughtful person.'

Gino told Adams he had never had mental health concerns, but had 'moments when I've been terribly down'. He denied that these moods were persistent or consistent with a mental illness. His mood was usually 'cheery'. He also denied abrupt mood changes. 'He believed he was able to adequately control his emotional state,' Adams wrote.

Gino identified his separation with Connie as the moment his anti-establishment beliefs escalated. He told Adams that he was bitter about the property settlement and Connie's infidelity, but no detailed discussion of either was included in Adams's report. There is no evidence that Connie profited unfairly from the settlement or was unfaithful.

Adams wrote, 'I asked him whether he found it easy to trust others, to which he replied, "Sometimes yes . . . I've been hurt a lot in that area." He related this to the relationship with his wife and the separation from her stating that this was "the biggest trust that got broken".'

The offending started when he and Mark became 'very disillusioned with the whole system', Gino told Adams. 'Mark and I decided we weren't going to pay for anything anymore . . . we just went off radar.'

Gino was, in some ways, relieved it was over. His time in custody was 'much more of a normal life', and he had been content. He and Mark were 'trying to set a role as being total model prisoners', Gino told Adams. They respected officers, and avoided threatening them or fellow inmates. They would continually back down from confrontation. He was prepared to accept whatever sentence he was given. 'A whole new chapter needs to start,' he told Adams.

Adams wrote that his assessment of Gino was limited similarly to his assessment of Mark, and recommended the same mental health treatment as he had in the other report. He accepted Gino's explanations for his crimes:

> *It appears a significant turning point in Mr Stocco's trajectory occurred at the time of his relationship difficulties with his wife and eventual separation in 2001.*
>
> *Mr Stocco highlighted his embitterment as a result, and specific frustration with the outcome of the property settlement. Prior to this time Mr Stocco revealed beliefs that could be considered mildly anti-establishment, although by his own account his value system became significantly more anti-establishment and anti-authority from this point on.*
>
> *In my view Mr Stocco's intensifying anti-authority belief system was not a product of a mental illness, such as a delusional system, but was a set of values and subsequent behaviour that developed over time, in conjunction with his son.*
>
> *Mr Stocco described always having a close bond with his son, which appears to have become closer in the context of his separation from his wife and their time spent together, frequently just the two of them.*

It is curious that Mark and Gino Stocco's lawyers requested a supplementary psychiatric report from Adams. It was requested less than two weeks after the other reports were delivered, and completed only days before the sentencing hearing.

The main motivation for this appears to be that it could expand on the exemplary behaviour of Mark and Gino in prison, and emphasise that the offending had been greatly influenced by their shared beliefs. Both points could lend weight to an argument for leniency. If Justice Davies accepted that the Stoccos' model behaviour showed they had a good chance of rehabilitation, and if he was similarly receptive to the suggestion that they had essentially fuelled each other's offending, and that, as individuals, they were unlikely to commit any such acts again, it would likely result in a reduced sentence.

Adams spoke to both men one more time via video link to complete the supplementary report. Mark gave more detail about the arguments between Cimone and Gino leading up to the shooting. Gino said he moved to the property to perform electrical and maintenance work, but then felt pressured to help with cannabis cultivation before claiming he was told, 'We could get rid of you and no one would notice.' He later admitted to police he was never told this.

Adams found that the pair had developed and shared an anti-authoritarian system that did not originate from mental illness. It had developed over a long period. Mark had not felt pressured into adopting this belief system by Gino. Adams appears slightly more guarded about their prospects of rehabilitation than in his earlier reports, writing that while their engagement in the corrections system, their apparent understanding of their offending and their levels of insight are positive factors, 'on the other hand, the chronology of their anti-authority belief system and relative social isolation for a number of years leading up to their arrest must be borne in mind'.

While attending her father's funeral, a woman meets a man she has never seen before. Despite the horrible circumstances, she finds herself captivated by him and becomes convinced he is her soulmate. But he has to leave abruptly, and she realises she does not know his name, or anything else about him. A few days later, she murders her brother. Why?

This riddle can, supposedly, detect whether a person has sociopathic or psychopathic tendencies. If a person quickly determines the solution, that the woman killed her brother because she hoped the mystery man would know him and come to that funeral as well, it indicates they are able to make horrific decisions utterly removed from emotion.

Mark and Gino Stocco have been described as sociopaths by their victims, their own family and the police who investigated them. One detective, admitting to using a definition found on Google, referred to Gino as a psychopath and Mark as a sociopath: the father was born mad, and the son had learnt it, was the detective's reckoning. But Adams found that neither of them had a mental illness. There is no doubt that mental illness is widely misunderstood in the community, and that many who are diagnosed with mental health conditions are unfairly stigmatised. Terms such as sociopath and psychopath are bandied about to describe someone who merely appears cold or lacks empathy; schizo, or schizophrenic, may be used to refer to someone who is aggressive. But some of the people who described the Stoccos as sociopathic had either known them for a long time or were experienced police, who had a reasonable working knowledge of the criminal brain.

It must be reiterated that Adams himself did note there were limitations to his reports and that it was possible that the Stoccos had mental illness that had gone undetected by him.

At a base level, the main reasons the Stoccos articulated for murdering Rosario – that he was going to boot them from Pinevale and they thought they could get away with killing him – certainly fall within the prism of what is considered sociopathic. This is without even considering their bizarre rationales for destroying the property of people after only petty arguments, which could also lend weight to the sociopath theory.

But, as author Kevin Dutton found while researching his book *The Wisdom of Psychopaths*, the funeral riddle drastically simplifies the sociopathic mind. When he asked diagnosed sociopaths the puzzle, none of them came up with the answer. 'I might be nuts but I'm not stupid,' one told him.

27

Senior Constable Matt Shaw, one of the officers Mark and Gino Stocco shot at, told me he was shocked at how unmoved the pair were the first time they came face to face with the family of the man they had murdered. When Rosario Cimone's family read their victim impact statement to the court, it was marked with unabashed sorrow, delivered tearfully from only metres away, and yet the Stoccos did not flinch.

The prosecution do not expect victim impact statements to have great sway on the decision of judges; no families of murder victims have anything nice to say about the killer, or declare they are coping with the loss surprisingly well. But these statements balance the procedural, clinical and often dehumanising accounts of crime that are common in court. And they implore judges to at least consider making a ruling based not only on which of the lawyers in front of them are more convincing.

Prosecutor Creasey would make other arguments in relation

to the sentencing of Mark and Gino – about their complete lack of empathy, the varying accounts of why they had shot Rosario, the risk to life caused by their arson, and the fear of police that the Stoccos were trying to kill them – which were no doubt given more weight by Justice Davies than the victim impact statements. But the words of Maria Perre, Vincenza Nasso and Filippo Cimone were what most people in court that day remembered.

The siblings told the court that their father's body had been so badly decomposed that they were told they would be unable to recognise him. When the coroner gave the body to them, they were told not to open the body bag and were therefore denied the 'cultural tradition' of burying him in an open casket.

'Our family cannot adequately describe in words the agitation, rage, anxiety and grief and the multiple ways in which all of these emotions have affected our lives and the lives of our own immediate families and our extended family,' the statement read. 'He was a central part of all our families in his own way and we just can't see how we will all overcome his loss as well as our absolute horror [at] the way he died. Death of anyone you love is a crisis but to have your father murdered in the circumstances reported to us is beyond belief.'

While these sentiments are not uncommon in the statements written by families of murder victims, there are some aspects that are highly distinctive:

> *While we have been told he didn't suffer and that he died instantly we struggle to trust this information. Even if this is true we continue to be plagued by questions such as why did these men target our father, was he terrified and psychologically*

tortured before he died and did these men treat him with cruelty and humiliate him? All of these unresolved questions continue to torment us alongside the haunting images of what we think he may have looked like after insects and wild animals attacked his naked body.

Frankly, we can't see how we will ever recover and be able to move on. Knowing so little about the circumstances of his death and in particular why he was so sadistically targeted by these two men means we have not, as yet, been able to let go of him – we haven't been able to let him rest in peace.

Other sections of the statement appear to acknowledge the more shadowy parts of Cimone's life: 'Dad was many things to many people – he was a wonderful father, grandfather, brother, uncle and partner. We can only speak about what he was like with us.'

Finally, the siblings finished with a message to Mark and Gino:

We are writing this so the men who murdered our father know just what they have done, the damage and devastation they have caused to real people. We feel they need to accept that their cruel and callous actions have affected all of our family and we believe we will never recover from the loss we have suffered. Our lives will never be the same again.

No one has the right to take another person's life. We believe these two men chose to callously take another person's life – our father's life – in a manner that showed total disregard for human life. We feel they have shown no remorse and it is as if their actions mean nothing to them. The irony is that they still have one another.

We are not vengeful people but our hope is that the horror of what they have done, the pain they have inflicted on us and our families will stay with them for each and every day for the remainder of their lives.

It is a statement that leaves no doubt about the horror that the Stoccos inflicted on the Cimones. Or so it seems. But police who investigated the case found the statement somewhat perplexing and disingenuous. For instance, the Cimones barely hint at their conspiracy theories about the case. There are some indications (references to struggling to trust information, and knowing so little about the death), but nothing that spells out what they told police: that they believe the Stoccos took the fall for a murder committed by Cimone's friends, or only pulled the trigger as part of a conspiracy involving those friends. The Cimones believe that the Stoccos did not act alone, and are frustrated that the police cannot satisfactorily answer the questions they have about the case, according to several officers. Why, for example, did it take so long for Rosario to be reported missing by his old friend the bricklayer? And why did he not, at the very least, report that the Stoccos were involved? Why would he not turn in two people he barely knew when it appeared they would know something about where Rosario had gone? It was a simplistic, albeit somewhat understandable, contention to draw from the evidence.

The bricklayer had been somewhat delayed in reporting Rosario missing. But, as already outlined, he seemed to have the right intentions. And any delay also had to be seen in the context of Pinevale being used to grow marijuana, and the bricklayer not frequently travelling there. It is unclear – given the Cimones did not wish to participate in this book – whether this conspiracy theory also had some basis in the notion espoused by a number of other people I spoke to, including Connie's relatives, and Graham and Peg: that the Stoccos weren't capable of murder.

Police also believed the statement somewhat overstated the relationship the family had with Rosario. He could hardly have been the exemplary father and grandfather they claim if it took them three weeks to report him missing, one detective said. 'They wouldn't see him from one Christmas to another.' But another detective believed this was unfair; Rosario had last seen his family only weeks earlier, at a christening.

Also overlooked was the impact Rosario's frequent dalliances with crime – and stints in jail – had on his youngest child, and only son. Filippo not only looks like his late father, with the same block head and enormous upper body, but has a criminal record to match. He was fifteen when his parents separated, the only sibling still living at home. It is impossible to say whether that separation had the same impact on him as Gino and Connie's separation had on Mark, but court records show that, by the age of eighteen, Filippo, known as Philip, was a drug addict with eleven prior convictions for malicious damage, obtaining money by deception and larceny. And he was soon to be convicted of other offences relating to a frightening robbery in outer Western Sydney. Filippo Cimone and three other teenagers ambushed a man at a railway station car park and forced him to drive to a park, where he was robbed at knifepoint and made to give them the PIN to his bank card. He was then held hostage by two of the teens while the other two, one of whom was Cimone, used the man's car to drive to an ATM and withdraw $500. They then returned to the park, picked up the others and left the man there, before fleeing in his car.

By 2012, Cimone was even more clearly following in his father's footsteps: he was charged with the cultivation of cannabis, after 1000 plants worth about $2 million were seized in northern New South Wales.

Senior Constable Matthew Shaw also gave a victim impact statement during the sentencing hearing. He starts by outlining his history within the force, and then his day leading up to the shooting, before detailing how it unfolded and the effect it has had on him, bringing him to tears for the first time during his career:

> *For the first couple of days after this incident I did not sleep very well and it was not until maybe three or four days afterward that I lay in bed and actually thought how serious this incident had been. I could have been seriously injured or killed.*
>
> *I remained in a state of high emotion whilst the offenders remained on the run. I was angry a lot of the time and was short with my wife and family and friends. The anger was not directed at my family and friends, but rather at myself for how I had done things, and I was angry with the offenders for what they had done and how it had affected so many people.*
>
> *This emotion would cause me to remain at home, and I isolated myself from others and continued to think about what I had done and whether I could have done something differently that would have apprehended the offenders.*
>
> *These emotions would push me to the point of me needing to find a quiet place or space where I could regain control of my emotions.*

> *On some occasions I would not be able to control the emotions and I would be brought to tears and, when I did cry, I would be asking myself why. It was not something that I was used to and not something I had experienced before during my service.*

Shaw said that the phone call he received two weeks later was one of the best he had ever answered. He was told, 'They've got them.'

'Immediately hearing those words, I felt a huge amount of emotional relief. I needed to know that the offenders had been caught and no one else would be hurt either emotionally or physically.'

Shaw – and the Cimone family – had poured themselves out in front of the court. All that was left was for Mark and Gino to be sentenced.

28

They look like relatives at a wedding who wished they hadn't come. Gino wears a dark shirt under a dark suit with a red tie, Mark a light grey suit with a white shirt and blue tie. Mark looks the more dishevelled: his tie is askew, his top button undone, his suit hanging from him almost comically. It is 31 March 2017: the day the Stoccos will be sentenced, in court LG4 of the Downing Centre, in the heart of Sydney.

In front of the Stoccos, across the courtroom, the press sit in the jury box. To the Stoccos' right, Justice David Davies. To their left, the Cimone family, Senior Constable Matt Shaw and the officers involved in investigating Mark and Gino. Behind the Cimones and others is a glass-walled seated area, filled with what appears to be a mix of curious onlookers, school students and reporters who may have to rush to another hearing. Between Justice Davies and the seating area sit the clutch of legal representatives for the Stoccos and the prosecution.

*

Senior Constable Shaw arrives at court about an hour before the hearing, heads down the street for a coffee and is back inside with at least forty-five minutes to spare. He is in uniform. Tall. Broad shoulders and a defined jaw, rising to sideburns cut at his ear line. He has thoughtful eyes behind wire-rimmed glasses. A bloke you'd pick as a copper even without the uniform.

We walk down the stairs to court LG4 and stand outside. He's got his police hat in one hand, which he places on a seat. He's talking about closure. About how he'd hoped for it after the sentencing hearing, but Justice Davies had wanted to spend more time getting his head around the sentence. Understandable, Senior Constable Shaw reckons – there's no need to open himself up to appeals. Best to get it right. Besides, after today, it's over. In about two hours, he will be driving back to Wagga, leaving Sydney and the Stoccos behind.

A sheriff comes to open the court. On the way back, he asks whether Shaw is one of the officers who was shot at. When Shaw confirms this, the sheriff extends his hand, and tells him he's lucky or brave or both: things Shaw has no doubt heard every week for the past eighteen months. Shaw softly thanks him, and tells him he tries not to think about it. We move inside, wanting to make sure we get seats.

The courtroom appears inspired by suburban council chambers of the 1970s. Strange tones of green and red. Wood panelling and scuffed walls. Patterned carpet and upholstery designed solely to hide stains – the type that induces nausea when it's wrapped around bus seats. At 1.52 pm, four members of Rosario's family walk into court, find seats together near Shaw, sit down and wait. His son is not with them. Soon after, Mark walks in, followed by Gino, flanked by two corrective services officers. They sit with a seat between them, but after Justice Davies enters, and the court stands, they change position and sit down next to each other.

The Cimone relative nearest to the Stoccos, the husband of Rosario's daughter Maria, is staring at them. It is a look challenging them to explain what they've done, a look almost tinged with disappointment, rather than with menace or disdain. His eyes do not waver for almost ten minutes.

Gino is slumped down in his chair slightly, his shoulders facing forward rather than towards the judge, his head straight. He stares blankly into the middle distance, but occasionally he looks to the judge, and then towards the back of the court, and the Cimone family and Shaw. Gino seems an old fifty-nine. His hair is grey and wispy, his face heavily creased, his body drawn and gaunt. But he does not look frail. He wears an expression of utter indifference. It is almost disconcerting how little he appears to care that he is likely to spend most of his life in prison; an almost adolescent nonchalance.

Mark, on the other hand, almost looks scared. He is reedy, and taller than his father. His head is barely wider than his neck and topped with a helmet of hair parted to the right. He moves his entire head when he looks, not merely his eyes, and spends more time looking at the judge than his father does. He watches curiously, like he's trying to learn something, as if having a good understanding of his sentence will better prepare him for it. Occasionally, his mouth will be stuck in a small 'o', like he's waiting for Justice Davies to finish speaking so he can say something. Other times, he has the same downturned mouth as his father. There are other things that father and son share, of course. Narrow lips. Almost reptilian noses. Longer than average ears. And eyes like buttons, irises as dark as their pupils.

Justice Davies is talking of burning and slashing and shooting and stealing and murder. Gino barely moves. At one point, he quickly scratches his left cheek. He remains unmoved when the Cimones start to react to Justice Davies' words. As the judge outlines Gino's police interview, his claims that he feared for his life when he shot Rosario, who had pulled a gun on them, and that he acted in self-defence, Maria shakes her head.

Justice Davies reads the details about the shotgun: a 12-gauge Remington model 870 pump-action shotgun containing five or six rounds of Diana BB and No 2 shot 12-gauge shotgun cartridges. Gino rolls his tongue around the inside of his mouth. Perhaps behind those button eyes he is thinking of the click the gun made when he flicked off the safety. Remembering raising the gun and pointing its barrel towards Rosario Cimone. Maybe he can still feel the sensation of his left hand sliding forwards and back to pump a cartridge in the chamber. The index finger on his right hand sliding in front of the trigger. Can he still see the look in Rosario's eyes the moment before he pulls it?

'Mark handed the firearm to his father and said, "Shoot him,"' Justice Davies continues.

'Gino replied, "No, tie him up, tie him up," but Mark said, "Just shoot him."'

Maria is crying now, using a tissue to dab her nose and eyes, as relatives on either side look towards the judge.

'Gino walked out of the house carrying the firearm, followed by Mark. The deceased was standing about two metres from his car,' Justice Davies reads. 'Gino removed the safety catch and actioned the shotgun by pumping it once. He approached the deceased from the front and shot him once to the stomach area from a distance of about two metres. The deceased doubled over and Gino actioned the shotgun again, expelling the spent cartridge and loading a new one in the chamber. He shot the deceased again to the stomach area. The deceased fell to the ground and died almost immediately.'

Gino and Mark are impassive. At one point, Mark looks out the corner of his eye down and to the right towards his father. He then looks blankly towards the Cimones and Shaw, before facing the front and then Justice Davies again. Gino stares straight ahead. If he were captured in a photo, he would look almost regretful. But that would be deceiving. Watching him, his small movements and the shape of his body and the flicker of his eyes, gives the opposite impression.

The hearing has been going for about fifty minutes, and Justice Davies starts to outline the objective seriousness of each charge. He will detail how the murder the Stoccos have pleaded guilty to, for example, compares with an average murder offence. This assessment of the objective seriousness is then used to explain the sentence; if a murder is found by the judge to be at the worse end of the scale, the offender will be sentenced to a penalty close to the maximum: life. As murder in New South Wales has a standard non-parole period of twenty years, Justice Davies has less discretion. He must decide where on a sliding scale from twenty years to life the murder of Rosario Cimone sits. He deals with the offences chronologically, starting with the arson at Canowindra, then the murder of Cimone, and finally the shooting at police.

Two months earlier, during the sentencing hearing, Crown Prosecutor Wayne Creasey SC submitted that the arson at Plenty, the Tidswells' property in Canowindra, was marginally above the mid-range. In relation to the arson, the Stoccos are charged with recklessly destroying property by fire, an offence punishable with an eleven-year maximum prison term. Creasey submitted that Davies, when weighing his sentence, should consider that the Stoccos trespassed onto the farm at night, originally to steal diesel, before setting out to destroy property that they knew was valuable and essential to the management of the farm. They lit fires in two locations and were motivated by 'an inexcusable desire to seek vengeance against the person whom they believed still owned the property'. Creasey rebutted the explanation given by the Stoccos to the psychiatrist, Adams, that they had not intended to harm anyone when they lit the fires, and had deliberately avoided setting light to the house or cottage, by submitting to Davies that all fires expose people, including firefighters, to a risk of injury.

Ian Nash, Mark's lawyer, accepted that vengeance motivated the fire, and that it was lit to damage valuable and important equipment. But he argued that trespassing, stealth and exposing people to risk of injury were factors common to most, if not all, offences of arson. Furthermore, he said, lighting a fire in sheds during winter, when it was unlikely to spread, could not be compared to starting a blaze in a suburban residential area. Mark Ierace SC, for Gino, said there had been a conscious decision by the duo to not set fire to the houses at Plenty.

Justice Davies considers three main factors. The first is the vengeful motive. The second is the intention to not harm others. And the third is the significant financial loss suffered by the Tidswells. The John Deere tractor that was destroyed was eleven years old and insured for market value. They were paid \$81 809 by the insurance company but had to spend \$223 000 on replacing the tractor – a loss of more than \$140 000.

'Although the owners of the property were entirely blameless victims, I do not think that that in itself is relevant to an assessment of objective seriousness,' Davies says. 'If it were, that would suggest that a similar offence was somewhat mitigated because of a perceived wrongdoing by the owner of the property. The particular significance of the present owners being blameless victims is the financial loss they have sustained. As far as financial loss is concerned, it should not be overlooked that it is also the present owners' insurers who are considerably out of pocket by the wrongdoing of the offenders. That is ultimately a cost to the community through increased premiums.'

Davies rules that the offence falls in the upper end of the mid-range. He then starts speaking about the murder, in a level voice that he skilfully raises, sharpens or lowers to match his words. He is nineteen pages into his thirty-one-page sentence, and these changes in pitch keep everyone listening.

Davies outlines Creasey's earlier argument that the murder was well above mid-range. The lack of premeditation was acknowledged, but it was a 'matter of great gravity' that the Stoccos had been motivated by anger and frustration, Creasey submitted. Nash and Ierace accepted the murder was above the mid-range. Davies again outlines the relevant factors: that the murder was committed with someone else, the use of a weapon, the killing of someone in a property that the victim would consider home, and the treatment of the victim's body. He rejects Nash's argument that because Rosario was growing marijuana at the property he could have no expectation of security in his home. Davies' consideration of the treatment of Cimone's body as an aggravating factor is not limited to its being dumped naked in the scrub, but also encompasses his boots and $50 cash being stolen from him.

'I accept that there was no planning or premeditation about the killing,' Davies says. 'Whilst not accepting that there can ever be a justifiable motive for murder, the reason put forward by

Mark Stocco and ultimately accepted by Gino Stocco after he put forward a false account of fear and apprehension of threats by an armed victim, that it . . . that they might be required to leave the property, was so trivial as to defy any rational assessment. The killing was coldblooded, callous and without any rational justification albeit it was not planned.'

Davies finds that the murder is high in the mid-range.

For shooting towards Constable Benjamin Kerslake, and then Shaw and Senior Constable Stephen Woolatt, during a police pursuit near Wagga, the Stoccos face two charges of discharging a firearm to prevent lawful apprehension. Like murder, and about thirty other offences in New South Wales, this carries a standard non-parole period. For this offence, Davies has to sentence the Stoccos to at least nine years. The maximum penalty is twenty-five years, and Creasey had submitted that the offences were at this high range.

Davies finds that shooting at the police 'enabled' the Stoccos to remain on the run for another twelve days. He says the pair had conceded that they caused psychological distress to the officers, but submitted that they had deliberately steadied the firearm before shooting to ensure an accurate aim that would not endanger the lives of those pursuing them.

'Too many films and television shows involving high-speed car chases with the wrongdoers shooting at the police have a tendency to inure the viewer to the real dangers involved,' Davies said. 'A viewing of the DVD from the video camera in one of the police cars involved in the present matter was a chilling reminder to all who viewed it . . . of the real danger in what took place and the real fear engendered by the shooting in the police officers concerned.'

I find myself thinking of that DVD footage. At the bottom of the frame, a slip of police car bonnet. A radio buzzing and a howling siren. A white ute barely visible through a cloud of dust as high as the gums overhanging the road. A 'do you copy?' over the radio, seconds before a faint crack is heard. The next sound is Kerslake's voice, the voice of a person who fears someone is trying to kill them. 'Urgent, urgent, urgent, urgent, shots fired, shots fired,' he shouts into his radio, before another bullet hits his car, letting off a dull thwack.

'Whilst it is accepted that there was no intention on the part of the offenders to cause personal harm to the police officers,' Davies says, 'not only was that not apparent to the officers concerned but the risk of serious injury or death to them was considerable either because of a ricocheting bullet or because the police car might have crashed.'

Davies says that the offence should be 'a useful reminder to the community of the dangers to which police are exposed in carrying out their duties on a daily basis for which they rarely receive acknowledgement'. He finds that the offences fall into the upper end of the mid-range.

The judge concludes by outlining the objective reasons for sentencing, and then moves to the subjective. As the Stoccos did not give evidence, Davies is largely relying on their police interviews and the psychiatric reports to determine their levels of remorse and gain insight into their offending and the factors in their lives that may have influenced their behaviour. He details their criminal records: Gino and his thirty-three-year history of lawlessness; Mark and his inexplicable slide from civil engineering student to murderer. He finds that while neither had previously committed offences as serious as those for which they are to be sentenced today, their records entitle them to no leniency in sentencing.

Davies appears somewhat perplexed by the impact that featuring on the Australia's Most Wanted television program had on the Stoccos, which he finds was a significant turning point. He looks towards the press in the jury box when he says, '. . . the justification for that is hard to fathom because their offending to that time consisted largely of relatively low-level property offences. Dr Adams said that being so characterised appeared to have heightened their anti-authoritarian stance and solidified their views of being unprotected by the legal system and the police.'

Davies and Adams are right to conclude that being two of Australia's most wanted was a turning point for the Stoccos. But they do not know that, firstly, it was a list reported on the news rather than an actual television program, and that its significance was about where the Stoccos were, and not just its contents. When Graham and Peg told the Stoccos to leave, it forced them from a place that was more like home than anywhere else they had stayed for more than eight years. By increasing their notoriety, it also greatly reduced the chances that they would find another place as secure as Wedderburn again. Being part of an Australia-wide campaign transformed them from being little more than a thorn in the side of Queensland Police and only really being vigorously pursued by farmers like Redding and Durkin, to criminals of national significance. It meant that when the bricklayer offered them a place to hide, albeit with the caveat they would have to harvest marijuana to live there, they were too desperate to say no.

Davies starts to address the question of remorse. By his second sentence, the Cimones are again shaking their heads. Davies refers to questions 153 and 154 of Mark's police interview, when he is asked about going to grab the gun, and about telling his father to shoot Rosario rather than tying him up. 'I said,

"Just shoot him." So, I couldn't be bothered tying him up,' Mark had told police.

'Whilst remorse must be judged at the present time, any expressions of remorse must be seen in the light of that statement with no regret attached to it,' Davies says. 'Further, as noted, neither offender gave evidence at the sentence hearing. Nor did they, through their counsel, offer any form of apology to the relatives of Mr Cimone or to the police officers. In those circumstances a court would be reluctant to accept any expression of remorse made to a doctor whose report was tendered.'

Even if Davies was to accept any remorse expressed to Adams by the Stoccos, he says there was only one statement in the psychiatric report about Mark that could be considered as possibly remorseful, where Adams wrote that Mark had accepted the impact of his offending on the victims.

Davies found a similar absence of remorse exhibited by Gino in Adams's psychiatric report: 'He reports Gino as saying that what they did was a "total misjudgement" and it was a "really bad call to do what we did". That may be some small indication of remorse but it is not clear. Gino also said that he recognised that damaging people's property would psychologically affect them and cause harm. Nothing was said about how killing people might affect those close to them nor how police officers might be affected by believing, quite reasonably, that they were being shot at by a high-powered rifle while trying to apprehend the offenders.'

Curiously, Davies says there is evidence that the Stoccos offered some assets, mostly $48 000 left over from a property settlement between Connie and Gino, to the Tidswells. He found that, given this offer, and the statements made to Adams by Gino regarding the arson, there was some remorse for the crimes at Canowindra, but not for others: 'I do not accept that the rather general statements made to Dr Adams by both Gino and Mark referred to above indicate any real remorse for the murder or the shooting offences.'

At the sentencing hearing, Nash said that Mark's early guilty plea and the comments to Adams showing that he took responsibility for the crimes were demonstrations of his remorse and contrition. He argued that, given a lack of significant incriminating forensic evidence, the case against Mark was not strong – a contention that is now rejected by Davies, who says it was possible a thorough forensic investigation had not even taken place, given the suspects confessed within hours of their arrest. Davies gives credit to the early plea, but he says this credit is 'negated' by Mark changing his explanation for the killing in the twelve months between confessing to police and being interviewed by Adams, when he suggested he feared Rosario and his partners.

'When the offenders were not prepared to give evidence and subject themselves to cross-examination at the sentence hearing, I cannot place any store on the justification provided to Dr Adams to the extent that it differs from what was said immediately after the offenders were arrested,' Davies says. There is some doubt as to whether Rosario had treated the men badly or was involved in growing cannabis, Davies says, but that is beside the point. 'He was a human being, a husband, father, grandfather, brother and uncle, and was someone whose family cared about him . . . I again extend my sympathy to the family for their loss.'

As Davies speaks of all the things Rosario was, Maria, his firstborn, bends at the hip, puts both elbows on her thighs and weeps into her hands.

Davies moves on to detailing his findings in regards to rehabilitation. He then gives his first implicit indication that the sentences will be significant. After saying that Adams was guardedly optimistic about the prospects of both men in his reports, Davies says, 'The issue of rehabilitation is of more significance for Mark Stocco because he is a relatively young man. Given Gino Stocco's age, the reality is that there is not a great likelihood that he will ever be released from prison.'

Gino was guaranteed a minimum twenty years, given the standard non-parole period for murder, the minute he pleaded guilty. But the matter-of-factness of Davies' remark, which effectively damned him to dying in prison, is stark. And yet Gino continues to stare into the distance, seemingly unmoved, while his son bends slightly forward and looks down.

'Two things encourage me to think that Mark Stocco's prospects of rehabilitation are reasonable,' Davies continues. 'The first is his immediate admissions and his truthful account of what happened. Secondly, when speaking with Dr Adams, he accepted the need to alter his anti-authority belief system and appeared to accept that he would need to continue to do so in order to lead a more stable existence in the community. His acceptance of that is shown to some extent by his reported behaviour in custody.'

The final two factors Davies has to address before handing down his sentence are deterrence and discount. Deterrence relates to the need to impose a sentence that will discourage those who may commit similar crimes. Discount relates to the sentencing reduction that the Stoccos could be granted because of their early pleas, which Davies determines should be 25 per cent. For deterrence, Davies is pointed about needing to send a message to those who, like the Stoccos, wish to lash out because of perceived wrongs. 'Committing offences as vengeance for perceived wrongs is a form of self-help against which the whole system of law, both criminal and civil, stands as a bulwark,' he says.

Finally, Davies moves to the sentencing itself. He says he accepts that Gino's age constituted a special circumstance that had to be considered, and gives another hint of what is to come, saying it is likely that Gino will spend his eighties in prison. He finds that no special circumstances exist for Mark. The sentences will be back-dated to 28 October 2015, the day the Stoccos were arrested.

Everything moves quickly now, as Davies rattles off the sentences he thinks appropriate for each offence, working in reverse chronological order this time, and assigning three numbers to each charge: the starting point, the indicative sentence with discount, and the non-parole, or minimum, period. For the arson, the sentence is five years and three months with no non-parole. For the police shootings, the sentence is nine years with a period of six years and nine months non-parole. For the murder, the sentence is twenty-six years with nineteen years and six months non-parole. He gives a short explanation of the aggregate sentence and high-risk offenders' laws, which the Stoccos are subject to, before Davies asks Gino Stocco to stand.

Gino does so, a man who looks even shorter when he stands, as there can no longer be any guessing at his height. Davies looks towards him as he rises, before returning to his notes and the sentence he is about to pass. Gino continues to look blankly ahead. Davies sentences Gino to forty years' imprisonment, with a non-parole period of twenty-eight years. He will be eligible for release on 27 October 2043 – five weeks before his eighty-sixth birthday.

Mark is asked to stand almost immediately after Davies finishes with Gino, that sentence – forty years – still shuddering through him. He quickly looks to the judge, but then drops his head before again raising his chin and looking at Davies. Then he looks to the same nothingness in the mid-distance of the court that occupied his father. Mark is also sentenced to forty years, but has a non-parole period of thirty years. He is given two more years because of his age, the reasoning being that he is unlikely to die in prison, so he should spend more time there. He will not be eligible for release until 27 October 2045. Three days earlier, he will turn sixty-six.

(Both men later appeal these sentences, on the grounds that they are manifestly excessive. The appeals were set to be heard on 24 March, 2018.)

The first thought that hits me is strangely sympathetic in the retelling, but at the time it is merely a question of practicality: what if Gino doesn't die in prison and is released into the world as an 86-year-old, with the only person who cares for him still inside?

The courtroom occupants are asked to be silent and then stand, as Davies leaves. The Stoccos leave the room next. Both walk with their hands in front of them, as if shackled, which they're not. There is an officer in front and another behind. They walk out the glassed room, down some steps, across a passageway and through an open door. Gino goes first, and Mark follows.

29

Senior Constable Matt Shaw is beaming as he walks out of court. He looks lighter, and appears to stand even more rigidly than before.

'Fair whack,' I half exclaim, half ask.

'Yeah. Yeah, definitely. Can't complain with that,' he says.

Shaw is pleased that the judge made reference to his victim impact statement – Davies described it as heartfelt – and that he acknowledged the risks police are put under every day but are rarely recognised for. It is also significant that the judge touched on the anguish experienced by Shaw's wife, Nicole, who was working the day Shaw was shot at and heard it unfold on the police radio. Shaw stays downstairs for a few minutes with police who worked on the case, including one who jokes that he's planning on having a beer for every year of the sentence that night. 'That's off the record,' he laughs, pointing at me.

The Cimones stand nearby. I ask again whether the family want to be involved in the book, explaining that it's important to me that they're a part of it. A son-in-law remembers me from the arraignment last year, but the answer is the same now as it was then. The only thing he offers is cryptic and somewhat conspiratorial. 'Even from what went on today, there was more questions than answers,' he says.

'What do you mean by that?' I ask.

'There's just more to it. I don't want to say anything else,' he answers.

Maria, Rosario's firstborn, who is standing further away, says, 'What's the point? He's not here to defend himself.'

I nod, say thank you, turn and leave them, thinking she has just answered her own question.

The Cimones leave the court about five minutes later, politely ignoring the pack of waiting journalists and cameramen, the only comment offered a quiet, 'It's a good sentence.'

Soon after the Cimones leave the Downing Centre, police gather on the forecourt outside the court complex. They are more willing to talk. 'Light or shade?' Detective Chief Inspector Mick Sheehy, from the state crime command robbery and serious crime squad, asks the cameramen. Sheehy has his back to the courtroom doors and is facing Liverpool Street, which is choking on mid-afternoon Friday traffic. Because of an awning, Sheehy can give his press conference either in the shade or with the late-March sun beating on his closely clipped head. He has given enough impromptu post-sentencing press conferences to know it's worth asking cameramen what they want.

Sheehy, a former homicide squad detective who has served for thirty-one years, has investigated the professional hit on businessman Michael McGurk, the fatal bikie gang airport brawl that claimed the life of Anthony Zervas, the 'coward punch' slaying of Thomas Kelly, and the accidental shooting death of Senior Constable William Crews during a police raid.

'Gino and Mark Stocco are callous and violent criminals who today have been held accountable for their actions in the cold-blooded murder of Rosario Cimone,' Sheehy says, from the shade. 'These individuals chose a path of crime due to a dispute, an ongoing dispute, they had over the illegal cultivation of cannabis. From our point of view, this is an exceptional sentence that's been handed down today. And from the family's point [of view], they are able now to rebuild their lives and move on from this terrible action.'

Sheehy mentions all the different elements of New South Wales Police that worked in unison to catch the Stoccos and build an 'exceptionally strong' brief. It is a necessary acknowledgement of the politics involved in modern policing, and shows his guile is not limited to detective work.

When he finishes, Detective Inspector Darren Cloake, to Sheehy's right, takes up the cudgels. Cloake says the Stoccos had 'not only taken one life, but they have seriously affected a number of families. We do hope that the sentencing . . . does bring some comfort to the family of the deceased person and the numerous other people that have been affected by them.'

Finally, the media, who shuffle to the left after Sheehy speaks, and then left again after Cloake, face Shaw. He has his hat on now, sitting just above his glasses, the brim jutting straight out from little higher than his eyebrows. 'Today was a good outcome,' Shaw says. 'It shows to people the job that the police do, and the judge touched on . . . just how inherent the dangers are out there for us.'

A reporter asks Shaw a lengthy question, which is essentially: do days like today bring up memories of the shooting?

'Absolutely it does,' he responds. 'It was difficult to come here again today. But from my point of view I wanted that closure, to actually see and hear the judge pass his comments and his judgment upon the two people today. I hope now to just move forward and just continue on in the job that I'm doing. It still continues to affect me today, it's daily – some days you wake up better than others. It's the nature of the job and that's what we choose to do. I very much enjoyed hearing the comments of the judge and him emphasising the dangers that we face every day.'

Shaw is asked whether he is bothered by the Stoccos' lack of remorse (he isn't) and what the day of the shooting was like ('surreal'). Then he is told what he has been told time and again since 16 October 2015: that he's incredibly brave.

'Not necessarily. I don't consider myself brave,' he answers, although it wasn't really a question. 'I just consider that I was doing a job on the day, that's all. And, yeah. I kept thinking back to the day, and days after it happened, all you want to do is prevent them from getting away and hurting someone else. That was probably the most disappointing thing about them when they did elude us, the fact that you think, "Well, maybe they're going to shoot at someone else." Thankfully they were caught not long after that.'

Behind Shaw, and to his left, Sheehy cuts in before another question is asked. 'That might do us there, guys.'

The sentencing of Mark and Gino Stocco did, for most people, bring an end to the fear and mystique that had surrounded them for the past fifteen years. But, for others, questions remain. There is a gnawing discomfort that, for the most part, what had caused Gino to spiral out of control, and take his son with him, is unclear. Some do not agree with the simple explanation that it was because Connie had left. There is, in their minds, a more sinister possibility.

There were limitations to the mental assessments carried out by Jonathon Adams, the forensic psychiatrist, which were mostly out of his control: the most obvious of these being the relatively tight timeframe he had to assess the Stoccos. Because of this, he was unable to question others or confirm what he had been told, some of which, it was later proven, was false. But there was one notable absence from his assessment, according to one expert I spoke to. The irrational way in which Gino reacted to minor slights appeared similar to the symptoms shown by some adults who were victims of sexual abuse as children. There is, however, no explicit mention of this in any of Adams's reports, although he does ask both Gino and Mark about the distinguishing features of their childhoods.

Gino attended Gilroy College, a Christian Brothers boys' school, in the 1970s, when, it would later be discovered, clergy-related abuse was rife. But there were no reported incidents at that college; the only confirmed abuse case involving a Christian Brother in the Ingham region during the time Gino was a boy was that of Terence Patrick Aquinas Kingston, who abused seven boys at a school in Abergowrie, about 40 kilometres from Ingham.

Nobody I spoke to had any information to suggest that Gino had been molested; certainly, his closest relatives, including his father, Peter, could only surmise that the separation with Connie was behind his mental disintegration. But did the break-up only expose a more terrible trauma that Gino had been suffering?

The family of Rosario Cimone were not especially concerned with what may have caused Gino's anger. But they wanted some answers. They were convinced, according to several sources, that there was more to their father's death than the court heard.

While the Cimone family did not wish to be interviewed, others who had spoken to them said they believed the men who had been on the dope plantation at Pinevale around the same time as Rosario Cimone and the Stoccos had something to do with his murder. Either the men – some of whom had known Rosario for many years, but whose identities are suppressed – killed him, and got Mark and Gino to take the rap, or they arranged for the Stoccos to kill him, threatening to either murder them or turn them in to the police if they declined.

The main fact that supposedly underpins the logic of this theory is that Mark and Gino had not killed before, and had no reason to kill Rosario. Why not just leave the property, as they had done countless times before, when they got in an argument? It is a valid point, but also a flawed one. The Stoccos' behaviour had gradually worsened in the fourteen years before they had met Rosario – a fact the Cimone family may not have been entirely aware of.

And, if they had been forced to either kill Rosario or take the blame, why not spill the beans after they were caught? Surely there was no point in maintaining the charade once the police had arrested them? If anything, it would have made some sense to try to strike a deal, given all the other charges the police would slap on the Stoccos; rolling over on some Calabrian Mafia figures, even middling ones, would no doubt have been viewed favourably. The counter-argument could be that the men had tentacles throughout the prison system, and the Stoccos feared reprisal should they give them up. But, again, this is far less likely than what we know to be true: Mark and Gino were consistently, from 2012 onwards, reaching the end of a shortening tether. And every time this happened, their actions got worse.

The Cimones' unwillingness to accept the police version of their father's death could, in some part, be explained by a general distrust of authority. It could also relate to a predisposition of some people with southern Italian heritage to more readily embrace superstition and conspiracy. This predisposition was echoed in the beliefs of one of Connie's relatives. During one of the many conversations I had with people who knew Connie, trying to get them to convince her to speak to me about her son and former husband, the relative said he did not think the Stoccos had killed anyone.

'But they confessed,' I protested.

'It's speculation, at the end of the day, unless there's CCTV and DNA,' he responded. 'Them confessing does not necessarily mean they've done it. Who knows what the police do these days.'

It is not just a chip on the shoulder about the police that has caused doubt, however. Connie's relative just did not think that the Stoccos, whom he described as petty and spiteful, and whom he had known for most of Mark's lifetime, were killers.

While some believed that Mark and Gino had possibly been put away for something they did not do, others were adamant that the pair were responsible for far worse. It is scarcely surprising that Doug Redding, the vigilante Darling Downs farmer, is a chief exponent of this view. He says that he had compared missing persons reports with details about where the Stoccos had been, and when. There were enough overlaps for him to strongly believe that the pair could have been responsible for murdering others they had met on the road and taken a disliking to. 'I've got no doubt about that,' Redding says. 'They murdered one bloke; they've admitted to that. There's god knows how many other disappearances that have been in places where they've been over the years. There's not a week that goes by where I don't find out about something else they've done. Surely to Christ, they will be questioned about everything they know.'

Police, on the other hand, think it unlikely that the Stoccos took another life. Dave Barron, the Ingham detective, says that Mark was incredibly forthcoming when he was interviewed. Darren Cloake, the Wagga detective, felt the same. 'He was quite forthcoming with his information and accounts. I think after eight years he was quite happy to get it off his chest.' Cloake says that Mark, somewhat obliquely, referred to not having killed before. 'He said he's never seen a man killed before, but when Gino shot the victim, he thought he would have had a bit more life in him. On face value, considering everything else Mark told me, I've got no other information to suggest any other deaths.'

Cloake acknowledges a small possibility that, because the Stoccos held vendettas for years after the original slight, links with potential victims could be ignored, or never even discovered. Should a farmer have been killed, for example, and he had hired dozens of workers over the years, keeping little record of any of them, how could you know whether the Stoccos had even been on the property, let alone had a dispute with the victim? There was also a minute chance that the Stoccos had been employed on other cannabis plantations before Pinevale – they had links to people in Ingham involved in cannabis cultivation, often worked in remote areas where other crops had been found, and had periods of several months unaccounted for in the time since their release from prison in Victoria. If they had tended other crops, the very clandestine nature of their work could have made it more likely they would commit murder, and less likely they would be caught. But Cloake was close to certain that Rosario was the only person Mark and Gino ever killed.

Other police – including Cloake's New South Wales colleagues, Banfield and Gorman – agree. They say it is unlikely that the Stoccos would have spent enough time with anybody, other than an employer, to become so agitated with them that they would resort to murder. And, if they had, someone would have reported the farmer missing. While the Stoccos' employers often lived on isolated properties, it would not have taken long for neighbours or suppliers, for example, to raise the alarm.

Another detective said it could not categorically be ruled out that the Stoccos may have picked up and then killed a hitchhiker, but there was nothing to suggest they did it, either. They were offenders motivated by either necessity, such as when they stole, or vengeance, in cases where they lashed out at those they felt scorned by. What would be their motive for killing a fellow nomad?

Redding is not entirely alone, however, in his belief that Mark and Gino Stocco were responsible for taking more than one life. Linda Stocco – the wife of Gino's older brother, Mario – believes the pair contributed to the deaths of Peter and Egidia Stocco. No one can say whether this is true; certainly they would have caused stress among the family, but Peter seemed to almost enjoy the visits from journalists, by all accounts, and Egidia had dementia and was in a nursing home, so was either shielded from much of it or did not even know it was occurring.

Mario and Linda live not far from the farm where the Fragapanes first settled, and then grew their multimillion-dollar business, in Werribee South. There is no doubt that Mark and Gino's gallivanting had an impact on them too, not least of all because they remain friendly with the Fragapanes, but also because everyone knew they were relatives, and those who didn't may have been able to guess, given they had a personalised numberplate reading 'STOCCOS'. Linda said the couple would not contribute to this book unless they were paid, and added that they still got along well with Connie, who lived nearby.

There are those who think the Stoccos have not killed anyone, those who think the Stoccos are serial killers, and those who know the Stoccos have killed but do not want to believe it. Graham and Peg, the retired couple living on the outer south-western edge of Sydney, seem to fall into the final category.

I first spoke to them the day before Mark and Gino's sentencing. They were worried about what the following afternoon would bring. They felt that Mark, particularly, did not deserve to spend some of his best years inside. And they pitied Gino, too. It was hard to avoid the notion that, should the Stoccos miraculously walk free the next day, they would be welcomed back to the house. After all, their room was still made up. And Graham still had some work for them.

'They promised to put a railing on here, but they never did,' he said, as he walked up the staircase to the top level of the shed the Stoccos called home, on and off, for two years.

When we got to the top, he showed me around the three rooms and then, finally, returned to the bedroom. Graham stood, slightly hunched from the decades of work that are now behind him, staring at the bed Mark and Gino shared. His hands were clasped behind his back, his eyes weary. 'It's all a bit sad, you know?' he said.

For the most part, Graham is alone in his sympathies for the Stoccos. It is the prevailing view that the world will be better with them ensconced in green tracksuits and concrete and metal. And it will be better still if Gino Stocco dies surrounded, not by an open road and his loving son and a stolen car, but by four cold walls.

That is the just and likely outcome, Darren Cloake reckons. But then he goes quiet, inhales, and says softly, 'Unless he escapes.'

Author's note

The Stoccos has been compiled through interviews over a period of more than two years, including with victims and their families, police, and those who knew the Stoccos. It has also relied on previously published material, documents obtained through freedom of information laws, and documents granted by the courts.

In the case of Mark and Gino Stocco, who would not be interviewed by the author, quoted material was mostly gained from two main sources: interviews with police, and interviews with a psychiatrist. As it was impractical, each quote by the Stoccos in the text is not attributed to the interview or report in which it was made.

All information gathered from other sources in the book has been attributed accordingly, to the best of the author's knowledge. The account of the police chase is based on the police statements of several officers involved in the incident.

Every effort has been made to ensure the accuracy of the content at the time of publication.

Acknowledgements

For trusting me to write this book, and being unfailingly generous while I did so, I wish to thank (in no particular order): Ian Durkin, Doug Redding, 'Graham and Peg', Dave Barron, Mick Wolfe, Darren Cloake, Liam Duffy, Matt Shaw, Fiona Duncan, Luke Tidswell, Peter Farley, Rick Nugent, Paul O'Halloran, Virginia Gorman, Mick Banfield, and the countless others who spoke to me but did not wish to be named, including victims or relatives of the Stoccos, those who had known them, and police. Thanks also to the wider Queensland, Victoria and New South Wales police forces for their assistance.

My former colleagues at *The Age*, where I worked while writing this book, were patient, encouraging, and offered guidance. Thanks especially to Chris Johnston, Tammy Mills, Cameron Houston and Tom Cowie. Thanks also to other journalists across Fairfax Media who assisted with the book, particularly at the *Sydney Morning Herald*.

At Penguin Random House, thanks to Cate Blake, Amanda Martin and Kevin O'Brien for all your work.

For teaching me the importance of words, I thank my mother and father. For being the first person I properly shared them with, I thank my brother. And for supporting me to keep trying to find them, and picking up everything else while I do, I thank my wife.